Praise for
Decoding the Divine

Leonard Sweet is an institution unto himself. He writes more books than I read. But nothing brings more joy to my heart than to see a conclusive work that brings together what's been going on in Len's mysterious head for years—a conclusive work around semiotics! No one exegetes the world better than Dr. Sweet. And this creative and masterful volume will feed the power of the church's imagination for an entire generation, no doubt. Read *Decoding the Divine* and the world will open its treasures to you. This book is a sweeping force.

A. J. SWOBODA, PH.D., UNIVERSITY OF BIRMINGHAM
Associate Professor of Bible and Theology at Bushnell University and author of *The Gift of Thorns*

To decode the complex signs of our fractured, contentious and anxious times, we need this book to follow the true master of semiotics—Jesus. This manual reveals the most essential, riveting, invigorating, sanctifying decoding keys for our culture, for the church, and for us deep cultural missionaries.

MAKOTO FUJIMURA
Artist and author of *Art and Faith: A Theology of Making*

Words fall short to describe the overwhelming effect that *Decoding the Divine: Unveiling the Sacred through Semiotics* has had on me. I started reading this long-awaited magnum opus by Len on semiotics during a recent holiday. But then *Decoding the Divine* turned into my holiday. After working through the twenty-three semiotic tells embedded in the book every day, I then repeated what I'd learned to my wife every evening. The following day I reread it again in order to fathom its sheer depth, beauty and truth. I'm still trying to process these twenty-three epiphanies, these twenty-three transcendent experiences of awe that changed forever how I perceive life and God's goodness.

I have been a friend, follower, and student of Len for many years. I have devoured his books, sat at his feet many times, and watched numerous of his teachings. But *Decoding the Divine* is far more beautiful and mind-stretching than everything I have ever experienced. I have become an undergraduate student all over again at the feet of the master who re-introduced me to the Master in so many indescribably fresh ways. Water has truly been turned into wine by the most important and prolific theo-semiotician on the planet.

STEPHAN JOUBERT
Extraordinary Professor in Contemporary Ecclesiology, University of the Free State, South Africa

I was first introduced to Leonard Sweet's "23 tells of semiotics" during my doctoral cohort's pilgrimage to Oxford ... and I was mesmerized. Len has a way of making the ordinary extraordinary, turning every moment into a sacred encounter.

Decoding the Divine is an invitation into the semiotic secrets that, until now, have been reserved for his doctoral students (except without a dissertation to write and at a fraction of the cost!). This book is playful, practical, and, as always, profoundly insightful. The maestro of metaphor, Len orchestrates a symphony of sacred signs that invites us to tune our hearts to hear the melodies of meaning he hears in the world.

Through Len's lens, life becomes a mosaic of meaning, where every sign points to the divine. With each page, you'll feel the veil between heaven and earth grow thinner as you learn to read the sacred language of God woven into creation. This book isn't just a read; it's a revelation. To study under Len is to be forever changed, and now, through *Decoding the Divine*, his wisdom is available to all who are ready to see and savor the beauty of God's sacred story.

>**DR. DUANE WHITE**
>Leader in O2 Network of Churches & Ministers,
>https://duanewhite.online

For more than three decades, Leonard Sweet has been a dear friend and mentor, profoundly shaping my understanding of applied semiotics and futures studies. I've also had the distinct privilege of having him as my doctoral chair during my studies in this discipline. To say that Len has been a consistent voice of wisdom and prophetic savoir-faire would be an understatement. With the release of his latest book, *Decoding the Divine: Unveiling the Sacred Through Semiotics*, Len has once again demonstrated why he stands as one of the few voices uniquely equipped to guide us in the sacred discipline of reading the signs of the times, Scripture, and culture.

Len's unparalleled ability to interweave the Scriptures, theology, and church history produces a tapestry of insights that is nothing short of revelatory. In this book, Len takes us by the hand and teaches us what he calls "brailling the culture"—helping the blind see by leading them through the signs, textures, and signals that God has placed in both the visual and linguistic worlds. His work is a masterclass in theo-semiotics, offering clarity and assurance where confusion and uncertainty often reign.

What sets Len apart is not just his depth of understanding but his relentless attentiveness. He does not let the grass grow under his feet. With an eye ever-watchful for signs, trends, trajectories, and possibilities, Len teaches us how to discern God's voice in the unexpected, the unnoticed, and the concealed. He challenges us to recognize that the God who speaks does so not just in overt declarations but in the subtle language of culture, symbols, and the overlooked dynamics of life.

Like a voice crying in the wilderness, Len calls us to prepare the way of the Lord by uncovering the ways in which Christ intentionally conceals Himself—inviting us to search, to see, and to discover His riches. As Len so brilliantly reveals, the signs are all around us. They are a trail that leads to Christ, the hidden wisdom of God. But only those willing to pay attention, to listen deeply, and to approach the sacred text and the culture with humility and curiosity will find the treasures He has left for us.

Decoding the Divine is not just a book; it's an invitation. An invitation to see the world differently, to listen for the whispers of God in places we might not think to look, and to follow the signs to the One who is present in ways more abundant and profound than we could ever imagine. Len Sweet's theo-semiotics is a vital key to unlocking this journey. With every page, he equips us to follow the signs that lead to the riches of Christ in all His glory.

For those seeking to see what others overlook, to learn how to read both the sacred and the secular with Spirit-led eyes, and to encounter Christ anew in unexpected places, this book is an essential guide. Len Sweet, in his brilliance and faithfulness, reminds us that God's signs are always pointing us home—if only we have the eyes to see.

> **MARK CHIRONNA**
> Bishop, Theo-Semiotician (PhD, D. Min), Psychologist (MA), BCC Coach, Musician, Senior Pastor (Church on the Living Edge)

The enduring legacy of Leonard Sweet's copious corpus may be the rescue of Christian faith from the irascible ideologies of the ivory tower and the discount bins of department stores. When you read Sweet, you discover the mystery of the living Jesus, human and divine. You hear the call to rediscover Jesus as "the living, breathing manifestation of God's presence."

And how do we best do this? We look for the living, both in the text and in the uncharted territories of our lives. Previously, you may have heard of "sacred semiotics" as the much less interesting "cultural commentary." But semiotics is so much more. As he colorfully explains in this overdue yet instantly seminal source on the subject, semiotics is no less than "the ability to interpret signs and symbols in ways that breathe new life into Scripture and alter understanding."

If you want to understand who Jesus is, and why it matters, you will benefit from the looking glass Len offers.

DR. LEN WILSON
Publisher, author, and Jesus follower

Len Sweet's *Decoding the Divine* is a transformative guide to discerning God's signs in Scripture, creation, and culture. In this super-intriguing and practical guide to semiotics, Sweet sharpens our spiritual vision, helping us see and embody the gospel in every context. *Decoding the Divine* isn't just a book—it's a poetic invitation to awaken to God's rhythms and align with His eternal purposes. A must-read for anyone longing to engage faith and culture with wisdom and grace.

ALAN HIRSCH
Award-winning author of books on missional spirituality, leadership, and organization. Founder of Movement Leaders Collective and Forge Missional Training Network

As they have been for hundreds of students throughout the decades, the years I spent studying semiotics with Dr. Sweet were transformative for my life and ministry. Until now, enrolling in a doctoral program was the only comprehensive way to learn from Len how to read God's unique "sign language" in the world, but with the arrival of this book, he is making it accessible for anyone. Employing his signature style of creative communication, Sweet teaches us how to perceive the timely truths of God's present-future Kingdom for those who have eyes to see and ears to hear the sights and sounds of the signs of the times, and to faithfully respond to the significant opportunities toward which they point.

ERIC E. PETERSON
Founding pastor of Colbert Presbyterian Church near Spokane, WA, and the author of *Wade in the Water: Following the Sacred Stream of Baptism*

Len's magnum opus *Decoding the Divine* is a masterpiece of insight, Biblical connective tissue and a crash course in decoding the Bible for all time.

DR. RICH MELHEIM
Dr. Melheim has written and produced 39 books, produced 24 music albums, and is a futurist, neuro-educator, entrepreneur, student of NFTs/Blockchain/Metaverses, semiotician, cartoonist, comedian, speaker, publisher, playwright, songwriter, family counselor, business systems consultant, log cabin builder, and preschool designer. Melheim has taught in 1000 cities on five continents.

Leonard Sweet delivers an opus on semiotics and does it in the melody of Jesus. Decades of work, countless students impacted (myself included), and now composed for the masses, this is a written legacy. No one blends depth with clarity like Sweet, and this volume exemplifies his signature "simplicity." Semiotics is key to understanding the future, and there is no better guide than Leonard Sweet.

BRYCE ASHLIN-MAYO
President of Ambrose University and author of *Digital Mission: A Practical Guide for Ministry Online*

Len Sweet is the only writer I know who can deliver on this book's promise: *Decoding the Divine*. At one level, God defies decryption. On another level, however, God communicates. The trick is developing the necessary receptors to detect God's relational overtures. *Decoding the Divine* is both an academic and engaging exploration of how signs, symbols, and metaphors shape faith and understanding. If you want to learn how to find God in all the places you never thought to look, this is the right book for you!

CHARLES CONNIRY
President, Western Seminary, Portland Oregon

For decades, Len Sweet has shown us how all of life and the things of God are presented to us in the semiotic—signs and symbols. In this book, Len brings together his tools, keys, and ciphers into one place. With this book, you will receive a gift and the handing on of ways to unlock scripture and your life's events, relationships, and encounters with God.

JASON SWAN CLARK, PH.D.
Lead Mentor, Doctor of Leadership, Portland Seminary, Director of the London Centre for Spiritual Direction

DECODING THE DIVINE

UNVEILING THE SACRED THROUGH SEMIOTICS

REVISED EDITION

LEONARD SWEET

The Salish
Sea Press
Orcas Island
Washington

Decoding the Divine: Unveiling the Sacred Through Semiotics

ISBN revised edition softcover: 978-1-63613-034-7

Published by The Salish Sea Press. Box 1492, Absecon, NJ 08201.
https://salishsea.press
https://www.facebook.com/thesalishseapress/

The Salish Sea Press is a program of SpiritVenture Ministries.
https://leonardsweet.com/

Copyright © 2025 by Leonard Sweet. All rights reserved.

Interior designed by Carmen Barber: keepingyouwriting@gmail.com
Cover designed by Michael Buckingham: michael@holycow.org
Tri-Donkey artwork by Bryan Butler: kados2000@gmail.com

Unless otherwise indicated, Scripture quotations are the author's own paraphrase. If the notation LIS is used, this also indicates the author's own paraphrase. Other versions are noted in the back matter.

The Salish Sea Press

Dedicated To My Students:

Past, Present, and Future

You are the signs I read,
The symbols I interpret,
The meaning I seek.

In your eyes, I see the future;
In your questions, I find my mission;
In your growth, I leave my legacy.

Together, we decipher the world.
It has been, is, and always will be,
An honor to study with you.

~ Leonard Sweet

The Three Donkeys

CONTENTS

Acknowledgments xvii
Preface 23
Introduction 27

Semiotic Tell #1
    The Living Tell of the Times 45

Semiotic Tell #2
    Water Turning to Wine
    (and Signs to Sacrament) 69

Semiotic Tell #3
    The Mirror's Blind Spot 97

Semiotic Tell #4
    Tongues of Culture 111

Semiotic Tell #5
    The Divine Constellation 127

Semiotic Tell #6
    The Elephant Unseen 147

Semiotic Tell #7
    The Cover's Deception
    (and the Sign Beneath) 159

Semiotic Tell #8
    Cosmic Curveballs 177

Semiotic Tell #9
    The Cyclops' Gaze 191

Semiotic Tell #10
- Storms of Signs...213

Semiotic Tell #11
- The Fog of Meaning..221

Semiotic Tell #12
- The Symphony of Differences...............................235

Semiotic Tell #13
- Tick Bites..249

Semiotic Tell #14
- Nets Cast Forward...263

Semiotic Tell #15
- The Truth in the Maze..279

Semiotic Tell #16
- The Reimagined Box..285

Semiotic Tell #17
- Symbolic Truffles...293

Semiotic Tell #18
- Semiotic Fool's Gold..305

Semiotic Tell #19
- Signs Under Pressure...323

Semiotic Tell #20
- The Navel's Pull..331

Semiotic Tell #21
- The Waltz of Memory and
  Pirouette of Imagination......................................341

Semiotic Tell #22
> The Levitation of Signs 369

Semiotic Tell #23
> The Sentinel's Threshold 377

Connect with Leonard 389

Scripture Versions.. 391

Notes 393

Acknowledgments

I am a historical theologian by academic training, a preacher by divine calling, and a semiotician by what can only be described as a glorious obsession. Like a child who sneaks into the cookie jar, I've helped myself to semiotics through rigorous self-study rather than formal training. I find myself in good company with novelist Walker Percy, who confessed to Peirce scholar Kenneth Laine Ketner, "As you well know, I am not a student of Peirce. I am a thief of Peirce. I take from him what I want and let the rest go, most of it."[1]

But perhaps semiotics runs in my blood. In 1630, my ancestor James Sweet sailed on the *Arbella* from Southampton to Salem Harbor with the Winthrop Fleet, bringing two ancient arts with him: craftsmanship and bonesetting. Think about it: the craftsman weaves external elements into shelters of beauty, while the bonesetter coaxes internal chaos back into harmony. Both arts transform fragments into wholeness—rather like what we semioticians do, though with considerably less splinting involved.

This book arrived like a summer thunderstorm—sudden and electric—but it's been gathering clouds for twenty-three years. That's how long I've been teaching these semiotic tells to doctoral students at George Fox University. This twenty-third cohort marks my final chapter at Portland Seminary (formerly George Fox Evangelical Seminary), where I've had the joy of collaborating with wizards of administration like

Loren Kerns, Cliff Berger, Jen McNab, and Heather Rainey. It seemed poetically right to transform my twenty-three tells into book form just in time for this last group.

What an extraordinary journey it has been. It began when David Brandt, George Fox's remarkable eleventh president, and Jules Glanzer, our imaginative seminary dean, invited me to join their dream of creating something special. Their vision drew me in to help launch the doctoral program, advise the president, and join the faculty as a distinguished visiting professor. The adventure continued under my friend Robin Baker, who took the helm as president in 2007. When Jules left to lead Tabor College in 2008, Charles Conniry stepped in as dean, becoming not just a valued colleague but a dear friend. Together, this remarkable quartet gave me the freedom to soar, often going to bat for innovation when traditional academic structures threatened to clip our wings. Their canopy of trust, protection, and friendship made this doctoral program possible, and my heart brims with gratitude for their gift.

While this book is dedicated to all my students, Cohort twenty-three holds a special place in my heart: Hailey Armoogan, Arron Chambers, Naomi Chong, Steve Chong, Justin Dishong, Joanne Hagemeyer, Trey Harris, Joel Johnson, Sung Kim, Chad McSwain, Derek Pritchett, Amanda Ross, Jeremy Saylor, Brad Sumner, Wade Swickard, and Lisa Taylor. A special tip of the hat to Joanne Hagemeyer, who saved me from including something that would have had me hiding under my desk in embarrassment for years to come.

St. Augustine once observed that "Nobody, after all, uses words except for the sake of signifying something" (*De*

ACKNOWLEDGMENTS

Doctrina Christiana 1.2.2).[2] In my case, the most profound meanings have sprung from the beloved meaning-makers in my own home. My ezer-wife Tia and our erudite son Jeremiah Luke have patiently entertained countless mealtime musings as these ideas tumbled out between passing the balsamic and buttering bread. And speaking of tables—they truly are magical places where wisdom often arrives in unexpected packages. Just this morning over breakfast, as I mentioned wrapping up my semiotics textbook with the working title "Decoding the Divine—In Twenty-three Commandments," eight-year-old Luke glanced up from his syrup-drowned pancakes with the kind of piercing insight only children possess: "Why do you need thirteen more commandments than God?"

My wife Tia is my perfect pitch pipe, always tuning my academic flights of fancy back to Middle C when I drift into the stratospheric registers of scholarly showboating. Speaking of which—have you ever noticed how academic writing often reads like an instruction manual for assembling quantum physics in Sanskrit? Take poor Rowan Williams (one of my intellectual heroes), who was once cruelly described as being "never knowingly understood." Ouch. That's not a moniker I want to wear. My writerly ambition is to be an anti-scholarly scholar, an academic acrobat who can flip between profound and playful without dropping anyone's attention. I aim for prose that sparkles rather than sedates, that makes unexpected connections dance together like old friends at a party. Think less ivory tower, more tree house with a really good view (which I came close to building at Sanctuary Seaside, and may still one day if enough of you buy this book). But sometimes I still get lost in the playground of my mind—and that's when

Tia gently (or not so gently) rappels me back down to earth. She's my built-in translator from academese to human, and this book is infinitely more readable because of her.

A sign, Umberto Eco once wrote, is anything one can use to lie with. Speaking of signs, when it comes to liturgical semiotics, my former student Dr. Kevin Olds knows his signs from his symbols, his bread from his wine—and he's never let me get away with fibbing about either. His expert counsel on the sacrament-and-sign chapter proved invaluable—though I'm still convinced he speaks in tongues when he gets really excited about ritual.

Now, as for editors ... every writer needs a Nathan in their life, someone brave enough to point that prophetic finger and declare, "Thou art the one who needs a do-over: do another draft." My two fearless Nathans were content editor Erin Healy and copy editor Carmen Barber. They returned my manuscripts looking less red-penned and more like crime scenes, but their ruthless caring transformed these pages. Some might call it editorial bloodshed; I call it grace. To Kevin, Erin, and Carmen: your fingerprints are all over this book, some of them actually in red ink, and I couldn't be more grateful.

The inspiration for the "Source Code" sections at the end of each chapter comes from George Robson V's online Bible study of the same name. These interactive prompts were born from a chorus of pastoral voices all singing the same blues: "It's tough out here in the local parish now. Folks are so detached from the source." Consider these sections your reconnection cables to the divine power grid.

Harold Bloom once noted that Nietzsche "attempted to

ACKNOWLEDGMENTS

live his life as a poem" before madness claimed him at fifty-five. I've embraced a similar poetic existence, though thankfully with better mental health outcomes (so far, at least—my family might beg to differ).

Like the Scottish poet Hugh MacDiarmid, I have little patience for mouse-sized efforts that yield only crumbs. Poetry—whether in verse or theology—should unleash cosmic forces: think less delicate snowflake, more avalanche of ideas.[3] This book aspires to be such a force of nature, hoping to fulfill Ecclesiastes 12:11b's vision of putting "the mind of one man into many a life" (MOF). Though in this case, the only "one man mind" I pray to have shared is the mind of Christ.

If my reach exceeds my grasp in these poetic aspirations, I seek clemency on these grounds: true poetry, like true theology, should aim not for the precious but for the revolutionary. It should catch the wild wind of the Spirit and spin it into new ways of seeing God's language-saturated world through sacred imagination.

And to all the unnamed saints, living and dead, in my celestial bleachers who kept shouting "swing away!" and "swing for the divine!" when I was tempted to bunt—this moonshot's for you.

Preface

The Lord himself will give you a sign:
The virgin will conceive and give birth to a son,
and will call him Immanuel.

ISAIAH 7:14 NIV

My beloved students,

For three decades, I've walked alongside you through the labyrinth of semiotics—the maze, haze, and daze of decoding the signs and symbols that shape our world. Now, as I commit these words to paper, I'm not merely writing a book—I'm unveiling my heart, sharing the secrets that have guided my journey with you.

Some of you have sat in my classrooms, Zooms, and Dolphin Cay living room, your avid faces illuminated by the light of discovery. A few of you have bowed down and stepped up to join me in my octagonal Star Chamber. Others have found me through the pages of my books, sermons,[4] or the digital threads of social media. But make no mistake:

All of you are my students.
All of you are my torchbearers.
All of you are my living legacy.

Whether we've met in person or only in the realm of ideas, you've each left an indelible mark on my spirit. You've challenged me, inspired me, and reminded me why this field of semiotics—this art of interpretation—matters so profoundly.

So lean in close, colleagues. Listen carefully. For in these pages, I'm whispering the secrets I've gleaned from a lifetime of studying the divine dialogue written in the very fabric of existence.

These are not just lessons.

These are not just theories.

These are the keys to unlocking not just the global but the cosmic conversation that surrounds us all.

Welcome to the inner sanctum of semiotics.

Welcome to my legacy.

Welcome to my secrets.

Welcome home.

Semiotics: Semiotics is the study of signs and symbols. And signs are God's celestial communication, sacred semantics, the language of the holy. If we can't read signs, we can't receive the bouquets of love God bestows on us in every day.

Decoding signs of love? My dog Windsor is the top dog in that department. In my family, there's a resident Sherlock Paws who puts even the greatest semioticians to shame. This semiotic genius anticipates my every move like I'm a particularly transparent cheese Danish. He can decipher my mood faster than a toddler deciphers a juice box—one tap at the door and he's on high alert, tail acting as a built-in emotional barometer.

Packing for a trip? Forget subtle hints. This family member launches a full-on guilt trip, an Oscar-worthy drama complete with hand-wringing and a soundtrack of sorrowful whimpers. Leaving the house? He's the first one to

PREFACE

"accidentally" trip me with a misplaced leg. Visitors? He's the epitome of a canine concierge, mirroring my enthusiasm (or lack thereof) with Swiss-watch precision.

This mastermind of mutt-communication and canine comprehension? None other than Windsor, my beloved Bernese Mountain dog. My life is a perpetual game of "decode the dog"—and I'm constantly losing. With his ever-wagging tail and eyes that could melt glaciers, he's become the undisputed semiotics champion of our household. His tail wags are a masterclass in signification—a single motion that can convey excitement, enthusiasm, or even a subtle warning.

I'm no Professor Charles M. Nielsen, the undisputed king of canine theology and author of one of the most barking mad yet brilliant religious satires ever penned. My mentor in historical theology famously argued that dogs, those four-legged philosophers, were far more deserving of communion than many of us humans. After all, as he sagely pointed out, we expect less of our dogs than we do of our fellow parishioners. Who, honestly, trains their kids better than they train their pups?

Nielsen's radical idea wasn't just about sharing crackers and grape juice with Fido; it was a paw-sitive statement about our lost innocence and the redemptive power of unconditional love. If dogs can be unfailingly loyal, adorable, and judgment-free, maybe they're more of a Christ figure than we imagined, and convey the semiotics of salvation in ways we've overlooked.[5]

Living with my semiotic savant is both a hallowed blessing and a hilarious curse. I'm pretty sure Windsor has a Ph.D. in Semiotics ... or at least a Ph.D. in making me feel guilty

25

for leaving him behind. His mastery of "the wag" and the "soulful stare" is so impressive, it's no wonder I suspect he moonlights as a dog whisperer (as my wife Tia moonlights as a whale whisperer—she can spot the orca whales off our deck better than the whale-watching boats). As we navigate the world of semiotics together, I'm grateful to have Windsor as our trusty sidekick. He may not be able to explain the finer points of Peirce's triadic model, but he's taught me that sometimes the most powerful signs are the ones that come with a wagging tail and a snuggle.

So, join me on this journey into the fascinating world of semiotics, the divine dialect where the lines between human and animal communication blur[6]—and the only constant is the joy of discovery, courtesy of my trusty furry guide, Windsor, who both interprets signs and symbols and is the source of signs and symbols. While I may never sniff out life's mysteries quite as well, I'm content to follow his lead (and hopefully avoid any suspicious "accidents" near the suitcase). That's why I considered titling this book, "Everything I Know About Life (Especially Semiotics), I Learned from My Dog (Except How to Resist Those Puppy Dog Eyes)."

Semiotics can teach you how you can "Watch-and-Pray"[7] Jesus even better than Sir Windsor can "watch-and-wag" me. Are you ready to decode the divine?

It brings me great pleasure to embark on this adventure together.

Your professor and fellow semiotic adventurer,

~ Leonard Sweet

Introduction

Welcome, my dear students, to the fascinating world of semiotics.

Imagine, if you will, standing beside me as we gaze upon Caspar David Friedrich's haunting masterpiece, "Monk by the Sea" (1809). There's a solitary figure on the shore, curved like a question mark against the vastness of a fog-shrouded sea.

This painting, colleagues, is more than just oil on canvas—it's a visual paradigm for the journey we're about to embark on together. Just as Friedrich's monk peers into the misty horizon, we too are about to venture into the cultural fog that envelops us. And let me tell you the first of many secrets: every society is a fog machine. It generates its own haze of assumptions, beliefs, and traditions that can obscure our vision of reality. We often look back on history with deceptive blue-sky clarity, but the present and future? They're shrouded in uncertainty.

This is where semiotics comes in, my brave adventurers. It's our compass in this fog, our tool for penetrating the mists of cultural meaning. Think of yourselves as cultural detectives, attuning your senses to the subtle birth cries of future paradigms, the rumble of approaching cultural storms, the thunderclaps at thresholds. Exciting, isn't it?

Now, I know what you're thinking. "But Professor Sweet, isn't semiotics just some dry academic subject?" Oh, how wrong you are. Let me let you in on a second secret: semiotics is everywhere in pop culture. It's like finding Easter eggs in your favorite TV shows.

Remember Sheldon Cooper from *The Big Bang Theory* referencing semiotic theory? Or that *Bones* episode titled "The Signs in the Silence"? How about Abed Nadir in *Community* analyzing everything through a semiotic lens? Even Will Graham in *Hannibal* uses semiotic analysis in his criminal profiling.[8]

Not high culture (elite brow), or folk culture (roots brow), but pop culture (street brow), my students, often carries the highest IQ. At its best, it is a master of the simplicity on the other side of complexity. When something starts popping up all over pop culture, you can bet it'll soon be a hot topic in many church pulpits and pews.

So, what's all the fuss about? Here's the scoop: semiotics is the science and study of "signs," or *semeia* (*semion*) in Greek. In the words of Charles Sanders Peirce, the godfather of semiotics, signs are "something which stands to somebody for something in some respect or capacity."[9] In other words, semiotics is a synoptic, synthetic subject that is all about relationships and connections. In this book, we're focusing on applied semiotics, not theoretical semiotics.[10] Don't worry, just as you don't need to know geometry to ride a bike, you don't need to do semantic somersaults or be a structuralist theoretician to master this.[11]

But here's something you might not know: you've already passed a semiotics test. Remember your driving exam? That was all about reading the signs of the highway. And Jesus? He insisted that his disciples pass a similar road test, knowing

INTRODUCTION

how to "read the signs of the times" not just "the signs of the sky."

This book, my dear students, is your induction into the tribe of Issachar, the tribe who "knows the times and knows what to do."[12]

Let me share another secret with you: God's grammar isn't found in texts. Our native theological tongue is a semiotic one. Divine discourse is sacred symbology, making culture a story language. Learning to decode that language of the earth and skies? That's what semiotics is all about.

We're living in an "iconomic" culture, where the major currency is signs, signals, and gestures. People communicate in hand gestures, emoticons and emojis, fashion and brandings, body language, traffic signs and symbols. It's a whole new world out there, and you need more than just the right words to navigate it. You need to uncover the right stories and metaphors behind the words that breathe life into language. Signs are not one-way delivery systems from addresser to addressee, but involve a complex system of context, code, and culture, to adapt linguist Roman Jakobson's famous model.[13]

Now, I know this might sound overwhelming. But remember, you're not alone in this journey. We're in this together, decoding the divine and the human, one sign at a time. And trust me, once you start seeing the world through a semiotic lens, you'll never look at things the same way again.

So, are you ready to embark on this adventure? To learn the secrets of decoding the hidden structures of meaning that shape our world and give life its purpose? I've written it as more of an impromptu spoken lecture than an academic paper or published monograph.

Let's dive in together and unlock the door to effective communication in the twenty-first century. The possibilities for influence and impact? They're truly limitless.

---

*The story of your life is not a drama. It's a musical.
And if you don't like the storyline, change the soundtrack.*

THEO-SEMIOTICIAN DUANE WHITE

Saddling Up for the Semiotic Rodeo: Picture this: You're at a rodeo, the air thick with dust and anticipation. But this isn't just any rodeo—it's the Semiotic Showdown at the Significance Corral, where meaning bucks wild and signs run free. I've been riding this bronc for years, not just eight seconds, and let me tell you, it's the ride of a lifetime.

Back in '99, I first mounted up with *Soul Tsunami*, lassoing the concept of semiotics and wrestling it into the cultural arena. It was more than just fancy rope tricks—it was a semiotic rodeo to help us wrangle "our sea-change future."[14] Twenty years later, I circled back around in an anniversary tribute with *Rings of Fire*, proving that this bucking bronc of cultural semiotics still had some kick left in it.

In 2010, I saddled up *Nudge*, my trusty steed for a semiotic stampede through evangelism. I wasn't there to show off my semiotics spurs, but to remind us all that Christianity itself is a symbol system—a semiotic network of stories and images, rituals and concepts, all embodied and enacted in our daily lives.[15] The key to riding this particular bull? Semiotic literacy—the ability to read the signs of divine presence without getting thrown.

INTRODUCTION

Just when you thought the dust had settled, along came *Telos* in 2022. My former student Len Wilson and I teamed up for a semiotic rodeo through the "last things." We weren't just kicking up eschatological and teleological dust—we were reading the signs of heaven's hoofprints on earth today.

But let me tell you about the wildest ride of all: *Giving Blood* in 2014. This wasn't just preaching—it was a full-on semiotic homiletic showdown. I declared it loud and clear: "Semiotics is the currency of the gospel." And who better to back me up than the original semiotic cowboy himself, Augustine?

Picture Augustine, not in his bishop's robes, but in Wranglers and a Stetson, laying out his Semiotic 5 P's:

> Pause: Hear the whisper of meaning in the wind
> Presence: Taste the flavor of significance
> Picture: See the image of understanding unfold
> Ponder: Touch the texture of interpretation
> Promise: Smell the aroma of revelation

In Augustine's own words (imagine them drawled around a campfire):

> You called and cried to me and broke open my deafness. You sent forth your beams and shone upon me and chased away my blindness. You breathed fragrance upon me, and I drew in my breath and now pant for you. I tasted you, and now hunger and thirst for you. You touched me and I burned for your peace.[16]

Now, beloved students, it's time to saddle up. The Semiotic Rodeo is about to begin, and you're invited to ride. Hold on tight—we're about to decode the signs of our times, and it's going to be one wild ride.

As we embark on this bucking, twisting journey you'll never forget, I want to share with you a story that illuminates the profound impact semiotics can have on one's life and faith. It's a tale of metamorphosis, featuring none other than the aforementioned African theologian Augustine (d. 430), architect of Western Christian thought.

Augustine, once a Manichean "hearer" and self-confessed libertine, finds his world turned upside down by an unlikely catalyst—Ambrose, the Bishop of Milan. Ambrose wasn't your run-of-the-mill bishop. His rise to the position was itself a testament to his character.

When Milan needed a new bishop, the people—in what some might call divine inspiration and others mob frenzy—demanded Ambrose. And how did he respond? By resisting with every fiber of his being. He even resorted to extreme measures like torture, solitude, and feigning a less-than-saintly lifestyle to escape the papal tiara.[17] Talk about dedication to avoiding promotion.

But here's where it gets interesting, my budding semioticians. Ambrose had two qualities that would change Augustine's life forever. First, there was his embodiment of virtue and humility—reluctantly accepting his fate only when cornered and exhausted. But more crucially, there was his approach to Scripture. Ambrose did something so novel, so revolutionary, that Augustine and others would watch in fascination: he read silently and to himself. Can you imagine? In

INTRODUCTION

those days, this would have been as strange as seeing someone use a smartphone in Ancient Rome.

But the real magic happened in Ambrose's sermons. He introduced what we today would call a semiotic reading of the Bible. Suddenly, the Old Testament wasn't just a historical document—it became a living, breathing narrative. This approach, my dear students, was the spark that ignited Augustine's imagination, illuminating his path from heresy to orthodoxy.

Now, I know what you're thinking. "But Professor Sweet, didn't Augustine and Ambrose have deep, long conversations about this?"

Well, here's a little secret: their interactions were actually quite limited. Ambrose was often too busy with his duties or engrossed in his silent reading. Yet, these brief mentoring encounters were enough to profoundly shape Augustine's faith, ultimately blessing the world with his theological insights.

Sacred Semiotics: This, my colleagues, is the power of semiotics—the ability to interpret signs and symbols in ways that breathe new life into Scripture and alter understanding. It's not just about decoding; it's about reimagining, reinterpreting, and revolutionizing our relationship with the divine.

You may have noticed that this second printing organizes its insights into "23 Tells" rather than "23 Commandments." This shift is deliberate. One of my doctoral students, David Sunde, challenged the original "commandments" framing when he received a copy of the book. He was right to call it out. After sifting through alternatives, I landed on "tells"—a term that resonates deeply with the practice of semiotics on multiple levels.

In poker, a "tell" is a subtle shift in behavior or expression that betrays a player's hand—an unconscious signal decipherable only by the keen observer. In archaeology, a "tell" (from Arabic) is a mound formed by layers of human habitation, each stratum unveiling the story of a buried civilization. In everyday language, to "tell" is both to narrate and to perceive ("I can tell something's off").

These layered meanings mirror semiotics itself—the craft of reading faint signs, excavating hidden depths, and weaving observations into insight. A semiotic practitioner attunes to the "tells" others overlook, unearths the cultural "tells" rich with untold histories, and "tells" these discoveries to the world. Unlike commandments carved in stone, tells are alive—dynamic, contextual, and ever shifting. They emerge from within rather than dictate from above. They sharpen perception rather than enforce practice. They're less about rules to obey and more about patterns to discern.

With this shift, I hope these "23 Tells" act not as rigid directives but as perceptual lenses—inviting you to see the world, The Story, and their intricate interplay anew. Like life's truest tells, they whisper instead of shout, beckon instead of command, and illuminate rather than prescribe.

So approach them not as commandments to follow, but as twenty-three tells to decode and deploy—signposts lighting the path to deciphering the divine.

John Wesley had a mantra: "Redeem the time." To truly redeem the time means remembering your telos—why you were placed on this earth to begin with, tracking the

INTRODUCTION

tides—monitoring the signs of your times, and embracing your tell—seeing each moment as a sacred opportunity.

Why twenty-three?

There are twenty-three pairs of chromosomes in human cells. These twenty-three chromosomes contain our genetic blueprint, carrying the DNA that encodes all of our inherited traits and biological functions. These twenty-three chromosome pairs determine everything from our physical characteristics like eye color and height, to our susceptibility to certain diseases, and even influence aspects of our behavior and development. They essentially serve as the instruction manual for building and operating the human body, with each chromosome pair containing thousands of genes that play specific roles in our biology.

These "23 Tells" form the genetic code for decoding the divine. They are the instruction manual for living and functioning as a semiotician, and especially a theo-semiotician.

If semiotics is learning to know the world as we don't know it, but actually is, theo-semiotics is decoding the divine unknown in what truly is. Or more succinctly: If semiotics reveals the world as it truly is beyond our knowing, theo-semiotics decodes the divine hidden within it.

So, what can these "23 Tells," The Code, do for you? Let me share some more secrets:

The Code will introduce you to the divine discourse of signs, symbols, gestures, and stories—God's primary love language. Imagine being fluent in the very dialect of the divine!

Like Augustine, you'll discover new ways to open up the Scriptures. #ICanSeeClearlyNow isn't just a hashtag—it's a promise.

You'll learn to "read the room," not just the text, of The Story. It's like upgrading from a black and white photo to IMAX 3D.

The Scriptures will become a cinematic experience in your mind, complete with a soundtrack. Who said Bible study can't be a blockbuster?

You'll master the art of meeting Jesus where He is, in the midst of people where they are. It's like having a divine GPS.

You'll become Grand Puzzle-Masters. The 31,102 verses of the Bible will transform from individual puzzle pieces into a breathtaking masterpiece spanning from the Pentateuch to the Apocalypse. Talk about the ultimate connect-the-dots.

You'll develop X-ray vision for God's work in the world and the church.

You'll master the art of crafting messages that resonate deeply with your audience.

You'll create compelling narratives that inspire agency and transfiguration.

You'll learn to rise above yourself to "read" pragmatically and prophetically what God is doing in the world and in the church.

You'll discover that the white spaces in life and Scripture—the silences, the pauses, the hushes and hums—can become as meaningful as the words themselves. You'll be reading between the lines like a pro.

You'll have sharpened skills at textual hermeneutics (reading the Bible as a literary text) while raising your contextual intelligence to the highest levels of cultural and biblical semiotics (reading the Bible as a contextual story).

INTRODUCTION

You'll see the world in harmony and contrast, uncovering hidden beauty in the everyday:

> A sonnet within a block of stone
>
> A symphony of flavors in a simple meal
>
> The silent orchestra of societal shifts
>
> The thorny rose of a wounded soul
>
> The flickering ember of hope in deception
>
> The true north when your soul's compass spins wildly[18]

You'll become a prophetic dot-connector, linking world events with the Word. It's like being a spiritual detective.

Your mind will shift from thinking in words to thinking in metaphors and narratives. Symbol gives rise to thought, and narraphors (narrative metaphors) become doors to the divine.

Your ministry will next-level up, equipped to build up the body of Christ for the twenty-first century mission field (and our twenty-second century kids!).

You'll develop superhuman senses—hearing the hush before a hurricane, the silence before the trumpet, the whisper before the roar. When a thought whispers, you'll be all ears.

Most importantly, you'll fall deeper in love with Jesus. And therein lies the heart of the matter, the crux of the cross.

And so, my beloved students, I charge you with what I call The Issacharian Blessing:

> May you be farsighted in a world of near-sightedness, followers of Jesus in a world lost in the short-sighted chase. In a world ruled

by signs and symbols, may you be weavers of meaning, mending the frayed tapestry of life and blessing the ties that bind not break. In a world whose currency is story and song, may you be the storytellers and songwriters of the soul, curating the narrative of Jesus, signing and singing His story into the hearts of the world.

Are you ready to decode the divine? Let's begin this adventure together.

Your Sherpa in this semiotic journey,

~ Leonard Sweet

INTRODUCTION

Source Code Interactives

1. Forget flashing neon and scrolling messages. The original signs were silent storytellers. A barber pole swirled red and white, an apothecary displayed a vibrant globe or a mortar and pestle, and a cobbler simply hung a worn boot outside his shop. While text dominates modern signage, symbols once reigned supreme. Symbols transcended language barriers, effectively communicating a trade. Images like a tankard (tavern), scissors (tailor), bushel basket (grocer), wooden Indian (tobacconist) later gave way to text-based signs, reflecting the rise of literacy. But even today, the prancing horse is known around the world as the symbol of speed, elegance, luxury, risk, danger, and adventure— even without the Ferrari name to go with it.

   Can you think of equivalents in church history and your church today?

2. How do symbols and images differ from text-based communication, and what advantages do they offer?

3. How did the rise of literacy impact the way businesses and trades communicate their identity and purpose? How might the current rise of graphicacy be shaping how we live and move and have our being?

4. What role do symbols and images play in church life and communication today, and why do they remain effective?

5. How does it hit you when you hear that God's Grammar is not found in texts, and that our native theological tongue is a semiotic one?

6. Is it thrilling, or chilling, or illing, to learn that divine discourse is sacred symbology, making faith and culture a story language, and that learning to decode that language of the earth and skies is what is called semiotics?

7. Discuss how we are perpetually signaling our intentions toward one another and expecting those signals to be picked up, translated and processed. Are you good or bad at this?

8. If growing up is learning to "read" the signaling in God's cosmic lexicon, how has your education dealt with the fact that 90% of communication is nonverbal (facial expression, body language, energy flow, etc.)? How do you feel about this book's argument that everyone needs semiotic training, not just communicators?

9. Do you think engineers, mathematicians, and scientists would agree that every word we use is more than just an assemblage of letters, but a picture, a visual narrative of a concept, idea, or experience? If you have STEM people in your midst, ask them what and how they think they think.

10. Cognitive science (a.k.a. "psychoneurolinguistics") reveals that every word has behind it a rich storehouse of back stories and every story has behind it a root metaphor. These "narraphors," as I like to call them,[19] form the very foundation of human communication and understanding.[20] What narraphors do you use to describe your life and tell your story?

11. Pope Francis has recently underscored the enduring significance of Romano Guardini's classic *The Spirit of the Liturgy* (1918), asserting that "the first task of the work of liturgical formation" is to restore our capacity for symbolism.[21]

    Do you agree that we've lost the symbolic richness of the liturgy, a language not of abstract ideas but of tangible elements: bread, wine, fire, water, space, time—physical realities that convey profound spiritual meaning? How might we recapture it?

12. Cognitive scientist John Vervaeke has proposed a comprehensive framework for understanding the nature of knowledge, suggesting that it comes in four distinct varieties: propositional, procedural, perspectival, and participatory.[22]

    Propositional knowledge is the realm of "knowing that"—the factual, declarative information we can articulate and share.

    Procedural knowledge, on the other hand, is about "knowing how"—the practical skills and abilities we develop through experience and practice.

    But Vervaeke's framework goes beyond these familiar categories, introducing two additional dimensions of knowledge that are often overlooked.

    Perspectival knowledge is the art of "knowing how to see and pay attention"—the cognitive lenses and frameworks that shape our perception and understanding of the world.

Participatory knowledge, meanwhile, is about "knowing how to be in relationship"—the interpersonal and relational skills that enable us to engage with others and the world around us in meaningful ways.

Vervaeke argues that Western culture has traditionally privileged propositional knowledge above all else, while acknowledging the importance of procedural knowledge in certain domains. However, our cultural blind spots have often prevented us from recognizing the profound importance of perspectival and participatory knowledge in shaping our experience and understanding. This is where semiotics comes in.

a. Discuss Vervaeke's thesis and his four kinds of knowledge. Can you see them in your own life?

b. Where are you strongest? Weakest?

c. How does semiotics—the study of signs and symbols and their use or interpretation—provide a powerful framework for integrating these four dimensions of knowledge?

d. Do you think by attuning us to the complex interplay of language, imagery, and meaning-making, semiotics helps us cultivate a more holistic and nuanced understanding of the world and our place within it?

e. Might semiotics not be just a tool for analyzing texts or decoding advertisements, but a means of expanding our cognitive horizons and deepening our engagement with the multifaceted nature of knowledge itself?

INTRODUCTION

f. By bringing together the propositional, procedural, perspectival, and participatory dimensions of knowing, how might semiotics offer a richer, more dynamic understanding of what it means to make sense of the world, find meaning in the world, and experience the world in all its wonderments?

Semiotic Tell #1

The Living Tell of the Times

GOD HAS CODED THE DIVINE into the human, which makes decoding the divine through semiotics an imperative journey of interpreting the sacred symbols embedded in human consciousness and culture. Humans were created to understand the divine through signs while being themselves bearers of divine signs. This is the mirrored nature of humanity.

Semioticians are honorary members of the biblical Tribe of Issachar. They are skilled at interpreting the Word within them and the world around them. Just as the Tribe of Issachar "understood the times and knew what Israel should do,"[1] semioticians analyze biblical and cultural signs and symbols to gain insight into the Word and world.

The plural use of "times," both in reference to Issachar and in Jesus' instruction to "read the signs of the times," is significant.[2] It suggests we should comprehend not just our current moment, but also the past and future. This holistic view of time is captured in the Aramaic word "Maranatha," which carries with it three tenses: "the one who was, is, and is to come."

In essence, semioticians strive to understand the interconnected nature of past, present, and future through the study of symbols and their meanings. They are at the same time a historian, sociologist, and futurist.

Only a church that lets itself be invaded by the Spirit, the Renewer of all things, and that is attentive to the signs of the times can become the new heaven that the new human being and the new earth need.

SPANISH-SALVADORAN JESUIT THEOLOGIAN
IGNACIO ELLACURÍA, MARTYRED IN 1989.[3]

What canaries are to coal mines, or crickets are to forest ecosystems,[4] semioticians are to cultures, and theo-semioticians are to churches and communities of faith.

Weather talk, the top topic of conversation in the world, is often used to avoid more meaningful or controversial topics. Jesus used weather lore to drive his disciples deeper into faith and thought, and to induct them into the Order of Issachar.

One day Jesus turns to his disciples, summons a cliché used by Greek and Roman sailors and farmers to predict weather patterns, and says: "Red sky at night, sailor's delight; red sky in the morning, sailor's warning."[5]

For the Ultimate Issacharian, this proverb was more than just a weather forecast from weather vanes and star gazers. It was a metaphor for the life of faith. Jesus was saying, "Pay attention to the signs, discern the times, and adjust your sails accordingly." Or in his exact words: "You know how to read the signs of the sky, you must also learn to read the signs of the times."[6]

When his disciples heard this, they didn't think of Virgil, who was the first to record these lines thirty years earlier in

SEMIOTIC TELL #1

his didactic poem *Georgics*, considered one of the greatest works of Roman literature. They knew the Scriptures enough to connect Jesus' words to the Tribe of Issachar, as reframed in 1 Chronicles 12:32. This Issachar story is the superhero origin story, the locus classicus, for theo-semioticians.

Issachar is a rawboned donkey
lying down among the sheep pens.

When he sees how good is his resting place
and how pleasant is his land,

he will bend his shoulder to the burden
and submit to forced labor.

GENESIS 49:14–15 NIV

I've told you this story many times, but repetition is the mother of retention, so here it is again. King David is throwing a massive rally, gathering troops from all twelve tribes of Israel. It's like an ancient draft day, with each tribe bringing their best to the table. But right in the middle of this list, we stumble upon something unexpected—the tribe of Issachar. While everyone else is flexing their muscles and rattling their swords, Issachar shows up with … smarts? The Bible says they had "understanding of the times, to know what Israel ought to do."[7] Of the twelve tribes, Issacharians stood out from the crowd as they stood in The Story.

Here's where it gets really interesting. Issachar wasn't known for being smart. Their name actually means "reward" or "wages."[8] Why this sudden wisdom glow-up? It's like they're getting a brand new identity.[9] Even crazier? They brought the smallest number of troops—just 200 chiefs. These 200 represented the entire tribe, ready to back David 100 percent. Once again, it's quality over quantity, smarts over swords and shields.

When the tribes gathered for David's coronation, Issachar (along with Zebulun and Naphtali) brought a unique form of wisdom. While others came armed for war, their food-laden donkeys and oxen demonstrated that true leadership requires both the sword and the table. They manifested the truth that deep spiritual and cultural insight, or what I call "sacred semiotics," often happens best around a shared table.[10] In this, Issachar showed that wisdom includes knowing how to unite people through hospitality. Sacred semiotics rises between bread and blessing—like a soufflé that needs both warmth and wisdom. If we fast forward to when this book of 1 Chronicles was written, we discover how Israel's been through some rough times. They're looking back at their history, dreaming of a new king (spoiler alert: they're talking about the Messiah). So when they talk about following David, they're really saying, "Hey, when the real deal shows up, we need to be all in!"

When you think of priests today, you think of highly educated scholars and theologians. When you think of priests in the Bible, you think of Levites. But Levites were basically "meat men" who spent their days presiding at altars of sacrifice where they slit the throats of animals. Who were the scholars of the Scriptures, the theologians, those called to connect the sacred texts to the daily terrains and trajectories of the times?

SEMIOTIC TELL #1

FedEx of the Ancient World: The Issacharians, the tribe of scholar-gardeners, is represented by the animal with such cognitive abilities that it has earned a reputation as one of the most intelligent animals in the animal kingdom—the donkey, the only animal who speaks in the Bible after the serpent.[11] The wealthy and the politicians rode horses. The wise, the judges, and the scholars rode donkeys.[12] Before shipping containers, there were shipping donkeys. The donkey was known for carrying two "burdens" (saddle bags): one burden for himself, the other burden for others, the burden of Torah. How interesting that many people today regard donkeys as simple, stubborn, stupid, when the opposite is the case. One wonders how many times we have made the same mistake with people as we've made with donkeys.

Carry each other's burdens, and in this way you will fulfill the law of Christ.

GALATIANS 6:2 NIV

Issachar was the tribe that tented in the middle on one side of the tabernacle in the wilderness, with Judah on one end (the leading tribe represented by the lion) and Zebulun on the other (the tribe of entrepreneurs, financiers, merchants represented by the wolf).[13] Jesus was born in Bethlehem but bred in Nazareth. Bethlehem belonged to the land of Judah, the most powerful tribe. But Nazareth belonged to the land Joseph originally allocated to Issachar, right on the border with Zebulun.[14] Issachar's lands were adjacent to those of

Zebulun, and Nazareth was situated near the boundary between the two tribes.[15]

Issacharians are not just scholars—they've got street smarts to match their book smarts. They were the ones who knew the story best. That enabled them to read the room (or the era) and know exactly what to do about it. It's a tribe linked to the prophetic tradition, with the prophet Issachar, son of Jacob, receiving a blessing that includes prophetic language.[16]

With apologies to the Shirelles and mamas everywhere, "Jesus said there'd be times like this, there'd be times like this, Jesus said." In a time full of noise and nemeses, we need Issachar energy—the wisdom to understand what's really going on, and the prophetic guts and agrarian gusto to get the hands dirty and do something about it. God sends Daniels for every Nebuchadnezzar. Semioticians are those called to the mission of defibrillating what debilitates and the debilitated.

One of the key semiotic challenges is to distinguish the difference between the "spirit of the age" and the "signs of the times." The "spirit of the age" is the voice of the world as expressed in fashions, fads, public opinion, advertisements, entertainment, values. The "signs of the times" is the voice of God as sounded in narratives, images, words and warnings. The latter is always life-giving. The former is sometimes lethal, sometimes life-giving.

Rejoice, Zebulun, in your going out [i.e., trading], *and you, Issachar, in your tents* [i.e., studying].

DEUTERONOMY 33:18 NIV

SEMIOTIC TELL #1

Surfing Cultural Waves or Swimming Against the Tide?
In the ocean of modern life, we're constantly bombarded by waves. Some are the frothy, ever-changing surf of trends and fads—the "spirit of the age." Others are the deep, powerful currents that have shaped coastlines for millennia—the "signs of the times."

The spirit of the age? It's the siren song of billboards, the whisper of your Instagram feed, the shout of the latest viral TikTok dance. It's Lady Gaga's meat dress and the Tide Pod challenge. Sometimes it's harmless fun, other times it's a riptide pulling you under.

The signs of the times? That's the GPS of the divine, guiding us through life's stormy seas. It speaks through the graffiti on urban walls, the tears of a child, the silence of a forest. It's always a lighthouse, never a mirage. Can you feel the ill winds blowing where they listeth?[17] Can you hear "the voice of the temple saying to the seven angels, 'Go your ways, and pour out the vials of wrath of God upon the earth'?"[18]

Semioticians as cultural navigators must discern when to ride the wave, and when to swim against the current; when are the "spirits" and "signs" life-giving or lethal? Another semiotic secret trick? True wisdom often comes at an angle. It's not about being a square peg in a round hole, but about being the trigonometry in a world obsessed with basic arithmetic. In relationship to culture, to be on the side of the angels is to always be on the side angles.

Or to paraphrase The Ultimate Fisher of Souls, "I will make you anglers of men."[19] Jesus didn't promise to make us net-dragging trawlers, scooping up everything in our path. He said he'd make us anglers—discerning, enduring, skilled in the art of reading the waters and knowing just where to cast our line.

Semioticians cast wisely. The cultural seas are teeming, but not every catch is a keeper.

How can you can tell if the tide is going out or coming in? You don't look at the water. You look at the moored boats, and the direction they are pointing overall. When the tide is coming in, boats will typically point towards the shore. When the tide is going out, boats will typically point towards the sea. Moored boats will naturally align themselves with the direction of the current to offer the least resistance. You don't look straight at the water. You look at the angles of the boats.

---

*This may be a wicked age,
but your lives should redeem it.*

APOSTLE PAUL[20]

Decoding the Divine: Beyond Headlines and Hashtags: "Reading the Times" means more than binge-watching FoxNews/CNN or doom-scrolling through X. Hearing the Spirit's whisper to the church takes more than a *New York Times* subscription or a BBC podcast addiction (both of which I have). Sometimes, these "readings" are more static than signal, more noise than news.

To tune truly in to the frequency of truth, theo-semioticians need a sound system: prayer as your subwoofer, fasting as your amplifier, study as your equalizer, Spirit-testing as your noise-cancellation, and community as your surround sound. Biblical semiotics isn't just reading—it's a "pneumatological"

SEMIOTIC TELL #1

party where the Holy Spirit is the DJ, teaching us to feel the beat of divine signs in the rhythm of culture.

Just as quantum mechanics speaks in mathematics, the divine converses in a symphony of silence and song. Prayer and praise are not merely how we speak to God—they are God's native tongue.

Like a missionary immersed in an unknown culture, we are called to become fluent in the language of light. Yet here lies the beautiful paradox: the Divine first bends down to whisper in our earthly dialects, meeting us in the humble grammar of our humanity.

But the invitation remains—to learn heaven's mother tongue:

> The whisper in the wind,
> The pause between prayers,
> The poetry of patience,
> The sacred syntax of silence.

This holy language cannot be rushed; it is absorbed through the slow osmosis of surrender, learned in the lectionary of listening, mastered in moments of mindful waiting. It is a lifetime's curriculum in the academy of the Spirit, where every quiet moment is a lesson, and every answered prayer, a word made clear.

Outlook and Output: If you're semiotic savvy, or want to drive legally, you don't get behind the wheel without passing a crash course in road-sign reading called a "driver's test." Life's highway is a whole lot trickier than I-5, or I-95. Even our silicon-brained friends struggle with this—it's why self-driving cars took longer to hit the streets than a teenager learning to parallel park.

There's more. Being a sign-reading savant isn't enough. The world—and yes, the church too—is crying out for more than just cultural weathermen predicting storms. The world needs storm chasers, tornado tamers, hurricane whisperers. It's great to interpret the shadow puppets on our cave walls, but let's not forget to find the exit sign. Semioticians do both.

A doctor who only says "Yep, you're sick" isn't winning any awards, or helping anyone. The real MVPs diagnose AND prescribe. That's semiotics with an Issachar swagger—not just pointing at the problem, but painting a path to the "know-what-to-do" solution. Verbalization is not the same as mobilization. Vocalization is not the same as vocation. Signs are not solutions. Signs are signs, which often point the way(s) to solutions but not always.

At the graveside of a parent, every child wishes they had asked more, listened harder, remembered better. But wisdom lies not in the wishing, but in the walking and doing. It's in the recognition that the conversations we have, the moments we share, and the memories we create are the signs and symbols that give life its meaning.

Theo-semioticians turn regret into resolve, and make semiotics not just a study of signs, but a way of life—where every moment is a message, every word a gift, and every memory a treasure to behold.

So, future semioticians, are you ready to graduate from headline skimmers to hieroglyph handlers? Strap in, tune up your human antennae, and let's decode the divine in the

SEMIOTIC TELL #1

everyday. The signs are all around us—if we are ready to read between the lines.

Guidelines: Italian semiotician Umberto Eco proposed guidelines for interpreting signs in his books, especially *The Limits of Interpretation* (1990). The guidelines are:

1. The danger of overinterpretation:
   Signs can't be read at face value. But we need to be cautious of excessive or forced interpretations that go beyond the text's or sign's literal meaning.

2. Contextualization:
   Consider the historical, cultural, and social context in which the sign or text was created and interpreted.

3. Denotation vs. Connotation:
   Distinguish between the literal meaning (denotation) and the associated or implied meaning (connotation) of a sign or text.

4. The intention of the author:
   Consider the author's intention, but also recognize that it may not be the only valid interpretation.

5. The role of the interpreter:
   Acknowledge that the interpreter's own biases and cultural background influence their understanding of the sign or text.[21]

These guidelines promote a sensitive and nuanced

approach to interpretation, avoiding excessive or misleading interpretations.

The Best Glass-case Exhibit of Tell #1? It's called the crown jewel of advertising history—the commercial that didn't just end a TV show, but became a cultural touchstone that still fizzes in murk and muck of memory.

Most of you, my students, have no memory of America in the 1970s. The country is more divided than a pizza at a Super Bowl party. Vietnam War raging, racial tensions boiling, protests erupting like popcorn kernels in a hot pan. Into this maelstrom of mayhem steps ... a soft drink commercial?

But not just any commercial. The Coca-Cola "Hilltop" ad, a.k.a. "Perfect Harmony," didn't just sell soda—it bottled hope, corked unity, and served up a heaping helping of "why can't we all just get along?" In sixty seconds flat, this ad did what politicians, peaceniks, and pundits couldn't—it brought the whole world together on a hilltop, singing in perfect harmony. It wasn't just selling bubbly drinks; it was peddling the American Dream, supersized and served with a smile.

Fast forward to today, and Coca-Cola's got a veritable army of anthropologists, ethnographers, and semioticians working to ensure that carbonated sugar water stays relevant in our increasingly complex world.[22]

But in 1971, when this carbonated catalyst first hit the airwaves during the Super Bowl, it wasn't just an ad; it was a shot of pure, unadulterated spizzerinctum straight to the global psyche. It lifted spirits higher than a helium balloon at a kid's birthday party.

Can you picture a United Nations of fresh-faced youngsters, perched on an Italian hilltop, belting out "I'd Like to

SEMIOTIC TELL #1

Teach the World to Sing" like their lives depended on it? This wasn't just a commercial; it was a semiotic sucker punch that positioned Coca-Cola as the unofficial sponsor of world peace.

In one fizzy, feel-good moment, Coke didn't just refresh the world—it reframed it. It gave us a common jingle when we couldn't find a common ground.

That is the power of knowing your times and knowing what to do. It's not just good advertising; it's Tell #1 in a bottle, ready to be shaken, stirred, and served to a world thirsty for connection.

Buckle Up! In one semiotic moment, the world needed a cold coke. In this theo-semiotic era, maybe this world needs something else that is cold. We're about to dive into a refreshing pool of biblical wisdom that's cooler than the other side of the pillow.

Jesus, the master of metaphor, is giving his disciples their marching orders. He's laying out a mission so big it could make your head spin. But just when you think he's going to drop the mic, he serves up this thirst-quenching gem:

> This is a large work I've called you into, but don't be overwhelmed by it. It's best to start small. Give a cool cup of water to someone who is thirsty, for instance. The smallest act of giving or receiving makes you a true apprentice. You won't lose out on a thing.[23]

Did you catch that four-letter word that's more shocking than a polar bear plunge? C-O-O-L. Or most translations,

C-O-L-D. The original Greek is *"psuchros"* (sounds like a sneeze, packs a punch like a tsunami).

Jesus could have just said "water" and called it a day. But no, he went full-on sommelier and specified "cold" water. In today's world of ice machines and refrigerators, we might shrug this off like dial-up internet. But in Jesus' time? This was bigger than the Super Bowl, the World Cup, and the Olympics combined.

Cold Water: The OG Luxury Experience: In Jesus' day, sipping cold water was like hitting the jackpot in the taste bud lottery. It wasn't your everyday joe; it was the Rolls Royce of refreshment. When it happened, it was a "pinch-me-I-must-be-dreaming" moment of pure, unadulterated joy.

Imagine a world without running water or fridges. Getting cold water meant someone pulled a Forrest Gump for you. They sprinted to the town well, probably dodging donkeys and street vendors, just to bring back nature's coolest cocktail. It wasn't just hospitality; it was a gold medal performance in the Kindness Olympics.

Move over, kale smoothies. Cold water was the OG wellness trend. It wasn't just more pleasing than room-temp H_2O; it was practically a fountain of youth compared to the lukewarm stuff that had been lounging around the house all day. No wonder Samuel Wilder Pease became the Aquaman of his time, inventing the first modern public drinking fountain in NYC in 1832.[24] The man knew his cool!

When Jesus drops this "cold water" bomb, he's not just talking about hydration. He's serving up a tall glass of semiotic significance with a twist of divine wisdom. He's saying, "Want to change the world? Start by being the ice cube in someone's day. Be the unexpected coolness that makes life a little more bearable."

In a world that's often hotter than a jalapeno's armpit, Jesus is calling us to be walking, talking refrigerators of refreshment. He's challenging us to go the extra mile, to make that sprint to the well, to serve up kindness so cool it gives people goosebumps.

Issacharians are sometimes tempted to phone it in with lukewarm efforts, but they remember: Jesus didn't call us to be tepid. He called us to be cool. Ice cold. Theo-semiotics is not just about meeting the moment with a story and song, but meeting the moment by cold-water practices like walking that extra mile[25] and giving that extra coat. Or as Jesus put it in his theology of more, "What do you MORE than others?"

Cold Coke quenches thirst and refreshes the body.

Cold Living Water heals and brings hope.

Living water is the "more" that matters. It's the only "more" that's more.

But there is more....

A command given by seventh-century ascetic St. John Climacus (also known as St. John of the Ladder) in his classic *The Ladder of Divine Ascent*: "If while you pray you find yourself in a state of rapture, of ecstasy, beside yourself, and yet you hear your neighbor asking for a cup of cold water, let go of your ecstasy and give a cup of cold water to your neighbor." Why? "Your ecstasy is private affair, while charity is divine."[26]

The fizz that truly pops: In a world thirsting for meaning, we're called to be more than just vending machines of virtue.

We're to be artesian wells of living water, gushing forth with a coolness that startles the soul.

Coca-Cola sold harmony in a bottle. Theo-semioticians offer eternity in a cup. That's the REAL "real thing." It's what the world really wants today.

So, dear semiotician-in-training, as you embark on this journey of decoding culture and encoding faith, remember:

Your calling isn't just about reading the signs of the times. It's about becoming a sign yourself—a neon-bright, can't-miss-it signpost pointing to the ultimate Source of refreshment. As I put it in another book, the ultimate witness is withness.[27]

The Issacharian mission is to:

> Know the times like a cultural sommelier.
>
> Know what to do like a divine barista.
>
> Serve it up ice-cold, with a side of sizzle and a sprinkle of holy mischief.

In the grand theater of life, where everyone's selling something, theo-semioticians are the ones offering the drink that truly satisfies—not just for a moment, but for eternity.

In God's economy, it's always happy hour, and the Living Water is always on tap. Cold.

Be a Sign of the Times.

SEMIOTIC TELL #1

Source Code Interactives

1. Peter Berger defines a "sign" as "something that stands for something else, and, more technically, as a spoken or written word, a drawn figure, or a material object unified in the mind with a particular cultural concept."[28] How do cultural concepts influence our interpretation of signs, and what happens when different cultures assign different meanings to the same sign?

    Consider everyday examples of signs that represent abstract concepts (e.g., national flags, logos, or emojis). How do these signs shape our perceptions and interactions, and what power dynamics or assumptions do they convey?

2. The donkey is the symbol of the Tribe of Issachar, the semiotic tribe: "Issachar is a rawboned donkey lying down between two saddlebags."[29] Alongside the ancient worship of donkeys, called onolatry, there was an opposing Greek saying, from the eighth to sixth centuries BCE, that portrayed donkeys in another light: "Gold's wasted on donkeys, their treasure is straw." The truth is in the acronym ASS: Acquired Savant Syndrome.

    There is a hidden joke in the biblical story of Balaam and his talking donkey in Numbers 22. The humor lies in a clever wordplay that only works in the King James Version (KJV) translation. When Balaam's donkey speaks, questioning its master's harsh treatment, Balaam responds with "Nay." In the KJV, this "Nay" sounds identical to a donkey's "neigh," creating an ironic echo of the animal's sound in Balaam's own response. Modern translations like the NIV, which use "No" instead of "Nay," unfortunately lose this playful linguistic connection. This type of wordplay was common in ancient Near Eastern storytelling, adding an extra layer of wit to the narrative. Without a semiotic ear and eye, biblical stories remain flat and lose their fun.

What role does humor and wordplay serve in storytelling, and how can it enhance or detract from the message?

How can exploring the historical and cultural context of a story uncover hidden meanings or jokes that might otherwise go unnoticed?

What insights can be gained from considering multiple interpretations of a symbol or story, and how can this approach deepen our understanding of the narrative?

3. Have someone check out Charles Perrault's French literary fairy tale called *Donkeyskin* (1695), a fascinating and complex morality play where a runaway princess hides beneath a repulsive donkey skin and discards it to reveal her true identity. Is it a simple tale of disguise and love, or does it delve into deeper themes like identity and appearance, female agency (the princess has the courage and resourcefulness to take charge of her own life), and the true beauty of donkeys?

4. Ignatian spirituality is known for its mantra "Finding God in all things." But "finding" is a big word. "Finding" requires seeking and study and research and reflection and debate and discussion. Knowing Jesus requires immersion

in the arts and sciences. This is why the tribe of Issachar were the scholars and intellectuals among the twelve Tribes of Israel. Priests (Tribe of Levi) presided at altars and slaughtered animals. Issacharians were the people who knew best the story of Israel so they could best "find" the way forward.

How might this perspective change our understanding of the life of faith?

What are the implications of viewing spiritual discovery as multifaceted, involving intellectual pursuit rather than just a purely emotional or intuitive one?

5. How does this parallel between the scholarly tribe of Issachar and the process of "finding God" challenge or enhance our traditional views of religious study? In what ways might the integration of arts and sciences into spiritual practice deepen one's faith or understanding?

6. How do you see these different approaches to spirituality, the priests (Levites) and the scholars (Issacharians) manifesting in modern religious practice? Is there a poise to be found between ritual observance and intellectual engagement in one's spiritual journey?

7. New England Patriot Malcolm Butler "read the field" better than anyone. The winning play of 2015 Super Bowl XLIX continues to inspire every semiotician: https://www.youtube.com/watch?v=U7rPIg7ZNQ8

Jesus demands that we "pay attention." Butler sure did. He said after-the-fact that he knew the play that the Seahawks were going to run from the formation that he saw. The fact that Butler had read the play and made this split-second determination was obviously true, as he crashed the play with authority, beating the larger Ricardo Lockette to the ball, jumping the route, knocking his manhandled opponent flat, and tearing the ball, and the title, from the arms of the crestfallen Seahawks.

"To the semioticians go the spoils?" Is it true? Discuss.

8. Discuss how semiotics is used in this clip from Season 1, Episode 5 ("The Tie on the Door") of *The Big Bang Theory*: https://www.youtube.com/watch?v=WRV9IH-wB1k&feature=youtu.be

9. "Babette's Feast" (1986) is an excellent case-study for semiotics students, either as a short story by Karen Blixen (writing under the pen name Isak Dinesen) or as a 1987 film adaptation.

Analyze the rich symbolic elements and metaphors through a semiotic lens. For example, the lavish feast can be seen as a sign system representing various cultural, religious, and philosophical concepts.

Discuss how the story prominently features food as a sign system, a means of communication and expression. Analyze how the preparation, presentation, and consumption of food function as signs within the narrative.

Discuss the deciphering of cultural codes and the clash between them—the austere Protestant culture of the small Danish village and the lavish French culinary tradition represented by Babette.

Analyze the story's structure, with its emphasis on the

SEMIOTIC TELL #1

transformative power of art (in this case, culinary art), as a semiotic system in itself.

10. Watch VulfPeck Live at Madison Square Garden: https://www.youtube.com/watch?v=rv4wf7bzfFE

    Why is this like taking a semiotic bath?

11. Check out the semiotics of Snarky Puppy's "Family Dinner" and Lalah Hathaway ("Something"): https://www.youtube.com/watch?v=crw_6bUCwvo

    Don't miss 6:13 into the video, where you will hear something very rare: polyphonic overtone singing. What is significant about this, besides being rare?

12. In Season 1, Episode 6 of *Emily in Paris*, Emily starts dating Thomas Leroy, a professor of semiotics at Université de Paris (also known as the University of Paris or Pantheon-Sorbonne University). He's a charming and intellectual character who shares a romantic interest with Emily and is her date to the ballet performance of *Swan Lake*.

    Can you think of any other characters, fictional or real, that specialize in "signs?"

13. Watch the Netflix drama *Diana*. It is two hours and seventeen minutes. Look for any images that stand out, especially about the mourning rituals.

    Did you notice the mounds of flowers? What did you notice about the mounds of flowers? It was less a mound of flowers than a mound of plastic. What does it say about western culture that we aren't able to put a tribute

65

of flowers on a memorial without separating them from everyone else's and wrapping them in plastic?

14. Ace of Base is a Swedish pop group comprised of three siblings and one friend. Their debut album was the best-selling album of 1994. If every story needs a soundtrack, listen to "The Sign" and see if it might be the theme song for semioticians.

> I saw the sign and it opened up my eyes I saw the sign
>
> Life is demanding without understanding
>
> I saw the sign and it opened up my eyes I saw the sign
>
> No one's gonna drag you up to get into the light where you belong
>
> But where do you belong

How does this fit or not as a semiotic theme song?

15. Semaphores are visual metaphors, signaling mechanisms used for communication. In the ancient world, semaphores were used widely. Tradesmen would be instantly recognizable by the symbols they wore. Carpenters stuck wood chips behind their ears, tailors stuck needles in their tunics, and dyers wore colored rags. On the Sabbath, these symbols were left at home.

Because the second commandment forbade "graven images," there are few Jewish portraits showing dress at the time. Also because of this prohibition, the Jews produced little in the way of paintings, sculpture, or carvings.

SEMIOTIC TELL #1

(Have someone read the story of a young Hasidic boy's passion for art named Asher Lev in Chaim Potok's semiotic masterpiece *My Name Is Asher Lev* [1972]). The masonry and carpentry of the day appear utilitarian. One notable exception to the commandment seems to be the tolerance of dolls for children.

a. What semaphores can you think of that we use today?

Let's prime the pump a bit.

Uniforms and logos worn by police officers, firefighters, company employees.

Traffic lights and signs: Red, yellow, and green lights direct traffic.

Hand signals: Police, construction workers, and cyclists use hand gestures to communicate.

Flag signals: Maritime flags convey messages between ships.

Emojis, Brand logos, warning labels, color coding (red for urgent), categories (blue for boys), or themes (green for eco-friendly).

b. How have semaphores evolved over time, and what drives these changes?

c. In what ways do modern semaphores maintain or depart from their ancient counterparts?

d. What cultural or societal factors influence the design and use of semaphores?

e. How do semaphores impact nonverbal communication, and what are their limitations?

f. What role do semaphores play in shaping identity, profession, or affiliation?

g. How have technological advancements impacted the use and design of semaphores?

h. What are the implications of the second commandment on Jewish art, architecture, and cultural expression?

i. In what ways have semaphores been used historically to convey social status or hierarchy?

Semiotic Tell #2

Water Turning to Wine (and Signs to Sacrament)

The rabbis of old used stories to guide their people, whereas we ministers often guide our people with ideas and theories. We need to become storytellers again and to discover that God's truth is revealed in the concrete and personal language of the story.

HENRI NOUWEN[1]

SEMIOTICIANS ARE ALCHEMISTS OF MEANING who turn signs into stories, stories into significance, and significance into sacrament.

Life is a series of signal moments. Each moment is laden with meaning. While perceiving these moments is one feat, truly comprehending their essence is another. Deciphering signs is challenging in itself, but discerning divine action in the world and recognizing the Holy Spirit's evangelizing work in popular culture and piety requires both training and faith. The ultimate goal in theo-semiotics is to transmute these signs into a narrative of profound significance, potentially evolving into a sacrament of divine presence.

This concept echoes in the Gospel accounts of religious

leaders challenging Jesus. They demanded a sign from heaven to validate his claims. Jesus urged them to observe the signs already present in their world rather than seeking new ones. He emphasized the futility of demanding fresh signs when numerous indicators already surrounded them. Gesturing towards the temple, Jesus prophesied: "All these things you see—the time will come when not a single stone will be left on another; every one of them will be thrown down."[2]

Amidst this array of significations, where does true significance lie? As Wheaton College's Crystal Downing puts it in her book that taught us Truth is not weights on either end of a bar bell, but opposite sides of the same coin, "semioticians analyze how signs make meaning and what gives them value."[3] This encapsulates the essence of the semiotic journey—from observation to interpretation, from meaning to sacred significance.

A sign has two aspects: a *significant* (signifier) and a *signifie* (signified). The *signifier* is a mental representation of a perceptible pattern of sound. The *signified* is the relational linguistic value of a sign, not a thing but the notion of a thing.[4] A sacrament is when the sign and signifier become one. Jesus himself is the biggest "SIGN"—he is our Ultimate Sacrament, the sign of the new people of God, the sacrament of God's salvation. Jesus is the primal or primordial sacrament, and his body the church.

The incarnation is the greatest semiotic act in history. In the words of David Bentley Hart:

> The incarnation is the Father's supreme rhetorical gesture, in which all he says in creation is given its perfect emphasis. This is particularly

evident in the Gospel accounts of Christ's miracles: the healing of infirmities, the raising of the dead, the feeding of the hungry, even the transformation of water into wine. These are not acts that manipulate or negate the order of creation in order to achieve an astounding effect; in them the goodness of creation is reaffirmed, its peace is restored: they repeat God's gift of creation by imparting joy in the good things of the world—food and wine, fellowship and rejoicing, life and vision and health—to those in whom such joy is lacking. Christ's miracles—as do all the aspects of his life and ministry—constitute a *semeiosis* (John's Gospel, in fact calls them *semia*) that restores the original semiosis of the world, the language of divine glory, and reorients all the signs of creation toward the everlasting sign of God who walks among them.[5]

The question is not, "Will Jesus show up today?" Or even worse: "What can I do to get Jesus to show up today?" Jesus is constantly present, forever near. He shows up in the quiet moments,

> in the quandaries of thought,
> in the chaotic times,
> in the midst of hardship,
> through acts of kindness.

He appears in unexpected places, and in the wounds of life and our world.

The real question is, "Will we show up where Jesus is showing up?" Will we open our eyes to see, and our hearts to embrace Him, wherever we may be? Every place we plant our feet, there is a sign: "Jesus Christ is here."

All my writing and research is based on a simple semiotic truth: We don't meet people; we meet God in people. You don't meet people where they are; you meet Jesus where he is in the midst of people where they are. These are the unspoken words at every encounter of a Jesus human during the course of a day: "What aspect of the Almighty are you revealing to me today?" "What divine drama are you staging?" Is God merely a character in our stories, or the author and protagonist? To discover Him, we must learn to read the Bible, and we must learn to read human narratives.

I feel the original Adam reviving within me.

NATHANIEL HAWTHORNE

AFTER RETURNING FROM BROOK FARM[6]

Story is the sacred script. Elie Wiesel intuited it: Israel, the world's first storytellers, were chosen to narrate God's epic because they loved stories so much. Jesus perfected the art, turning parables into portals to the Kingdom.

All Jesus did that day was tell stories—
a long storytelling afternoon.

MATTHEW 13:34 MSG

SEMIOTIC TELL #2

Jesus was the consummate storyteller. A master of the parable, He transformed ordinary tales into profound revelations. His words, like seeds scattered on fertile soil, took root in the hearts of listeners, sprouting understanding and transformation. Through His narratives, the Kingdom of God became tangible, a realm accessible to all. Jesus' approach to encountering the divine through stories and signs invites us to look for God's revelation in the everyday narratives of those around us, echoing the semiotics of meeting Jesus in the midst of the signs and stories of people where they are.

St. Thomas Aquinas highlighted the role of sensory experience and imagination in human understanding. He wrote, "Man cannot understand without images."[7] Ironically, in 1966 *Time Magazine* published the first cover in its history with no image on it. The magazine cover carried only three words on a black background: "IS GOD DEAD?" But God has such a sense of humor. In five short years (1971), a cover of *Time* magazine proved Aquinas right and carried the title "The Jesus Revolution."

The Thing's the Thing: The highly-charged, hotly-contested word "sacrament" comes from Latin *sacramentum*, and Latin is not one of the original languages of New Testament. Translators of the Greek New Testament started rendering the Greek "*mysterion*" (or transliterated into Latin *mysterium*) as "sacrament." None of these translations involve a "rite" other than making a sign or a brand or a seal in the flesh (tattoo) that showed you had "sacramented" yourself, pledged your loyalty and allegiance, to a commander. In other words, "sacrament" and "mystery" were interchangeable in the first couple of centuries, with the added component of some kind of maturity that meant being sacramental.[8]

One of the great saints died a few years ago. His name was Mr. Rogers. When Mr. Rogers arrived in heaven, God greeted him personally and said, "Welcome to my neighborhood."

And God gave him a sweater.

Interesting how one artifact can sum up a life. I've wondered what artifact might represent mine. A boarding pass—the symbol of spending too much of my life being, not water-boarded in dark rooms, but wind-boarded strapped in planes?

People need thingies. Matter matters. Every religion has to have its holy things … its holy objects, its sacred relics. Matter has a granular texture, and the semiotic significance of tangible objects cannot be overstated.

From a semiotic standpoint, the best gifts are used items, heirlooms haloed with memories, artifacts "stuffed" with stories. We think we are being cheap if we give someone a used item. But we express less care if we gift a story-less, store-bought item with no significance or provenance other than the store. The store is not a story. It's hard to make a storybook Christmas out of storyless presents. When our homes or our churches stop being a storehouse of stories and become a treasure trove of silver and gold, gadgets and gizmos, pots and pans, points and props, it ceases being a Jesus dwelling.

Semioticians would do well to acknowledge the profound impact of the physical world. By sacramentalizing material objects, we don't seek to possess them, but to infuse them with meaning. Sacraments elevate the mundane, revealing the intricate integration of the spiritual and the physical.

SEMIOTIC TELL #2

Semiotics is the lens that turns life into a living Sacrament. Through semiotics, every sign is sacred, every symbol a sacrament. What if every moment was a Mass? Welcome to the world of semiotics.

Sacrament of the Table: Take, for instance, the sacrament of the table. Food and drink transcend mere sustenance; they become vessels of grace, as exemplified in the communion ritual. Jesus' parting words, "Do this in remembrance of me," underscore the importance of embodiment. The Eucharist is more than a reenactment, it is a re-enchantment that weaves together the spiritual and the material, reminding us that our relationships are inextricably linked to the physical world.

That is why semioticians sacramentalize the material, not for purposes of ownership but for meaning. Sacraments elevate matter, testifying to the degree to which relationships require the physical and the material.

In the grand theater of faith, we've been staring at the wrong prop as the centerpiece of worship. Spotlights blind us. Curtains conceal. But the real action?

It's happening offstage, where the aroma of authenticity wafts from a wooden surface we've literally looked over but often overlook: the table. Welcome to the semiotics of supper, where meaning isn't just served—it's shared.

Stage Fright vs. Table Rights: The stage screams, "Look at me!" The table whispers, "Let's look at each other."

One is a monologue, the other is a trialogue.

One is a performance, the other is a potluck.

We've become experts at stage management, but amateurs at table manners.

It's time for a cosmic change.

Jesus—The Original Table Turner: The Messiah wasn't just flipping tables in the temple; He was flipping our understanding of sacred space.

His pulpit? Often a dining table.

His sermon? Usually a shared meal.

His altar call? "Pass the bread, please."

The Table is the "source and summit" of life, and the eucharist is the "source and summit" of the life of faith and the church. Where is Christ most present and likely to be discovered? Not sitting at conference tables, or convention gatherings or even church pews. But at the table of the eucharist where the church family gathers and at the table of the home where the family gathers to eat and at those public tables where the community gathers for the common good.

What if our semiotic spotlight swiveled? From floodlights and footlights to candlelight? Instead of decoding the dramatics, let's decipher the place settings. Instead of analyzing the applause, let's interpret the "Mmms!," "Amens," and "Heavenly" between bites. The stage may sign autographs, but the table signs hearts.

Want to cook up a revival? Start with your dining room.

Swap the spotlight for candlelight. Trade monologues for "pass the salt-of-the-earth" dialogues. Exchange standing ovations for seated conversations. Those might be the best "signs" of revival and revolution.

The table isn't just a sign—it's an invitation. To authenticity. To community. To a feast where the menu is meaning, Jesus is Honored Host, and everyone's both host and guest. So, Seminarians, are you ready to trade your stage fright for some table rights? The next act of faith might just start with these four words: "Dinner's ready. Come eat." The church bell is a dinner bell.

The Symbol as Real Presence: Let's dive into this rich feast of symbolism and semiotics, shall we? Imagine we're at a grand table, laden with the history of church debates and sprinkled with the spice of Greek wisdom. On one end sits Ulrich Zwingli, adamantly pushing away the bread and wine, insisting they're mere placeholders. At the other, we find John Calvin, savoring every morsel, his palate detecting nuances his contemporaries missed. Martin Luther and John Wesley are at another table entirely because they don't like the way the others were using the word "symbol." A few times Luther carefully used the German word "*Zeichen*" or "*Sinnbild*" to describe the Lord's Supper, but he was extremely cautious and critical of its use in relation to the sacrament.

The bread we break and the wine we drink are more than just symbols—they hold the power to unite us with the divine. To grasp this truth, let's break bread together and explore the true meat of the matter: the original meaning of the word "symbol."

Imagine two ancient Greeks, each clutching a shard of pottery. These fragments weren't mere trash; they were promises made tangible, commitments held in the hand. When entering a contract or covenant, instead of signing a document, they'd break a prized vessel, and each party would take a shard. When reunited, these shards—called *symbolon*—served as visible evidence that the contract or covenant had been honored. Symbols often speak louder than words, whispering of shared purpose and unbreakable bonds.

This ancient understanding of symbols has profound

implications for a semiotic understanding of sacred rituals, such as the Lord's Supper. We often mistakenly reduce the bread and wine to mere symbols, devoid of any substantial reality. However, a symbol's potential need not be limited to representation; it can be recognized as a physical manifestation of a transcendent reality. True liberation lies in living through living, life-giving symbols.

In the Lord's Supper, the bread and wine are tangible expressions of Christ's real presence, not just metaphors for His body and blood. Just as the broken shards of pottery symbolized a shared purpose and unbreakable bond, so too do the broken shards of bread and poured-out drops of wine symbolize the unity between Christ and the disciple. This understanding of symbols transforms our understanding of the Lord's Supper, inviting us to experience the profound reality of Christ's presence in the simplest of elements—bread and wine.

The biblical accounts of the institution of the Lord's Supper provide compelling evidence for the idea of real presence. Jesus' words, "This is my body broken" and "This is my blood poured out" are not mere poetic expressions but rather a declaration of the profound reality that the bread and wine are truly shards of His body and blood. The idea of real presence is not only consistent with Jesus' divine nature but also with the transfigurative power of the Lord's Supper.

A symbol is more than just a representation; it is an instrument for evoking emotions, re-membering the past, inspiring action, and creating a sense of community. As disciples gather around the table, partaking of the bread and wine, they are not merely engaging in a symbolic act; they

SEMIOTIC TELL #2

are entering into a communion with Christ and with one another. It is not merely a ritual to be performed or a representation of a memory but a sacred symbolic encounter with the divine—real presence in real time, an "outward and visible sign of an inward reality and grace."

Let's express it in terms of our metaphorical menu. Symbols aren't just appetizers; they're the main course of human communication. They're also the secret sauce that adds flavor where words fall flat. Think of a lion—not just any lion, but the Lion of Judah. In one image, we taste power, victory—and paradoxically—the gentle sacrifice of the Lamb.

Symbols are the comfort food of ideas, easy to digest where pointed arguments might stick in our throats. They're the bread and butter of explaining the inexplicable—like the Trinity, a concept so complex it begs for visual aids.

And for dessert? The sweet, sometimes bittersweet, emotional punch that symbols pack. But beware! Like a family recipe passed down through generations, symbols can lose their potency. What once exploded with flavor might, for later diners, taste as bland as unseasoned mashed potatoes. Semioticians call for a quickening of symbols, a contextualization that tantalizes a twenty-first century palate.

The profound influence of table fellowship in my life traces back to my mentor, historical theologian and semiotic satirist Charles Merritt Nielsen. When he received a modest inheritance from his father, Nielsen made a choice that embodied deep wisdom: rather than pursuing material luxuries or personal comforts, he invested in life-changing relationships. Several times each week, he would gather his seminary students around restaurant tables across Rochester,

New York, creating vibrant spaces of dialogue reminiscent of Martin Luther's famous *Table Talk* (*Tischreden*).

What made these gatherings particularly remarkable was Nielsen's generous spirit. Despite being a committed TULIP Calvinist, he welcomed students of every theological persuasion to join him at some of Rochester's finest establishments. There, over carefully prepared meals, he served up something far more nourishing than just food—he offered wisdom, perspective, and life-changing conversations that I still remember to this day. This profound example of intentional table fellowship has shaped my entire ministry and writings, flowering into works like *A Cup of Coffee at the SoulCafe*, *SoulSalsa*, *The Jesus Prescription for a Healthy Life*, and *From Tablet to Table*—not to mention my hospitality sanctuary and "advance" center Sanctuary Seaside (Orcas Island, Washington). Nielsen's legacy showed me how a simple table, even one prepared by someone else, could become sacred space, where food and fellowship merge to nurture for a lifetime mind, body, spirit.

So, as we clear the table, let's never forget something, my budding semioticians: in the great banquet of ideas, symbols are both the dishes we serve and the shared act of breaking bread together. They connect us, nourish us, and invite us to taste the divine in the everyday.

The Lord's Supper invites us into a sacramental way of life, where symbols are not mere representations but vehicles of divine grace and vows of allegiance. Just as the bread and wine become channels of Christ's presence, our daily actions and encounters can be infused with sacred meaning. This sacramental worldview transforms how we perceive and interact with the world around us. Through repeated participation in these sacramental symbols, we're not just remembering a past event, but actively participating in an ongoing mystery.

A sacramental approach to symbols doesn't just change our understanding—it changes us, molding us more into the image of Christ and binding us closer to our communities of faith. Or as Dr. Kevin Olds, who also teachers semiotics at Kairos University, likes to remind his students, "You are what you eat."

Abductive Method as Hoisting a Hypothesis: Understanding the abductive method is crucial to semiotics because it is the foundation of how meaning is generated from signs and symbols.[9] For the godfather of semiotics Charles Sanders Peirce, abduction is the primary mode of reasoning that drives the interpretation of signs because it allows for creative insight.[10]

Abduction is the process of intuitively guessing or proposing a tentative connection between a sign and its possible meaning, based on incomplete information. Rather than starting from established facts (deduction) or gathering data to establish patterns (induction), abduction deals with forming explanatory hypotheses that can later be confirmed or refined. This process is essential for uncovering deeper layers of meaning, connecting seemingly disparate signs, and understanding how meaning evolves within different contexts. Without abduction, the flexibility needed for interpreting complex, evolving systems of signs would be severely limited.

Imagine a scientist raising a flag (the hypothesis) on a flagpole to see how it flies in the breeze of inquiry. In abduction, the hypothesis is not a certainty but a creative, informed guess designed to explain surprising or puzzling observations. Just like hoisting the flag to assess its visibility and reaction to wind, the scientist lifts up and spins the hypothesis to see if it holds up under scrutiny and aligns with available evidence. The key is that abduction is the first step in reasoning, where ideas are proposed to generate explanations that can later be tested (through deduction and induction) to refine or discard them.

In the same way, if you want to see the invisible you hoist a sail or throw up a flag. Suddenly the invisible becomes visible, and the wind becomes watchable. In life you see the shape of the invisible by hoisting hypotheses and launching adventures and risking safety. The shape of the invisible is found by looking at the visible with discernment, discretion, and care. If you want to see God in your life, put some wind in your sails. Let your guard down. Be open to all manner of abductive adventure.

Could comfort and convenience of deduction and induction be killing us?

Second Life Learning: That spirit of adventure took me, and some of you, to Second Life, the online virtual world, which was launched on 23 June 2003 by Linden Lab. As some of you will remember, my doctoral students at George Fox University were the first to use Second Life as a "classroom" for learning as part of a degree program. Each student had to create their own avatar, interact with others online, build virtual learning environments (Ocean, Mountain, Desert campuses), and engage in various activities within the digital space. Your avatar could pull a book off a shelf, peruse its table of contents, and then order it directly from Amazon through

SEMIOTIC TELL #2

Second Life. You knew there was a metaverse before most had heard the word "meta."

At about the same time, the lack of a sense of openness to the future led a group of students at another university to petition the Dean of the Seminary to take a required course on evangelism at a different seminary because their professor (me) had integrated social media engagement into the syllabus. Social media was ostensibly "elitist, racist, classist" they declared in their petition, and should be eschewed and denounced by clergy.

Semiotics is a reminder that the challenge of life is to live before you die. Life isn't a dress rehearsal—it's a one-time performance. Use it or lose it. Live fiercely. Love deeply. Learn fearlessly. Dream relentlessly. Or risk becoming a ghost in your own story, sleepwalking through the greatest gift you'll ever receive.

The homeless crisis? It's not just about mental health. It's a meaning crisis, a semiotic breakdown. Loss of meaning comes when you no longer see essence behind existence, referent behind sign, or subject behind object. When we lose our sense of trust, our ability to "read" the signs of life, our minds crumble. Society's breakdown isn't just in our synapses—it's in our souls.

So semiotics is a wake-up call to find your fire. Because life's meaning isn't hidden in some distant philosophy—it's forged in the crucible of adventurous, abductive, semiotic living. Don't just exist in a world that offers "meaning" about as meaningful as "Your call is important to us, please hold."

The meaning of life is living like you mean it.

This isn't just a catchy phrase I made up. It's a semiotic

revelation. In semiotics, we study how meaning is created and communicated. Semioticians help others apply this to life itself.

Life as a sign: Your existence is a symbol, constantly interpreted by others and yourself.

Missional living as signification: When you live missionally, you're actively creating meaning, not just passively existing.

Authenticity as the signified: "Living like you mean it" signifies authenticity, passion, and deliberate choice.

Actions as signifiers: Your choices, your pursuits, your relationships—these are the signifiers that point to the deeper meaning of your life.

Cultural context: The interpretation of a "meaningful life" varies across cultures, but the act of intentional living transcends these boundaries.

In essence, you're not just interpreting the signs around you—you're creating them. You're writing the text of your life, and "living like you mean it" ensures that text is rich with significance, not mere noise in the semiotic landscape. By living semiotically, you're not just existing in the world of signs—you're actively shaping it, adding layers of meaning to the complex web of signification that is human existence.

EPIC Life:

Story+Imagination+Play = Beautiful Life:

Roberto Benigni's cinematic equation isn't just celluloid magic—it's a blockbuster blueprint for living large.[11] Let's roll the highlight reel:

Story: Your life's not a dry documentary, it's a

page-turning thriller. Every scar, every triumph, every plot twist—they're all chapters in your bestseller.

Imagination: Crank up your mind's green screen. Dream in IMAX, create in 4K, and find meaning that's Oscar-worthy. Your brain is the special effects department of your soul.

Play: Life's playground is always open. Whether you're swinging from the monkey bars or conquering the jungle gym, keep that recess bell ringing in your heart.

Mix these blockbuster ingredients and—BAM!—you've got a life that's not just beautiful, it's box office gold.

Benigni's formula isn't just clever. It's a universal remote for tuning into life's HD channels. We're all storytellers, spinning yarns around the campfire of existence. Our imagination? It's the ultimate streaming service, broadcasting hopes and fears in surround sound. And play? It's not the opposite of work, as you've learned from me before,[12] it's the antidote to a grayscale world.

So grab your director's chair and megaphone. It's time to shout "Action!" on the set of your beautiful life. Remember: in this production, you're the star, Jesus is the screenwriter, and the Holy Spirit is the special effects wizard. Now that's what I call a Hollywood ending.

Power and Peril, Diagnosis and Prescription: In the intricate web of meaning that surrounds us, semiotics emerges as both a lens and a tool. It is not merely about deciphering signs and signals; it's about navigating the complex semiosphere that envelops human existence, transforming mere signifiers into profound significances that shape our collective "lifeworld" (*Lebenswelt*).

Signs are not solutions in themselves, but rather portals to potential resolutions. They are the very fabric of our perceived reality, the building blocks of meaning (as posited by Ferdinand de Saussure's dyadic model of sign).[13] The true power of semiotics lies not in passive observation, but in active engagement with the sign systems that construct our social, cultural, and personal realities.

Through the lens of semiotics, Rob Henderson's *Troubled* (2024) examines how abstract ideological signifiers have supplanted material symbols in elite status marking. His analysis reveals how the upper class has shifted from conspicuous consumption to what he terms "luxury beliefs"—a complex system of ideological signs that simultaneously mark social distinction and function as barriers to class mobility. These belief-signs operate as powerful semiotic markers, with the privileged class encoding status through ideological positions rather than material displays. These "beliefs" are more preached than practiced, with devastating social consequences as these semiotic status symbols that signify membership in the elite club "trickle down" and ripple through class hierarchies, with the working class bearing the burden of elite signification systems that privilege high-brow values over health and wellbeing.

Henderson's *Troubled* traces how a troubled childhood illuminates the deeper troubles of a society where elite "luxury beliefs" have become both symptoms and sources of social disruption and disfunction.[14]

Semiotics, like any powerful tool, is morally ambivalent. It can be wielded for enlightenment or manipulation, for liberation or oppression. The application of semiotic knowledge in financial markets or political propaganda demonstrates its potential for both creation and destruction. As Umberto Eco warned, we must be vigilant against the "semiotic guerrilla warfare" that can subvert meaning for nefarious ends.

The Shadow Side of Semiotic Mastery: The most effective semioticians in history often operated from the shadows of moral ambiguity. The Third Reich's mastery of symbols, images, branding, and propaganda serves as a chilling reminder of semiotics' potential for evil.[15] Their understanding of what Roland Barthes would later call "mythologies"—the cultural connotations that transform signs into powerful ideological tools—allowed them to craft a narrative that resonated deeply with collective unconscious desires and fears. The swastika is a powerfully allusive symbol. Nazis had the most impressive military uniforms ever conceived by the human imagination. They knew what they were doing. They fought for souls as well as war booty.

The notion that "God has planted the future in the present" aligns with Charles Sanders Peirce's concept of "unlimited semiosis"—the idea that every sign points to another sign in an endless chain of meaning. Our task, then, is not to predict the future, but to engage in "abductive reasoning"—making the best hypothesis based on limited information, and continually refining our intuitions and empirical understandings as new signs emerge.

Theological Roots of Semiotic Thought: Augustine and Aquinas, in their explorations of signs and sacraments, laid foundational concepts for what would become modern semiotics. Their insights resonate with contemporary semiotic theory:

Augustine's assertion that "things are learned by means of signs"[16] anticipates the twentieth-century "linguistic turn" in philosophy and social sciences, recognizing language and symbolism as the primary mediators of human understanding.

Aquinas's definition of sacraments as signs that "make men holy"[17] prefigures the performative aspect of signs—the idea that signs don't just represent reality, but can actively shape and transform it, a concept later developed by J. L. Austin and John Searle in speech act theory.

In conclusion, semiotics is not just an academic discipline, but a powerful praxis for understanding and shaping the world. It requires us to be both keen observers and ethical actors, constantly negotiating the boundary between interpretation and creation, between decoding the world and rewriting its narrative.

Turn water into wine, and signs into sacrament.

SEMIOTIC TELL #2

source code interactives

1. If humans are indeed sign-making creatures, and we live in sign-making communities, what kind of a sign-maker are you? What kind of signs are you making? We express our identity, our "selfhood," in the making of forms and signs.

2. Is a sign still a sign if no one can read the sign?

3. Irish essayist Chris Arthur, in his book *Reading Life* (2017), tells the story of a lifetime of omnivorous "reading" (poetry, prose, memories, natural histories, essays), that also includes the process of "reading" aspects of life. For example, he "reads" his ten-year-old daughter's feet ("Where will they take her?") or his four antique walking sticks. He "reads" a whale's tooth, a path near the University of St Andrew's between a fence and a hedge. He reads tracks in the snow at Lumb Bank, just beyond the house where a photograph of Ted Hughes presides over gatherings of students and tutors.[18]

    What are some things that you "read"? What books? What bibelot? What beliefs? What activities?

    Here are two things that I'm always reading: tags on towels (which I then remove), and powerlines and telephone poles (which I hate).

4. Like the scribes of Jesus' day, we admire deeply our prophets, erecting memorials to revere them and sponsoring pilgrimages to enshrine them in our memories. But who are the only prophets we so honor? Dead ones.

Have we ever met a living prophet we didn't persecute and hate and try to bring down?

Martin Luther called his seal, a rose, "a symbol of my theology."[19] Here are his words to a friend explaining the meaning of the colors and forms of his emblem:

> There is first to be a cross, black [and placed] in a heart, which should be of its natural color, so that I myself would be reminded that faith in the Crucified saves us ... Even though it is a black cross, [which] mortifies and [which] also should hurt us, yet it leaves the heart in its [natural] color [and] does not ruin nature; ... Such a heart is to be in the midst of a white rose, to symbolize that faith gives joy, comfort, and peace; in a word it places the believer into a white joyful rose; for [this faith] does not give peace and joy as the world gives and, therefore, the rose is to be white and not red, for white is the color of the spirits and of all the angels. Such a rose is to be in a sky-blue field [symbolizing] that such joy in the Spirit and in faith is a beginning of the future heavenly joy; ... And around this a gold ring, [symbolizing] that in heaven such blessedness lasts forever.[20]

What seal might symbolize your theology? Can you together sketch out a seal that might symbolize the uniqueness of your church?

5. Read in unison the following passage:

And God said, "Let there be lights in the

SEMIOTIC TELL #2

firmament of the heaven to divide the day from the night; and let them be for signs and for seasons, and for days and years" ... And God made two great lights: the greater light to rule the day, and the lesser light to rule the night. He made the stars also (Genesis 1:14, 16 NKJV).

Discuss how our agrarian ancestors took those words seriously, "let them be for signs," and "planted by the signs." They planted crops that would produce their fruits above the ground during the waxing moon (the time between a new moon and a full moon—when the moon is getting bigger), while plants that produce their crop below the ground were planted during a waning moon (the time between a full moon and a new moon—when the moon is shrinking).

Do you know of any other stories of how the lives of our ancestors depended on "reading the signs"?

6. Some people can't get "signs" ... and they never will. Do you know of anyone like this?

Ever see Jesus put up for rent? Well, I have! Picture this picture I took: a good ol' barn roof proudly declaring "Jesus is Lord." But wait, there's more! Slapped right on top is a "For Lease" sign with a phone number. Now we've got ourselves a holy real estate opportunity: "Jesus is FOR LEASE"! Call now, limited time offer!

I couldn't help but wonder on Facebook: Is this what happens when the church falls on hard times? Are we now outsourcing our savior? Is it "Jesus is Lord" or "Jesus is For Lease"? And here's the million-dollar question: Is leasing Jesus a step up or down from selling Him outright? At least with a lease, you get Him back eventually, right?

Some folks, "Bless their heart and gizzard" (as my Appalachian gramma used to say), couldn't play with the sign or see the forest for the trees. While most of us were having a theological yard sale of ideas, dear old Ethel (let's call her that) was busy posting and defending the barn owners' sign-placement skills. "Well, they had to put it somewhere!" she exclaimed, while the rest of us were debating whether Jesus prefers month-to-month or long-term contracts.

It's like watching someone bring a spoon to a knife fight—well-intentioned, but hilariously off-target. Poor Ethel stood there, puzzled as a penguin in a palm tree, while the rest of us metaphorically rolled in the aisles.

So, next time you're driving by and see "Jesus for Lease," remember: some see sacrilege, some see a bargain, and some ... well, some just see a barn with an identity crisis!

What would you see?

7. How do you personally experience the difference between "table" and "stage" in your religious or community gatherings? Can you share examples of each?

8. In what ways does the metaphor of the table represent intimacy, equality, and shared sustenance in your life or faith community? How does this differ from your experiences with "stage" environments of flood lights, fog machines, etc.?

SEMIOTIC TELL #2

9. Consider the idea of boundaries dissolving at the table. How might this impact our understanding of roles like "leader" and "follower" in religious contexts?

10. Jesus often used table fellowship in his ministry. How do you think this approach challenged the religious norms of his time? How might it challenge our current practices?

11. What "hidden meanings and power structures" do you think are reinforced by emphasizing stage-centric religious gatherings? How might these impact different members of the community?

12. Imagine your faith community shifted focus from "stage" to "table." What specific changes might occur in:

    a. Worship practices?

    b. Leadership structures?

    c. Community relationships?

    d. Outreach and mission work?

    How might emphasizing "table" over "stage" change our understanding of spiritual authenticity? What new opportunities or challenges might this present?

13. In what ways do you see the "spectacle of the stage" manifesting in modern religious practice? How does this align with or diverge from your understanding of your faith's core teachings?

14. Consider the phrase "genuine over performative" or "participative over performative?" What does this mean to you in the context of your spiritual life? Can you share

an experience where you've felt the difference between these two approaches?

15. How might a "table-centric" approach to faith change the way we interact with those outside our religious communities? What new forms of outreach or dialogue might emerge?

16. What potential drawbacks or challenges do you see in emphasizing the "table" over the "stage" in religious practice? How might these be addressed?

17. Reflect on a meaningful "table experience" in your life. How did it differ from a "stage experience"? What made it significant?

18. How might the concept of "table as primary signifier" reshape our understanding of sacred spaces? What would a worship space designed around this concept look like?

19. In what ways does your faith tradition already incorporate "table" elements? How might these be expanded or emphasized?

Consider Sweet's phrase "radical reinterpretation of religious practice." What does this mean to you? What aspects of your faith might be transformed by a shift towards table-centric semiotics?

20. What if semiotics is like X-ray vision for the soul, revealing the sacred beneath the skin of the everyday?

21. How can semiotics help you see God's fingerprints on every page of life's story?

SEMIOTIC TELL #2

22. When you see this list of words "Metaphors, Mantras, Memes and Shemas," how surprised are you to see "Shemas?"

    A Shema (Hebrew for "Hear") is the Jewish confession of faith made up of three scriptural texts (Deuteronomy 6:4–9, 11:13–21; Numbers 15:37–41). Together with appropriate prayers it forms an integral part of the evening and morning services. Pious Jews hope to die with the words of the Shema on their lips.

    Paul Patton has encouraged Christians to create their own "Shemas," their own summarial statements of faith, or what he called "hubs of the cognitive wheel." What if every month or every change in the liturgical calendar we were to compose a new shema worthy of reciting it or meditating on its two to seven times a day. By the way, if you can't memorize it, it's not a shema.

    Can you compose one? Might not the first shema be Adam naming the animals, creating categories and constructs and concepts.[21]

23. One author has suggested that the opposite of play is not work, but sadness, because play is another word for joy. What do you think?

Semiotic Tell #3

The Mirror's Blind Spot

WHAT IS MOST IMPORTANT IS not always what is in the mirror in front of you. The silver mirror reflects only a sliver of reality. It's the world behind and around and beyond the glass that shapes the true narrative. Semioticians illuminate the grander story, "reading" and revealing how the divine is at play in the larger story of the world and the church.

Opportunities often hide in plain sight, invisible to those who see only through the filter of their profession, preferences, or politics.

> We do not have to discover in which of several people Christ is to be found; we must look for Him in them all. And not in an experimental spirit, to discover whether He is in them or not, but with the absolute certainty that He is. Christ does not choose to be known through outward appearances—even the appearance of virtue.[1]

This quote (and the next one) from British Catholic artist and mystic Caryll Houselander (d. 1954) is part of a chapter titled "The Hidden Christ," a chapter of her book *The Reed of God* (1944). In this chapter, Houselander discusses the importance of seeing Christ in all people, regardless of their outward appearance. She argues that Christ is not limited to the religious or the virtuous, but is present in everyone. She writes:

> Christ is not a possession of the religious; He is the possession of the whole world. He is not a possession of the virtuous; He is the possession of the whole human race. He is not a possession of any one group or class or nation; He is the possession of all.

Read the Room: Semiotics is the art of "reading" all ... all of life ... and the Spirit. The church's hapless reading of the world is only outmatched by its haphazard reading of the Word: failed cultural exegesis, flawed biblical exegesis. All of these come into play as we look at what the church will be facing in the next two decades and beyond.

To help people see beyond themselves to what they cannot see and if they are still not seeing it, then just keep describing, holding forth, and loving them toward visions and vistas they do not know exist: this is the theo-semiotic challenge.

New research has revealed how it is easier to speak honestly, and hear the truth, unadorned and unadulterated, in a car journey because the driver and passenger look straight ahead, not at each other. The setup of sitting side-by-side in a car rather than face-to-face somehow facilitates more direct, unvarnished communication. The car journey allows for a kind of emotional distance or indirectness that paradoxically enables greater truthfulness and openness between the occupants.[2]

SEMIOTIC TELL #3

Semiotic "reading" is more a matter of the ears than the eyes, of picking up the vibrations and the frequencies and the silences than the chatter and the clatter or the appearances. Two to one, Pentecost is more about the gift of ears than the gift of tongues.

Early in the movie *Oppenheimer*, the father of quantum physics Niels Bohr, known by his colleagues as either "The Pope of Physics" or "Uncle Nick," encouraged Oppenheimer to study with Max Born. Born was a mathematician, a pioneer of wave theory, and incidentally the grandfather of Olivia Newton John. Here is why Bohr wanted Oppie to study with Born:

> Algebra is like sheet music. It is one thing to read the notes. It is another to hear the music.

It is one thing to read the words of Scripture. It is another to hear the music of the spheres. It is one thing to read the sheets and turn the pages. It is another thing to hear the score and turn the music up.

Exegete the white space. The silences, the pauses, the dashes and ellipses, the fractures in language—they speak volumes. Consider Van Gogh's paintings: a brilliant study of his background elements—fog, windmills, gaslights, lampposts, quarries, chimneys, fences, dykes, railway carriages, earth piles—reveals how the backdrop as much as the frontal plane is the key to understanding the painter's vision and values.[3] Similarly, in text or in talk, what's unsaid often carries as much weight as what's explicitly stated. In Japan, there are said to be (I have yet to personally verify this) rare but special business meetings where two stenographers are present. One takes down all the words that are spoken. The other keeps track of the silences and the spaces.

What is keeping us from looking ahead, scoping the territory, and moving forward in a hope-filled trajectory that fits our turbulent terrain? Why is it so hard to identify signals from the Scriptures, from the culture, from the future?

The church has its own unique blinders and blinkers. We all can saddle our hobby horses and lay down the battle lines. We all come encased in reality distortion fields that allow us to ignore inconvenient facts. What fish are to water, humans are to culture, and it is hard to see something so fundamental and all-encompassing as culture is to human life until we step outside our familiar cultural context.

That's why, in every doctoral defense, I am on the lookout for observational bias that comes in many forms, six of the most common being:

1. "Confirmation bias," where you find what you're looking for.

    Did your findings "find" you? Or did you "find" your findings? One of the greatest examples of confirmation bias is the Warren Commission, which focused on a single gunman and disregarded everything else related to the assassination of President John F. Kennedy, including Parkland Hospital doctors and nurses of Dallas, to reach their conclusion. Feigned ignorance is the natural state of mind for a semiotician.

2. "Blind spot bias," where your new-found

SEMIOTIC TELL #3

expertise blinkers you to believe you are uniquely exempt from bias or partisanship. It is important to know the essence and extent of your "scotoma" (blind spots). We all have them, just different ones, and they change over a lifetime. If someone were to ask you "How's your scotoma?" could you answer? We don't see things/others as they are, we see them as we are. That's a pretty big blind spot.

3. "Backfire effect," where your "defensive" postures lead to a hardening commitment to views that have been disregarded, discarded or discredited. You can tell if you're suffering from the "backfire effect" if you're always on the intellectual defensive.

4. "Availability heuristic," where we naturally recall not what is important but what is mentally available and quickly retrievable. What comes to mind quickly is an immediate issue but may not be a big issue. What is most available is often what is most recently "viral" on social media, which can poison discourse by promoting logical fallacies. As the saying goes, "The plural of 'anecdote' is not data."

5. "False dilemma fallacy," where a manipulative tool is designed to polarize an audience, promoting one side and demonizing

another. It's common in political discourse as a way of strong-arming the public into supporting particular candidates or controversial policies.

6. "Fallacy of mood affiliation," where you find facts/stats/views that fit a mood even if those facts/stats/views may be risibly, provably false. Rebecca Solnit uses a beautiful metaphor to describe her writing that fits this fallacy: "the art of picking out constellations in the night sky."[4]

In a more philosophic bent, British philosopher A. C. Grayling warns of the distinctly "human" limitations to the search for knowledge.[5] First there is Maslow's "Hammer Problem": "If all you have is a hammer, everything looks like a nail." On top of our hamhandedness there is the Drunkard's "Streetlight Effect" or "Lamplight Problem": we look for lost keys in places we can see or where it's easiest to look; we ask questions of things we know to ask questions of. There is also the "Pinhole Vision Problem": the data we have available to us is circumscribed by our sensory capacities and contextual tools.

All of these come into play as we look at what the church will be facing in the next two decades and beyond. Partly to limit my own limitations, I have identified three semiotic scenarios for our consideration.

1. Future wintering trends and trajectories where creativity has chilled into compliance. Whenever cliches harden into

SEMIOTIC TELL #3

conventions, pet phrases are stroked into iconic mantras, consensus frosts into icy orthodoxy, and sentiments coagulate into canons with all the attendant cants and chants, it is time to chip away at the frozen surface of the lake.

2. The ephemeral zeitgeist. Today's obsessions and trending topics will fade into obscurity within decades. A semiotician, then, ponders: What conversations and fixations will captivate future generations? This forward-looking fixation embodies the essence of "Carpe Manana"—seizing tomorrow's significance today.[6] We kowtow to sacred cows at the price of seizing the future—as well as stifling our ability to lift up a gospel (and craft a message) that performs reconnaissance missions behind the lines of each new generation.

◇

When the whole world is running toward the cliff, those few who are running the opposite direction appear to have lost their mind.

ANON, MISATTRIBUTED TO C. S. LEWIS

3. In the beginning, a garden. In the end, a garden city. And in between, a gardener's calling. For we are born to birth—to conserve and conceive, to bring forth life.

Our gardens may vary—a window box whisperer, a pet parent, a project pioneer, an idea innovator, a word weaver, a tech tender. But our mission remains: to turn deserts into paradises, swords into swards, Sheols into Shilohs.

The question echoing through eternity, the Pearly Gates shibboleth, may not be "What did you achieve?" or "What influence did you have?" but "Show me your hands!" Hands that have dug, planted, pruned, and harvested. Hands that have gotten dirty, been scarred, and worn the badge of beauty.

For in the garden, we find our truest selves—our creativity, our curiosity, our capacity for wonder. And when we tend the earth, we tend our souls. When we get our hands dirty, and in the dirt, we discover our divine design

Four short months before his death, C. S. Lewis wrote this note dated 28 June 1963 to Mary Willis Shelburne, an American widow with whom Lewis had a long correspondence in the later years of his life.

> Think of yourself just as a seed patiently waiting in the earth; waiting to come up a flower in the Gardener's good time, up into the real world, the real waking. I suppose that our whole present life, looked back on from there, will seem only a drowsy half-waking. We are here in the

SEMIOTIC TELL #3

land of dreams. But cock-crow is coming. It is nearer now than when I began this letter.

Of course, the "Gardener" in this metaphor is our Creator, who in God's own good time will bring us from this dreamlike state into the true waking life.

Seize Your Crystallizing Moment: Ever had that "Eureka!" moment? That split second when the universe's jumbled puzzle pieces suddenly snap into place? What's been bothering you and confusing you all comes together. Welcome to the wild world of crystallizing moments.

These aren't just "aha" moments. They're life reset buttons. One minute you're on autopilot, or in a tailspin. The next you're elatedly careening down a whole new highway of existence. A word, a glance, a bite of dubious gas station sushi—the tiniest spark can ignite these perspective-shattering revelations that change you and your relationships forever.

The Semiotician's Sixth Sense: For us semiotics nerds, it's all about staying primed for these cerebral supernovas. We're like intellectual storm chasers, sensors on high alert for that telltale crackle of impending enlightenment.

But here's the kicker: When that moment hits, you've got to move in two ways. First, crystallizing moments are like caffeinated cheetahs—blink, and you'll miss 'em. Second, you need to act quickly on that illumination or you'll loose 'em. I call it the "First Dibs Principle of Influence."

Ever try imagining "Over the Rainbow" without Judy Garland's voice? It's like picturing the Mona Lisa with a handlebar mustache—possible, but deeply unsettling. That's because whoever plants their flag on that mountain of inspiration first, gets to keep the view. Marlon Brando is the Godfather. Julie Andrews owns Mary Poppins. And don't even get me started on Johnny Depp's Jack Sparrow—that's a whole pirate ship of weirdness no one else can captain. Whoever gets there first owns it, sometimes to the point where ownership becomes oneship.

My punch-in-the-mouth epiphany about "First Dibs Influence" came in Australia, in a converted sports arena, me sandwiched between speaking giants like Robert Schuller. I swagger in fresh off the plane, ready to drop some freshly penned wisdom bombs from a chapter in a book I had just published a few months before.

But as I'm speaking, the crowd starts squirming, then fleeing faster than kangaroos from a dingo convention, zinging me with dirty looks on the way out. It is so disconcerting I almost decide to publicly take the sacrament of failure, shake the dust off my feet, and bring my time on stage to a crashing close by fumbling the mic. After the speech, I'm confronted by an angry mob on the arena floor, accusing me of intellectual theft, spiritual piracy, and other things that came out of nowhere.

It turns out, the previous night's headliner had delivered the exact same sermon using my exact same words. No amount of pleading or promising to show my name on the book I had written could assuage this posse of the raging redeemed. They had been moved to an experience the night before by the celebrity speaker, and resented anyone soiling and stealing that moment from them, even the real author of the sermon. I had shown up fashionably late to my own party, that had already become someone else's party.

SEMIOTIC TELL #3

When inspiration strikes in a crystallizing moment, don't dawdle. Dash. When clarity comes knocking, don't ask it to wait on the porch. Grab that moment by its metaphorical lapels and run with it. In the race to truth, the early bird doesn't just get the worm—it gets to be the worm. A really famous, influential worm that everyone else wishes they could be. Dare to share your ideas, and you'll be the one influencing the conversation. But always remember that the taller your ego stands, the more you live in your own shadow. Paul declares that all that matters is that truth is preached (Philippians 1:17–18). Sometimes we need to get out of our own way in service to the truth.

Hence the importance of keeping those semiotic antennae up and twitching. The next lightning-in-a-bottle moment could be lurking just around the corner, waiting to zap you and others into your next great adventure.

See beyond yourself. Don't be blinded by your own reflection.

source code interactives

1. If the first singer claims the song, what does this say about Jesus? Jesus, the perfect singer of God's melody for humanity, has made Life itself His signature tune. What do you think of this statement: "To truly live is to harmonize with His key"?

2. Check out the Red Heifer and Donkey in the nativity painting from the Besancon Book of Hours, a fifteenth-century book of hours found at Fitzwilliam Museum, Cambridge. Here is Mary tucked into a blanket, reclining and reading while Joseph is at her feet, taking care of Jesus. He has his slippers on, and the donkey is nibbling on his halo. The red heifer has a magnificent alpine bell, while there is a rare image of Joseph cradling his son, a swaddled Jesus.

   What else strikes you about this image?

3. When John Wesley used the word "discipline," it didn't mean habits or procedures but channels for divine-human interaction and life-giving deep breathing exercises that would heighten one's relationship with God and others.

   a. How does Wesley's conception of "discipline" as channels for divine-human interaction differ from modern interpretations of the word?

   b. In what ways might viewing spiritual disciplines as "life-giving deep breathing exercises" change one's approach to religious practice?

c. How does the semiotic shift in the meaning of "discipline" reflect broader changes in religious thought and practice over time?

d. What other religious or spiritual terms have undergone similar semantic shifts, and what might this reveal about evolving relationships between humans and the divine?

e. How might Wesley's understanding of discipline as a means of heightening relationships with both God and others inform contemporary approaches to spirituality and community?

f. In what ways does the metaphor of "breathing exercises" or "deep breathing" illuminate the intended function of spiritual disciplines?

g. How does this interpretation of discipline challenge or complement other religious traditions' approaches to spiritual practice?

h. What semiotic implications arise from framing religious practices as channels for divine-human interaction rather than as rules or obligations?

i. How might this understanding of discipline influence the way pastors and others teach and encourage faith formation in their communities?

j. In what ways does this concept of discipline as a connective channel relate to other semiotic systems within religious contexts?

k. What if disciples of Jesus were called

"Breatharians"—those who breathe deeply from the oxygen of the Spirit: "Breathe on Me Breath of God?"

4. Corporate guru Kenneth Blanchard is famous for his acronym for EGO—Edging God Out. Would you agree that the wider your EGO (Edging God Out), the narrower your view? To what extent do egos turn mirrors into walls?

5. We all have blind spots. What are yours?

6. Have someone tell the story of Narcissus. To what degree do we live in a narcissistic culture, as Christopher Lasch first suggested in his "The Culture of Narcissism" (1979). Have someone read Jimmy Carter's "Crisis of Confidence" nationally televised address from the Oval Office on 15 July 1979. Maybe there is someone in your group that remembers watching this "Malaise Speech"?

Semiotic Tell #4

Tongues of Culture

Culture is a language. Every missionary must learn the language of the culture to which they're sent, as well as its vernacular language.[1] This is why missionaries often themselves were used as diplomats—they knew the culture so well. In Persia they were the official representatives of France until the early nineteenth century.

For example, take something as simple as a smile. In some cultures, and even with some people, mouths turn down at the corners when they smile. This is often referred to as a "sad smile" or a "smirk" but it can be a genuine smile. There are some cultural and social factors that may contribute to this facial expression. In some cultures, such as certain Asian cultures, a slight smile or a neutral expression is considered more polite and appropriate than a wide grin, which may be interpreted as insincere or foolish.

The key phrase for learning the cultural vernaculars and codes is "AS THEY WERE ABLE TO HEAR IT." We need to speak "as they are able to hear it," as in the biblical reckoning for why Jesus spoke in stories: "With many such parables he spoke the word to them, AS THEY WERE ABLE TO HEAR IT; he did not speak to them except in parables."[2]

Our ableness must be contextualized according to "as they were able to hear it." This requires high contextual intelligence,[3] which is knowing the ph factor of every situation you are in so that you know when to add more theology or more narrative to make it more alkaline or acidic. Much of the church is too ph acidic, which leads to diabetes (too much sugar) and obesity (too little exercise and too many empty calories).

> *It is as though the ability to comprehend experience through metaphor were a sense, like seeing or touching or hearing, with metaphors providing the only ways to perceive and experience much of the world. Metaphor is as much a part of our functioning as our sense of touch, and as precious.*
>
> CONCLUDING WORDS TO *METAPHORS WE LIVE BY* (2003)
> BY GEORGE LAKOFF AND MARK JOHNSON[4]

The vernacular of this culture is image, story and song. Bind them together as metaphors, memes, and mantras, and they become the mitochondria of change.

The transition from Gutenberg to Zuckerberg means that images and metaphors is how the culture of the West communicates. In fact, if you are being heard at all in today's culture, whether you know it or not, you are already fluent in a language you don't know you speak: images.[5] But this expansion from being wordsmiths to imagesmiths must be conscious and intentional. Ironically, this returns us to the mother tongue of humans, which is narrative and metaphor.

St. Thomas Aquinas highlighted the metaphoric role of

SEMIOTIC TELL #4

sensory experience and imagination in human understanding when he wrote, "Man cannot understand without images."[6]

The basics of knowledge are found where? "It is pictures rather than propositions, metaphors rather than statements, which determine most of our philosophical convictions" argued Walter Raushcenbusch's grandson, US philosopher Richard Rorty.[7] German philosopher and intellectual historian Hans Blumenberg (d. 1996) conducted a metaphorical project where he proposed that "metaphorology" is what is behind advances in all human endeavor, especially science and including philosophy.[8] He names "absolute metaphors"—what Carl Jung would call "archetypes"—images that are at the root of all thought yet are beyond logic and rationality. For example, "light" as truth or understanding runs so deep in human thought that it's nearly impossible to talk about knowledge or comprehension without invoking it: we "see" the truth, have "illuminating" insights, experience "dark" times of confusion, or have ideas "dawn" on us.

Alles Vergängliche ist nur ein Gleichnis—GOETHE
"Everything transitory is but a metaphor"
Alles Unvergängliche ist nur ein Gleichnis.—NIETZSCHE
"Everything eternal is but a metaphor."[9]

Remember Thomas Aquinas' guideline about translation: equal respect is to be paid to the receptor's and originator's languages.

The Sweet family has table rituals, one of which is to find out what happens at school every day. The queries are not always met with excitement, but one evening my eight-year-old son Luke sparkled with excitement at the question.

"Dad, guess what?" he exclaimed. "During Lent, our entire school is spending time each day praying in chapel!"

Intrigued, I asked, "That's wonderful, Luke. What else happens in chapel?"

He sat up in his chair, put his fork down, and said, "Well, the pastor talks about a Bible verse and tells a story about it."

Curious to learn more about his faith journey, I prompted, "What was today's verse?"

Luke's brow furrowed as he thought hard, trying to recall the words. After a moment, he looked up at me sheepishly. "I don't remember," he confessed.

Undeterred, I tried a different approach. "That's okay. Do you remember the story that went with the verse?"

Luke's face lit up, and he launched into an animated retelling of the pastor's story. For the next ten minutes, he regaled me with every detail, his hands gesturing wildly as he described the characters and their antics. He even imitated the laughter that echoed through the chapel as the story unfolded.

As I listened to my son's enthusiastic recounting, a realization dawned on me. While Luke couldn't remember the Bible verse, the story had captured his imagination and stuck with him. It was a poignant reminder of the power of storytelling in teaching life's lessons, even if the story itself wasn't from the Bible.

Narrative is our cultural nuclear football. But while nuclear codes can only destroy, stories have the power to either save or shatter our world. Control the story, control reality itself. Control the story, and you hold the master key to all forms of power.

And perhaps nowhere is this power more poignantly missed than in Christianity's central narrative. We've taken the most compelling story ever told—a divine being who chose humanity over heaven, love over power, sacrifice over domination—and dismantled it into bullet points and bloodless propositions. We've turned a revolutionary drama of cosmic proportions into a theological textbook. The Jesus story isn't just another tale. It's the ultimate subversion of power itself, where the Author steps into His own story to rewrite its ending. But we've lost the plot, quite literally, by reducing this world-changing narrative into memory verses and moral lessons. To reclaim its transfigurative power, we must first reclaim it as a story—one that has already changed the world before, and will do it again if we will only "Go Tell It On the Mountain."

Metaphor is the witness of language that spirit and matter are congruent. Metaphor uses the language of sense experience to lead us into the world of the unseen: faith, guilt, mind, God. The visible and invisible, put asunder by sin, are joined by metaphor.

EUGENE PETERSON[10]

Unveiling the Hidden Power of Words: Critical Metaphor Analysis

Imagine a world where words are not just symbols on a page, but powerful tools that shape our reality. This is the world we live in, and this is the realm of Critical Metaphor Analysis (CMA), a revolutionary method that peels back the layers of language to reveal the hidden structures of power beneath.

In 2004, Jonathan Charteris-Black introduced CMA in his groundbreaking book *Corpus Approaches to Critical Metaphor Analysis*, igniting a paradigm shift in how we understand the role of metaphor in discourse.

CMA isn't just about identifying pretty turns of phrase. It's rooted in cognitive linguistics, which posits that metaphors are the very scaffolding of our thoughts. When we say "time is money," we're not just being poetic—we're structuring our entire concept of time around economic value.

CMA argues that metaphors are far from innocent. They can be wielded as weapons in the arena of power relations:

> Dehumanization: By comparing people to objects or animals, metaphors can strip away their humanity.
>
> Legitimizing Inequality: Metaphors can make unfair systems seem natural and inevitable.
>
> Creating Superiority: Through careful metaphorical framing, one group can position itself above others.

While CMA can be a powerful tool for uncovering hidden biases in everything from political speeches to advertising slogans,[11] it's not without its critics. Some argue that CMA is a double-edged sword:

> Prioritizes ideology over linguistic context
>
> Lacks empirical rigor

SEMIOTIC TELL #4

Oversimplifies complex social dynamics

Assumes conflict where cooperation might exist

As with any analytical tool, CMA requires careful, nuanced application. When used thoughtfully and without ideological bent, it can illuminate the subtle ways language shapes our world. But we must always be mindful of its limitations and potential biases. In a world increasingly divided by rhetoric, understanding the power of metaphor has never been more crucial. CMA offers us a lens to examine not just what is said, but how it's said—and the profound impact those choices have on our shared reality. Ironically, the misuse of CMA can become a prime example of the very power dynamics it was designed to expose.

Metaphor is the Creator, not the Caretaker, of Thought: C. S. Lewis' essay "Is Theology Poetry?" delivered to the Socratic Club at Oxford in November 1944, is contained in a volume delightfully called, *They Asked for a Paper* (1962), his last book published in his lifetime.

> We are invited to restate our belief in a form free from metaphor and symbol. The reason we don't is that we can't. We can, if you like, say "god entered history" instead of saying "god came down to earth." But, of course, "entered" is just as metaphorical as "came down." You have only substituted horizontal or undefined movement for vertical movement. We can make our language duller; we cannot make it less metaphorical. We can make the pictures more prosaic; we cannot be less pictorial.

Language matters. That's why if I hear that word "volunteer" one more time in a church setting, I'm going to officially nominate the word for the "Annoying Word of the Year" award. The church is the work of the Holy Spirit bringing Christ to life, not through "volunteers" but through "members" and "ministers" of the body of Christ. The world has casual helpers called "volunteers" that come and go. The church has committed members and dedicated disciples, active participants in the Lord's mission who are united in their devotion to Christ and each other.[12]

Before The Salvation Army was called TSA, they were the Christian Mission. William Booth's son was preparing an annual newsletter in 1878 and used the term, "volunteer army" to describe the people that comprised the Christian Mission. William Booth saw it, crossed out the word volunteer and wrote Salvation instead. It's been that way ever since.[13]

Metaphor isn't just the poet's plaything—it's the mind's metamorphosis machine. It doesn't just paint pretty pictures in our heads; it's the silent puppeteer pulling the strings of our actions. From the spark of a simile to the inferno of innovation, metaphor is the alchemist turning abstract gold into concrete consequences.

So the next time someone says to stop speaking in metaphors, it is the responsibility of semioticians to remind them that's like asking a fish to stop swimming or a bird to clip its own wings. We don't just speak in metaphors—we live them, breathe them, and let them choreograph our goings out and comings in.[14] The plainest way to speak is in narraphors (narrative + metaphor).

SEMIOTIC TELL #4

It is this that makes Christianity a faith that "acts." Acts speak the faith: "DO THIS;" "DO LIKEWISE;" "DO UNTO OTHERS;" "DO GOOD;" "DO NOT WORRY;" "DO NOT JUDGE:" "DO NOT BE AFRAID." Semioticians don't look for what people say so much as what they do. Jesus illustrates this method when the jailed John the Baptizer sends his disciples to ask Jesus, "Are you the One we've been expecting, or are we still waiting?"[15]

Jesus responds not with words, but with evidence of action:

Go back and tell John what's going on:

> The blind see,
>
> The lame walk,
>
> Lepers are cleansed,
>
> The deaf hear,
>
> The dead are raised,
>
> The wretched of the earth learn that God is on their side.[16]

In the end, the best metaphors are not mere figures of speech. They are blueprints for action. They bridge the gap between thought and deed, between faith and practice. Just as Jesus answered John with a litany of transformative acts, we too are called to embody our metaphors, to make them flesh. For in the interplay between language and action, between symbol and substance, we find the true power of faith: not just to speak, but to DO—and in doing, to change the world.

The Power of Metaphor: Reimagining Our Blue Planet: In our quest to understand the world around us, we must turn to metaphors to reach the world around us. In our attempt to comprehend the universe, metaphors serve as bridges between what we know and what we seek to understand. These linguistic bridges connect the abstract to the tangible, shaping our perceptions and, ultimately, our actions. But what if I told you that the metaphors we choose aren't just descriptive—they're decisive, determinative, and even definitive?

The language we use to frame our world becomes the lens through which we view it, and over time, we find ourselves inhabiting these metaphorical spaces.

Consider the iconic "Blue Marble" photograph taken by the Apollo 17 crew in 1972. This image of Earth suspended in the inky void of space has become a powerful symbol of our planet's beauty and apparent fragility. But is this static snapshot truly representative of our dynamic home? Is it a good or bad metaphor?

The "Blue Marble" metaphor, while visually striking and powerfully portraying Earth as small in relationship to the vastness of the universe, falls short in capturing the true nature of our planet. It presents Earth as a motionless object, a serene sphere floating in space. But this couldn't be further from the truth. Our planet is a whirling, churning cauldron of activity—a complex system of interacting forces and energies. A whirling dervish of dynamism.

Imagine if we could see the Earth as it truly is: swathed in swirling clouds, bathed in the intense heat of the sun, alive with countless biochemical reactions. This is not a fragile ornament dangling in the darkness, but a powerful, turbulent entity that both awes and frightens with its raw energy.

So, semioticians, we must ask ourselves: Is our planet

SEMIOTIC TELL #4

best understood as a spinning ball that merely rotates? Or is it more akin to a shimmering blue viburnum that reveals its true nature to those who draw near and look lovingly?

Perhaps an even more profound and biblical metaphor awaits us as we attempt to express this image in the language of the culture. What if we saw the Earth as a burning bush, aflame with the resplendent presence of the divine? This image captures not only the dynamic nature of our planet but also infuses it with a sense of the sacred. It challenges us to look at life sacramentally, to perceive our world through sacred hues. This perspective invites us to recognize the holy in the familiar, the transcendent in the turbulent.

But if our world truly glows with such significance, what blinds us to this radiance? The very metaphors we've chosen—suspended globes and glass marbles—may be obscuring our vision. They lull us into a false sense of complacency, suggesting that our planet is a fixed, unchanging entity rather than a living, breathing system that demands our engagement and trusteeship.

To truly see the "flames" of our vibrant world, we must first recognize the power of our chosen metaphors. We need to consciously select and cultivate imagery (especially biblical ones) that captures the dynamism, complexity, and wonder of our planetary home. By doing so, we can nudge each other towards a more profound understanding of our place in the cosmos.

As we stand at this critical juncture in human history, facing unprecedented environmental challenges, the metaphors we choose matter more than ever. Will we continue to see Earth as a distant, still, static marble? Or will we embrace a vision of our planet as a living, breathing miracle—a burning bush that demands our bowed-head respect, bare-foot attention, and beholden care?

The choice is ours, and the consequences of that choice will shape not only our perception but also our actions for generations to come.

So semioticians, choose your metaphors wisely, for in doing so, you choose the world you will willy-nilly inhabit.

Speak in Tongues. Learn the vernacular and its cultural codes.

SEMIOTIC TELL #4

source code interactives

You're my students, so you can learn some new words.

Ready? Here it comes: Images exist not to propugn or impugn or repugn, but oppugn.

1. What does this mean? How many of these four words did you need to look up? Do you like to play with words and learn new words? What does this suggest about the primary function of images in discourse or debate?

2. How does the use of "oppugn" (to call into question or dispute) differ from the other terms (propugn, impugn, repugn) in terms of how images might be used in argumentation?

3. In what ways can images challenge our preconceptions or beliefs more effectively than words alone?

4. How might this one sentence statement relate to the use of visual rhetoric in media, advertising, or political campaigns?

5. Can you think of specific examples where an image has served to "oppugn" an idea or belief effectively?

6. How does this perspective on images align or conflict with the common saying "a picture is worth a thousand words"?

7. What ethical considerations might arise from using images primarily to question or dispute rather than to support or attack?

8. How might this view of images influence our understanding of visual literacy in the digital age?

9. In what ways could this statement apply to different fields such as journalism, science communication, or art criticism?

    How might understanding images as tools for "oppugning" change the way we create, consume, or interpret visual media?

10. Check out an episode of *Star Trek* titled "Darmok" (aired 09/30/1991). It shows the humans in The Federation meeting "The Children of Tama", the Tamarines. The races have crossed before, but fruitlessly, because the Tamarine language is incomprehensible. (We are equally incomprehensible to them.) The translator works and the words are translated into English, but they convey no meaning. How do you communicate when the nature of language itself is different?

    Through the course of the episode, Captain Picard discovers that the reason neither can understand the other is that the Tamarine language is based totally in story and imagery, narrative and metaphor. He begins to learn the stories and images, and by the end of the episode, breaks the communication barrier, speaking to the Tamarine ship "in their own language."[17]

    How does the episode "Darmok" challenge our understanding of language as a universal tool for communication? In other words, what does it suggest about the

SEMIOTIC TELL #4

limitations of language when it's based on cultural and conceptual frameworks that are fundamentally different?

What role does narrative, metaphor, and semaphor play in shaping our perception of reality? How does the Tamarines' reliance on these elements suggest a different way of understanding the world?

Can communication be achieved without a shared understanding of the world? If not, how can we bridge the gaps created by different cultural and conceptual frameworks?

11. When Jesus quotes Isaiah 61 about himself here, there is one line Jesus leaves out of the Isaiah quote: "to proclaim liberty to the captives." According to teacher and author Ray Vanderlaan, when John heard this message he learned two things: first, Jesus was indeed who all Israel was waiting for; second, because Jesus left out the phrase "to set the captives free," John understood he would not be getting out of jail alive.

    What do you think?

12. In what ways does our current, media-rich culture echo medieval modes of understanding and communication that used the five senses to the max? How might our immersion in stories, images, soundscapes, and sensory experiences align more closely with pre-Enlightenment epistemologies than with purely rational modernist approaches?

Semiotic Tell #5

The Divine Constellation

Fascia Seers: Nothing in life is "just" anything. No moment, event, or happening. Nothing in life "just happens" alone. All is connected, a cosmic song.

The challenge we face as semioticians: To listen in to the links, tune into the connections, and hear the symphony that weaves time and space.

Semioticians, masters of signs, symbols, and connections, are the true Fascia Seers, revealing and interpreting the intricate web of meaning that underpins and overarches our world. Just as Fascia connects and supports the body's systems, semioticians unveil and clarify the hidden patterns and relationships that bind language, culture, and reality.

The future belongs to those who are deeply connected—to God, themselves, each other, and the universe. They are the Fascia Seers.

The Bible as a Jigsaw Puzzle: The Bible has become a vast, intricate jigsaw puzzle with 31,102 pieces—each piece representing a verse. To lay all the pieces out on one table, you would need it to be at least 30–40 feet (9–12 meters) long, and 8–10 feet (2.4–3 meters) wide.

There are three well-meaning culprits behind this slicing and dicing of the story—the best and worst thing that ever happened to the Scriptures. Stephen Langton, Archbishop of Canterbury in the early thirteenth century (around 1227) divided the Latin Vulgate version of the Bible into the chapters we use today. When it comes to the verses, we have Rabbi Isaac Nathan ben Kalonymus to thank. In the fifteenth century he divided the Hebrew Bible into verses for a concordance he completed around 1448. Then there was "Stephanus" (a.k.a. Robert Estienne), a sixteenth-century printer and classics scholar who came up with the verse divisions we still use today in his Greek New Testament (published in 1551).

About twenty-six years after Stephanus' chapter-and-verse New Testament, the Geneva Bible was first published (1560). The Geneva Bible was the first complete English Bible to use both chapter and verse divisions. It was the Bible the Pilgrims brought with them on the Mayflower.

You say: so what's the problem with all that? Well, if you like the "Skin Project" writings of Shelley Jackson, who had each word of a short story tattooed separately onto the bodies of 2095 volunteers, nothing. If you like fragmented narratives spread widely across space and time, with the story constantly changing as the participants come and go, then you'll never be averse to verses.

But Bible teacher Warren Wendel Wiersbe (1929–2019), mostly ignored by university biblical scholars, got it right. The Bible is basically a "picture book," a masterpiece of semiotics. It uses symbols, similes, metaphors, typology, numerology, hyperbole, allegory, personification, and other semiotic devices to get its message across.[1]

Versus Verses: At least three things should give us aversion to verses, according to what the don of semiotics, Charles Sanders Peirce, has taught us.

First is holism: systems and wholes are more fundamental than their individual parts.

Second is relations and patterns: to understand reality, you need to see the patterns in relationships. In fact, humans have built-in automated pattern-recognition systems if we only use them.

Third is emergence: complex systems exhibit properties that cannot be reduced to their individual components. The whole shapes its parts, not the other way around. Just as a jigsaw puzzle's image guides the placement of each piece, the overall pattern defines its elements. You can't grasp the big picture by studying the pieces in isolation—it's the complete design that gives meaning to each component.

When we approach the Bible verse by verse, we're essentially trying to understand a grand masterpiece by examining each brushstroke individually. This approach comes with more than its fair share of hurdles:

1. Loss of Context: Each verse, like a puzzle piece, was meant to fit into a larger narrative. By isolating verses, we risk misinterpreting their meaning or significance. Most "Intelligence Failure" comes not from lack of information, but from inability to connect the dots of the information that we already have.

2. Missing Themes: The Bible contains overarching themes and narratives that span multiple books and chapters. Focusing on

individual verses can cause us to miss these broader messages. When we don't know the missing parts of the story, we are prone to fill in the blanks with doctrines and dogmas. We don't so much connect the dots of the story as the dots of the doctrines. We need to derive our theology out of the story, not deliver our theology from the story.

3. Fragmented Understanding: Without seeing "The Big Picture," we might struggle to connect seemingly disparate parts of scripture, missing out on the interconnectedness of biblical teachings. We don't start reading The Story of Jesus with theories about the Bible. We read The Story first and then deduce biblical theology.

4. Misinterpretation: Just as a puzzle piece's shape or color might be misleading when viewed alone, a verse taken out of context can be easily misunderstood or misapplied. Semioticians trust the Story to tell the truth.

5. Overlooking Structure: The Bible's structure—its division into Old and New Testaments, the grouping of books, the progression of narratives—all contribute to its overall message. This structure is often overlooked in a verse-by-verse approach. But it's a division and organization (and

compilation) decided upon by people just as human as those who numbered chapter and verse, or who devote themselves to holistic Bible study today.

By reading the Bible as one story, semiotics enables us to see "The Big Picture"—the overarching narrative of God's relationship with humanity—and better understand how each "puzzle piece" fits into this grand design.[2] Even if you can't draw—and I failed the HTP (House-Tree-Person) test as a kid because no one could tell the difference between my house, tree, or person—you can at least paint by numbers and connect the dots.

Heartbeats Over Hoofbeats: Transcendence is found in unexpected connections that pop out and burst forth like a jack-in-the-box, revealing hidden truths with surprising clarity. Yet, it's the Spirit that opens our senses to discern these revelations. Why did John lean against Jesus at Last Supper? To "hear the heartbeat of God," Celtic legend tells us. For Jesus is as "close to the Father" as one can get—the very heartbeat of the divine.[3]

Theo-semioticians learn to attune their ears to the pulse of the Eternal, so they may better hear the heartbeats resounding throughout our world. In those sacred moments of enlightenment, the veil parts, and we glimpse the luminous interplay of heaven and earth. When John Wesley published his own annotated version of the New Testament in 1755, which became one of Methodism's historical doctrinal standards, he wrote in the preface: "The Spirit of God not only once inspired those who wrote it, but continually inspires, supernaturally assists, those that read it with earnest prayer."[4]

Wesley talked about the necessity of grasping the "general tenor" or the overall narrative and message of the Bible, from the first page to the last. Biblical semiotics trusts the ongoing inspiration and assistance of the Holy Spirit in understanding Scripture and speedballing truth.

To be sure, this is not as easy as it sounds.[5] Trust and truth can become perilously corroded by ratcheting terrors. We can easily see connections between things that are unrelated, and we quickly conclude causation where there is only correlation. Humans are, as Aristotle's categories and Linnaeus' taxonomies make clear, more splitters than lumpers. We love to take apart, parse, perfect precise definitions, assign to categories, as the first Adam did in the naming of the animals.

That is why semioticians always need to question what is there, what is not there. To be a skeptic about some things is not septic or dyspeptic but sceptic, healthy, and prudent, ensuring that one does not accept ideas uncritically.

My favorite TV detective Harry Bosch's advice to "Look for what's not there" resonates deeply, as absence can be a more revealing presence than what's overtly present. This is exemplified in the story of the healing of the paralytic, where the absence of the disabled man's family, particularly his father, speaks volumes. Furthermore, the use of the Greek word τέσσαρες (*tessares*) to describe the anonymous caregivers who carried the paralytic, rather than highlighting family or friends, underscores the significance of unseen or overlooked elements. By acknowledging these absences, we can gain a deeper understanding of the narrative and uncover new insights.[6]

The account of Jesus walking on water is incomplete

SEMIOTIC TELL #5

without acknowledging the omission of Peter's role in walking on water in two of the three gospels that tell the story, notably in the Gospel of Mark, where Peter is a primary source and protagonist. It's striking that Peter's most notable miracle, which showcases his faith and abilities, is absent from his own narrative.[7] This omission invites a closer examination of the story through a semiotic lens, potentially revealing a more profound narrative about "Doubting Peter" that rivals the famous story of "Doubting Thomas."

Semiotic Integrity: Integrity means integrated. And semiotics is nothing if not about the power of integration.

Semiotic integrity is about integration, and the story of Jahi, a teenager from California, perfectly illustrates this concept.[8] Though their daughter was declared "brain dead" by standard criteria, Jahi's parents chose to maintain life support, and her body surprisingly underwent puberty. Further examination revealed that her hypothalamus was still functioning, and her body continued to operate with proper care.

This remarkable case highlights that human life is more than just the sum of its parts. It's about how those parts integrate to form a cohesive whole. Similarly, semiotic integrity relies on the integration of six essential components, which I call The Semiotic Sextet Matrix:[9]

> Storify, not Versify
>
> Make the Story a Movie in Your Mind
>
> Trust the Story
>
> Receive the Story First, Theologize Last
>
> Every Story Contains the Whole Story

Live the Story

Just as Jahi's body functioned when her parts were integrated, even though some parts were broken, semiotic integrity is achieved when these six components work together in harmony. By embracing this matrix, we can unlock a deeper understanding of ourselves and the world around us.

1. Storify, not Versify:

    We've seen how verses can be an imposition, severing narrative threads and reducing the story to disjointed bits. Initially, chapters and verses were meant to guide us through the story, but they've become tools for dissecting it instead. As Len Wilson aptly puts it, "Verses turn stories into propositions, favoring lawyers over storytellers." This reductionism isn't just a loss of literary flair; it's more than the verve of verse has gone. The default mindset of verse is a form of biblical abuse.

    That being said, I'm all for story, even to the point where I argue that Paul makes you think you are listening to theology but you are really listening to story. But I also recognize story's time and place. Moses didn't descend from the mountain with a collection of anecdotes or poetic hints. There's a time for narrative unfolding and a time for declarative clarity; a time for metaphors to inspire and a time for direct prophetic declarations. Semiotics must not confuse the two, lest we forget the power of story and the weight of divine proclamation: "Thus Saith The Lord."

2. Make the Story Cinematic: Awaken to The Living Story

The vernacular of contemporary culture is narraphor (narrative + metaphor) with a soundtrack. The Story is alive, pulsing with meaning. Our challenge is to come alive to it, to internalize its rhythms and rhymes. The ancient rabbis' wisdom echoes: "Turn it over, turn it over, for everything is inside." As we delve into The Story, it beckons us to "turn, turn, turn"—to surrender, to see, and to be turned around and changed inside. The Jesus story makes us spanking new.

Envision The Story as a motion picture in your mind, unfolding before your eyes, and let its living narrative reshape you.

3. Trust the Story: Embracing Narrative Authenticity

Renowned author Israel Joshua Singer advised his brother, Nobel laureate Isaac Bashevis Singer, to avoid "zugerts"—explanations and interpretations that dilute the story's power. Instead, let the story speak for itself. This wisdom extends beyond literature to the semiotics of faith and identity.

True faith isn't about pretending a story is true; it's about staking your life on its authenticity. We've been taught to trust the Bible's words, but it's time to trust its metaphors and stories as equally authoritative.

In a world where stories are commodified and commercialized, our identities become shape-shifters, morphing with each narrative trend and tic. Identity requires narrative form.[10] Amidst the noise, only one story is worth trusting and living: the Jesus Story. When you trust this story, you'll find yourself saying, "That's not my story," when tempted by other competing world views and conflicting narratives.

Like the Appalachian phrase "My dog is not in that fight," semiotics helps us deflect distractions and stay anchored to the Jesus narrative. Trust the story, stay in the story, and it will chart your course. Meaning in life is found in the narrative's depths, not in detours to elsewhere.

Trust, but Verify. No better conceptual verifications have been proposed than Jonathan Edwards' five "tests of the Spirit."[11] But there are perceptual as well as conceptual tests of whether the story is true and of the

Spirit. In the words of 1 John 5:8 NIV: "The Spirit and the water and the blood; and these three agree." Trust the Story, but verify by filtering it through the Wind, Water, and Blood Tests.[12]

4. Receive the Story First, Theologize Last.

Let the story work on you before you work on any story. Let the Story Shape You.

Allow its beauty to seep into your spirit, like a sunrise slowly painting the sky. Don't rush to dissect and analyze; let the narrative work its magic on your body, mind, and spirit.

As Calvinist philosopher Paul Ricoeur so eloquently put it, "The symbol gives rise to thought." Let the story be the spark that ignites your imagination and reflection.

A true story is a precious, fragile gift. Your life is constantly changing, yet it remains uniquely yours. Similarly, the sacred stories of Scripture are timeless, yet they reveal new meanings with each encounter. As you revisit them, they resonate differently based on your current life experiences, offering deeper truths and insights.

Let the story be the master artist, shaping and reshaping you with each brushstroke of its wisdom. Only then, when your spirit has been transformed, can you truly theologize—reflecting on the beauty that has already transfigured you.

Open now the crystal fountain,
Whence the healing stream doth flow;
Let the fire and cloudy pillar
Lead me all my journey through.

"GUIDE ME, O THOU GREAT JEHOVAH" (1745)[13]

---

5. Every Story Contains the Whole Story: Crystal Fountain

Within every biblical narrative, no matter how small, lies a crystal microcosm of the entire story. Each story is a thread that weaves together with others, revealing the broader narrative. You can't tell one story without, in some way, telling the whole story. Whenever we read the Bible with our whole body, mind and spirit, we kneel at the manger and welcome the incarnation. And every time we do, we uncover new meanings and insights from the same mysterious and ever-flowing crystal fountain.

Every preacher preparing a sermon knows what Argentinian novelist/librarian Jorge Luis Borges is talking about in his essay "Partial Magic in the Quixote" (1949): "Every novelist has felt on writing a novel that the story he is telling could go on forever if he expanded on its loose ends: it would be the novel of novels, with all its stories interweaving to infinity."[14] Every story contains the DNA of the whole story.

6. Live the Story: A Manger Epic

You can't escape living in and through a story. We're all protagonists in some unfolding drama. The question is: whose script are you following? Are you starring in Madison Avenue's consumerist drama, Wall Street's high-stakes roller-coaster ride, Hollywood's glitzy spectacle, or Bethlehem's manger epic? Semioticians help others embrace their true narrative.

This culture is not hungry for a world view, but a life story. Our culture craves more than abstract philosophies—it hungers for a compelling life narrative. The greatest story ever told often remains untold, half-told, or distorted because we've lost touch with our own narrative arc. Semioticians help people to revolutionize their life by rewriting their story and reimagining their metaphors.

What makes a tale irresistible isn't the theology lurking in the background, but the vibrant testimony center stage. As Ivan Illich, a thinker with whom I often clash but find common ground on this matter, is widely attributed as saying:

> Neither revolution nor reformation can ultimately change a society. Instead, you must weave a new, powerful narrative—one so persuasive it sweeps away old myths and becomes the preferred story. It must be so inclusive it gathers all the fragments of our past and present into a coherent whole, illuminating a path forward into the future. If you aspire to transform a society, you must first tell an alternative story.

Here's the question every semiotician asks of every subject: Your life is the pen; the world, your parchment. What epic will you inscribe upon it?

Cognitive Crossfit: Semioticians are the weightlifters of meaning, sculpting their hippocampi into cognitive Atlases. Just as bodybuilders transform biceps into bulging symbols of strength, these masters of signs flex their hippocampi to hoist entire worlds of interconnected significance.

In the gymnasium of memory, the hippocampus isn't just another muscle—it's the cerebral spotter that helps us recognize, spatially map, and meaningfully connect our experiences. But for semioticians, it becomes something far greater: a neural Rosetta Stone, translating fleeting perceptions into a robust lexicon of lasting symbols.

SEMIOTIC TELL #5

As the hippocampus works overtime, consolidating fresh insights into long-term understanding, the semiotician's mind transforms into a bustling metropolis of signs. Each memory isn't merely filed away, but becomes a living, breathing part of this cerebral cityscape. New experiences are rapidly integrated, forming vibrant districts of meaning where every street sign, building, and passerby resonates with layers of cultural, historical, and personal significance. In this neural New York, Times Square billboards of immediate perception connect via cognitive subways to the Museum of Cultural History and the Skyscraper of Personal Experience, creating an ever-growing, three-dimensional matrix of interconnected meaning.

In this cognitive CrossFit, semioticians don't just exercise their hippocampi—they transform them into meaning-making powerhouses, capable of benchpressing entire semiospheres of human experience. You are what you remember more than what you experience. And what you remember most is what you did last.

Meaning is accrued through time and memory, multiplied by loss. Or to put it differently ... We are not merely the sum of our experiences, but the curators of our memories. Through the act of remembering and re-membering, we continuously reconstruct our identity. Meaning accumulates over time, its essence distilled by memory and deepened by loss. In this way, we are perpetually reborn through the alchemy of recollection.

I am my remembering self, and the experiencing self, who does my living, is like a stranger to me.

NOBEL LAUREATE ECONOMIST DANIEL KAHNEMAN[15]

Time as a River: Think of time as a river with three key insights:

> First, tomorrow's waters can only flow from upstream—the future emerges from the patterns of the past.
>
> Second, what really matters are the moments when the river changes course—those pivotal points where the present starts carving new channels different from the past's familiar flow.
>
> Third, to navigate this river well, you must be like a skilled captain, constantly looking ahead to approaching bends, checking your current position, and remembering the routes you've traveled before—your mind moving fluidly between future, present, and past.

This metaphor captures the essence of theo-semiotics: the past as our guide, change as our focus, and the need to constantly shift our gaze across time's horizon.

This metaphor also captures the essence of life: living in the "here and now." There are two words that crack open the universe. "Here" and "Now." Two words that always belong together: "Here and Now." You can't have one without the other. No escape. No detours. No exits. They are twin anchors to our ultimate truth. In the "here" of the "now," we find our commands, challenges, invitations to fully inhabit our one wild and precious life, and incarnate love. This "Here and Now" is not a cage. It's a commission. Here and Now. The only address where life actually happens.

Moishe and the Pope: There is an old tale about the time, many, many centuries ago, when the pope decided that it was time to reclaim a synagogue the Jews were using in Rome that really belonged to the Vatican. So he told them to move. Rightly, there was uproar from the Jewish community. So the pope made a deal. He would have a religious debate with a member of the Jewish community. If the Jews won, they could stay in their space. If the pope won, the Jews had to leave.

The Jewish community realized that they had no choice. The problem was that no one wanted to debate the pope. The only volunteer was a poor, simple old man named Moishe who opened the door to the synagogue each Friday night. Not being used to words, Moshe asked for only one addition to the debate—that neither side would be allowed to talk. The pope agreed.

The day of the great debate came. Moishe and the pope sat opposite each other. The pope raised his hand and showed three fingers. Moishe looked back at him and raised one finger. The pope waved his hand in a circle around his head. Moishe pointed to the ground where he sat. The pope pulled out a wafer and a glass of wine. Moishe pulled out an apple.

The pope stood up and said, "I give up. This man is too good. The Jews can stay."

Later, the pope explained what happened: "I held up

three fingers to represent the Trinity. He responded by holding up one finger to remind me that we believe in the same one God. Then I waved my hand around my head to show that God was all around us. He responded by pointing to the ground, showing that God was present right here. I pulled out the bread and wine to show that God has given us the Eucharist. He pulled out an apple to remind me of original sin. He had an answer for everything. What could I do?"

Meanwhile, Moishe explained to the Jewish scholars how he won the unwinnable debate. "Well," said Moishe, "First he said that the Jews had three days to get out. I told him that not one of us was leaving. Then he told me that this whole city would be cleared of Jews if we didn't leave the space. I let him know that we were staying right here."

"And then what clinched the debate?" asked the rabbis. "I don't know," said Moishe. "This was the strangest thing of all: he took out his lunch, and I took out mine!"[16]

This tale reveals a profound truth about human understanding: meaning often lies in the eye of the beholder. What the pope saw as deep theological discourse, Moishe interpreted as practical negotiations. Both men connected different dots to create entirely different pictures—yet somehow, their mismatched interpretations led them to the right outcome. Perhaps this is why we must always remember that the connections we see may not be the only ones possible, and that wisdom sometimes comes from unexpected sources and unconventional ways of thinking.

The same set of points can create countless constellations—and sometimes the simplest way of connecting them turns out to be just as valid as the most complex.

SEMIOTIC TELL #5

Source Code Interactives

1. Sweet suggests that verse-by-verse Bible study can lead to "fragmented understanding." How might studying the Bible as one continuous narrative change our interpretation and understanding compared to a verse-based approach? Give specific examples.

2. Here is a contentious quote from the chapter: "Every [Bible] story contains the DNA of the whole story." How does this principle apply to biblical narratives, and what implications does it have for how we interpret individual passages within the larger biblical context?

3. The Moishe and Pope story illustrates how different people can derive completely different meanings from the same signs and gestures. How does this relate to the chapter's broader discussion of semiotics and biblical interpretation?

4. This chapter presents the "Semiotic Sextet Matrix" as a framework for interpretation. Which of these six principles do you find most challenging to apply, and why?

5. Sweet argues, in opposition to many other scholars, that "This culture is not hungry for a world view, but a life story." How does this observation challenge traditional approaches to religious teaching and evangelism?

| SeMIQTIC Tell #6 |

The Elephant Unseen

It is only with the heart that one can see rightly; what is essential is invisible to the eye.

ANTOINE DE SAINT-EXUPÉRY[1]

The Art of Seeing the Unseen: Our world is a text, a sacred script, but we've lost the language. Semiotics isn't just the study of signs and symbols; it's the art of resurrection, of giving life to the dead letters around us.

The semiotic mission? To see the unseen, to observe the obvious, to illuminate the overlooked, to reveal the profound insights hidden in plain sight. Semiotics is about seeing what is seen, but even more it is about seeing what is still to be seen.

The invisible doesn't lurk beyond the horizon of human experience—it pulses at its very center. It reveals itself not in spectacle but in subtlety: through whispers that penetrate deeper than shouts, through questions that illuminate more than answers, through the spaces between things rather than the things themselves. The invisible isn't the absence of reality but its foundation; not emptiness but fullness speaking a language our eyes alone cannot comprehend. It's the eternal breaking through into the temporary, inviting us to see with more than sight, to perceive with the whole of our being what cannot be contained by mere vision.

> *So we fix our eyes not on what is seen, but on what is unseen, since what is seen is temporary, but what is unseen is eternal.*
>
> APOSTLE PAUL, 2 CORINTHIANS 4:18 NIV

Semiotic Tell #6 invites us to explore a fascinating paradox of human perception. How is it that we can be surrounded by meaning, yet fail to see it? Why do we sometimes need others to point out what should be glaringly apparent? From the grand halls of Downton Abbey to the subtle carvings on medieval church seats, from the blindness of Saul to the prescient warnings of George Orwell, we embark on a journey to uncover the art of seeing the unseen.

This ability to observe the obvious, to overcome "inattentional blindness," is not just a semiotic exercise, but a vital skill in our increasingly complex world. It challenges us to question our assumptions, to look beyond the surface, and to find meaning in the mundane. In doing so, we might just unlock a deeper understanding of ourselves and the world around us.

British philosopher Owen Barfield wrote, "The obvious is the hardest thing of all to point out to anyone who has genuinely lost sight of it."[2] Sometimes, the most profound insights lie hidden in plain sight.

This notion is illustrated in a pivotal moment from Downton Abbey's sixth season. The aristocratic Crawley

SEMIOTIC TELL #6

family, hosting an open house for charity, suddenly find themselves thrust into the role of amateur tour guides. As visitors eagerly explore the grand halls of their ancestral home, a surprising revelation unfolds: the Crawleys themselves are largely oblivious to the treasures surrounding them.

Mary, Edith, and Cora stumble through explanations, unable to answer basic questions about their own heritage. They're unaware that Highclere Castle earned its 'Abbey' moniker from its monastic past, or that a priceless Renoir hangs casually on their walls, its significance lost on them.

In sum, the Crawleys are aristocrats of ignorance. Their castle, a cathedral of history, was a barren wasteland to them. We're all a bit Crawley, sleepwalking through our own lives, surrounded by masterpieces and mysteries, yet blind to their brilliance. What stories, what wisdom, what beauty might be staring us in the face, patiently waiting for us to truly see it?

During "advances" at my home on Orcas Island, I like to play "The Misericord Game." A prize is given to the first advancer who can find all six misericords scattered throughout our small home. A misericord (literally "mercy seat") is a small wooden platform on the underside of a folding seat in a church which, when the seat is folded up, props up the inhabitant for long prayers and liturgies. Underneath these medieval misericords are highly carved ornaments depicting biblical scenes or humorous scenarios from everyday life. That humble seat of solace in medieval churches holds secrets. Carved into its wooden heart are stories of the human condition, etched in the language of symbol. To find them is to discover a hidden world, a world right beneath our noses. Yet the hardest misericords for my students to discover are the two right where they are supposed to be: under the flip-up structure of a two-seat pew in my study/studio.

Philosopher and cognitive scientist Andy Clark says that seeing and thinking are so inseparable that "we are never simply seeing what's 'really there.'"[3] We are basically oblivious to the obvious, so we need people to help us observe the obvious, to see slowly, to read slowly, to look at life slowly or to, in the words of Mark Chironna, "slow down to the speed of revelation." British biographer and historian Lord David Cecil (d. 1986) was famous for saying, more than a bit condescendingly, that only second-rate minds are afraid of the obvious.

Our culture is a coal mine, dark and dangerous. Canaries drop like flies, warnings ignored. We need new eyes, a spiritual EKG to detect the rhythms of the unseen. Social media is a hall of mirrors, distorting reality, making it harder to see the truth staring us in the face. How many dead canaries (or dead churches) on the floor of a coal mine do we need before we see that something is wrong in what we are doing? Semioticians serve in some ways as the coal-miners lifting up canaries in a toxic world.

Saul needed to be blinded first because he needed new eyes, the eyes of faith, the eyes of the original garden. He took a three-day journey into eye surgery where his eyesight was re-engineered. We all need new eyes to see what is in front of us. But sometimes, like Paul, we need to be blind enough to want to see.

Wittgenstein famously asked one of his classes, "Why did people used to think that the Sun went around the Earth?" One of his students replied, "Because it looks as if the Sun

SEMIOTIC TELL #6

goes around the Earth." Wittgenstein commented: "And how would it look if the Earth went around the Sun?" The obvious answer is: exactly the same. The mind can be as deceiving as the eyes. Our observations alone do not always lead us to the correct conclusions, and that the same observational evidence can be consistent with multiple, contradictory theories.

You have to believe that there's something to see before you can decide to look.

ASTRONOMER GUY CONSOLMAGNO SJ
DIRECTOR OF THE VATICAN OBSERVATORY[4]

The hardest thing to see is what is right in front of us. And it's getting harder in a world where many of our news sources have gone from getting us "the facts" to comforting us and confirming our assumptions in the hopes of getting more eyes and likes. Much of social media and mainstream media is skewed, selective, malicious and mendacious. That makes the struggle more constant and concrete "to see what is in front of one's nose," as George Orwell liked to put it. He was so concerned about this in his day he wrote a whole article on it.[5]

We live in a world drowning in data, yet thirsting for meaning.

We live in a world with unstable borders between fact and fiction, information and disinformation, myth and reality. Access to wild and wacky "facts" is at an all-time high. Wisdom is rare. We're surrounded by noise, desperate for silence.

Semiotics is the art of finding silence in the storm, of discovering the sacred in the superficial. We must become iconoclasts, smashing the idols of the spectral. Semioticians learn to see like children, with wonder and without prejudice. The world is a sacrament, a gift wrapped in mystery. Semioticians help unwrap it.

The world is a riddle wrapped in a mystery inside an enigma, as Churchill once said. But perhaps it's simpler than that. Maybe it's just a story, waiting to be read in forensic focus. And every life is a chapter, filled with plot twists, heroes, villains, and redemption.

To see is to believe, they say. But what if seeing is actually about reseeing? About letting go of what we think we know to embrace what we don't. It's about losing it to find it, about dying to live. The mystic Meister Eckhart said, "The eye with which I see God is the same eye with which God sees me."[6] In the same way, the eye through which we see the world is the same eye through which the world sees us. When we see the world with semiotic eyes, we begin to see ourselves with new clarity. We realize we are not just observers, but participants in a cosmic chorus.

In the sacred art of semiotics, the most profound revelations often come from the simplest of observations. We must be ever-present, sometimes sitting in silence, resisting the siren songs of distraction, to truly listen to the still, small voice within. We need to cultivate a holy curiosity, an insatiable desire to know the unknown, and learn from the tapestry of life around us. Even from a nine-year-old, Luke, my son.

Luke's world is one where Minecraft and Roblox reign supreme, not because they dazzle with visual sophistication,

SEMIOTIC TELL #6

but because they are sanctuaries of community and creativity. Here, players are not seduced by Disney-level graphics but are instead enchanted by worlds that are almost cartoonish in their simplicity, yet rich in meaningful connections and authentic experiences. What then, can a nine-year-old teach us? My son has opened my eyes to what I've coined "The Fidelity Fallacy," a lesson I first glimpsed through the wisdom of experience designer Edwin Schlossberg, who noted back in the '90s that true excellence was shifting from the quality of the performance to the depth of participation.

From the obvious all around us, we awaken to the seismic shifts in the markers of authenticity. In the realm of gaming, high-fidelity production no longer automatically signals quality or value. Oh, there will always be a market for such spectacles. But the real signs of authenticity now? They are found in participation, in the weaving of community, in the purity of genuine interaction. Just as video game companies have learned that photorealistic graphics do not guarantee success or satisfaction, so too must faith communities realize that the demand isn't for theatrical worship or polished presentations but for genuine community, for faith practices where everyone can participate, for an authentic engagement with the divine narrative.

The gaming industry's wrestling with adaptation to these changing preferences is a parable for the church in our times. Sadly, while some game developers double down on graphical fidelity to fend off the AI wave, some churches also amplify their spectacle, neglecting the core human desire for community and participation. Here lies the heart of the Fidelity Fallacy—the misguided belief that our spiritual lives can be enhanced by mere surface-level improvements rather than by deepening our devotion, biblical knowing, and communal experience.

Theo-semiotics, then, calls us, whether we are gamers or worshipers, to seek the profound over the superficial, to value community over spectacle, and to choose authenticity over artifice. Let us take note of what is plainly obvious, for in doing so, we might just find the divine whispering through the pixels and prayers of our daily lives.

This is the work of the semiotician: to be a detective of the soul, a priest of culture, a prophet of possibility. To see the world not as it is, but as it could be. To dream a world into being.

Semioticians create a world where the obvious is extraordinary and the invisible is palpable. After all, the obvious is that which is never seen. In the words of the famous mysterious message given to the protagonist by a blind old man in Jules Verne's novel: "Look with all your eyes, look."[7]

Observe the obvious.

SEMIOTIC TELL #6

Source Code Interactives

1. "The Invisible Man" (1911) is one of G. K. Chesterton's most famous stories. The murderer enters the house of the victim, observed by several witnesses, but all claim they saw "nobody." The "nobody" that entered the house was dressed like a postman, but the phenomenon of a postal carrier in uniform delivering mail was too common to even register as an event. Chesterton's hero, Father Brown, specializes in noticing the commonplace things that nobody else can see because they have become too familiar, too ordinary, too obvious. Watch any episode from the Father Brown series on PBS, and talk with one another about what it is to be amazed by what is around us, and dazed by wonders so familiar we do not even notice them.

   In order to see the unseen, you have to let things get cloudy and fuzzy. We like to teach the atom by picturing the solar system and the planets in orbit, but electrons move in clouds of probability, not in neat planetary orbits. So reality itself is a blurred picture of probability clouds. But there is good fog and bad fog. Sometimes, when one is dissembling, or unsure of what to say, that is when the fog seems to set in ... and the fog gets so thick the birds start walking.

   There is "good fog" that leads to insight and "bad fog" that comes from evasion or confusion. How can we tell the difference between productive uncertainty and unproductive confusion in our thinking?

   Sometimes we need to let go of our desire for perfect

clarity to see deeper truths. Do you agree? What are the risks and benefits of this approach?

2. How does embracing uncertainty and 'fuzziness' sometimes lead to deeper understanding? Can you think of examples from your own life where accepting ambiguity led to greater clarity?

3. Here is a Frog in the Kettle story:

> In 2013, twenty-five conservation bodies in Britain collaborated to produce a comprehensive "State of Nature" report (updated in 2016), recording in meticulous detail the changes in status of some 3,400 species in Britain, including mammals, plants, fungi, butterflies, dragonflies and, of course, birds. It was a sober, scientific compilation, but the results were startling. Over the past fifty years, 60 per cent of all wildlife species had declined, many of them sharply, to the point where a number of much-loved breeding birds are at risk of becoming extinct: skylarks are down nationally by 61 per cent, cuckoos and curlews by 62 per cent, lapwing by 64 per cent, corn bunting by 90 per cent, grey partridge by 91 per cent and turtle dove by 96 per cent (so now almost gone); and the figures for flowers, butterflies, moths and other insects are as bad or worse. The dimensions of this crisis have still not impinged on the general consciousness, however, and are

SEMIOTIC TELL #6

scarcely even mentioned by mainstream political parties.[8]

Why do you think such dramatic wildlife declines (60% across species) haven't 'impinged on the general consciousness'? What might explain this disconnect between the severity of the crisis and public awareness?

How might our perception of environmental change be different if it happened suddenly rather than gradually? For instance, how would public reaction differ if 60 percent of USA's wildlife disappeared overnight versus over fifty years?

4. Have someone read out loud the short essay "The Student, The Fish and Agassiz": https://firstdrafts.net/physicalscience/wp-content/uploads/2015/09/Scudder1879_The-Student-the-Fish-and.pdf .

5. Discuss the acronym PEBKAC, a customer support term which means "Problem Exists Between Keyboard and Chair" (PEBKAC). How does it apply to this conversation?

6. As much as John Ruskin hated the railways, or Robert Louis Stevenson hated the telephone, I hate telephone poles and power lines. Why are they so hard to get rid of?

Innovators are not always welcome. In 1589 William Lee made his way to the English court, hoping to be granted a patent for his invention, a knitting machine. Queen Elizabeth I turned him down: "Consider thou what the invention could do to my poor subjects," she enjoined.

"It would assuredly bring to them ruin by depriving them of employment."

This is the same argument Orcas Power and Light made to me for not putting power lines underground on Orcas Island. "What would our linesmen do if we did that?" I wonder where we would be today if we protected from technology the lamplighters, ice cutters, switchboard operators, knocker-uppers, pinsetters, elevator operators, typesetters, log drivers, etc.

Have you ever been bothered by those ubiquitous telephone poles and power lines that no one sees but are everywhere chopping up our trees and our views of the landscape as well as causing power outages in storms? What are some other reasons why the USA is one of the last in the world to put power lines underground?

7. How many of us have the BMB Syndrome (Behold Me Busy)? Also known as the White Rabbit hurry sickness: "I'm late, I'm late, for a very important date. No time to say hello—goodbye—I'm late! I'm late! I'm late!" How severe is your BMB syndrome?

semiotic Tell #7

The Cover's Deception (and the Sign Beneath)

JUST AS WE CAN MISS the obvious, we can miss the spaces, the silences, the what-isn't-there that often is as important as what is there. In fact, George Orwell predicted that telling the whole truth would become a revolutionary act one day.[1]

Nothing is ever as it seems, not even the obvious. Our loudest virtues often mask our deepest flaws. You can call it "Sweet's Law:" The sins we shout against are the ones we shelter within. The virtues we peddle are the first we betray. Just ask Peter, who vowed his life but couldn't risk his pride. The pinnacle of my character and the pit of my failings share the same foundation. My halo and my shadow are cast by the same light.

Voltaire is often attributed with the definition of a bore as someone who leaves nothing out. In fact, for a writer to leave nothing out means you have put nothing in of yourself. And what is left out is often more important than what is put in.

The distinction between appearances and things-in-themselves is one of the most basic in philosophical circles. Semioticians are not afraid of the "via negativa" ("negative theology") which says that God's transcendence is such that God can best be explained in terms of what God is NOT.[2] But what is often forgotten about apophatic theologians, whether in the Eastern Orthodox tradition (Gregory Palamas, Maximus the Confessor, Symeon the New Theologian (my personal favorite) or in the Western Tradition (Meister Eckhart, Johannes Tauler, John of the Cross) is that they combined apophatic methods with cataphatic (affirmative) approaches to offer the most complete understanding of the divine.

Semiotics is the art of noticing what's not there. In a world where nothing is as it seems, the most profound truths often lie hidden in the silences, the empty spaces, the gaps, and the gasps—these are the secret languages that whisper *important* messages. Semioticians are the masters of decoding these unseen narratives, seeking the tells, the tics, the grimaces, the gestures that reveal a hand in poker, or the unseen hand.

These often-overlooked aspects of communication can carry profound meaning:

> Silences: What's left unsaid can be as important as what's said.
>
> Empty spaces: In visual arts and music, negative space can define the composition.
>
> Gaps: The intervals between notes in music or pauses in speech can convey emotion and emphasis.
>
> Gasps: Involuntary reactions can reveal hidden thoughts or emotions.

Backmasking: Hidden Messages in Music: Backmasking is a perfect example of how hidden meanings can be embedded in art. This technique involves reversing audio or placing reversed audio within a recording. Notable examples include:

> The Beatles' "Revolution 9": Often cited as an early example of perceived backmasking.
>
> Pink Floyd's "Empty Spaces": Contains an intentional backwards message.
>
> Electric Light Orchestra's "Fire on High": ELO includes a deliberate backwards message in response to backmasking controversies.
>
> Weird Al Yankovic's "Nature Trail to Hell": parodies the concept
>
> Led Zeppelin's "Stairway to Heaven": Allegedly contains a backwards message praising the highway to hell.

Hidden messages in music aren't limited to reversed audio. They can appear in various forms:

> Lyrical metaphors and allegories
>
> Visual symbolism in album artwork
>
> Musical motifs and leitmotifs
>
> Subtle references to other works or cultural phenomena

Applying semiotic analysis to music reveals layers of meaning beyond the surface level of lyrics and melodies. Consider:

> The choice of instruments and their cultural associations

The use of silence or dissonance to create tension

The structure of a song and how it relates to its message

The performance style and how it informs interpretation

The intersection of semiotics and music, particularly through techniques like backmasking, highlights the multifaceted nature of artistic expression. This practice of seeking out "unseen narratives" enriches our understanding of both the art itself and the cultural context in which it was created.

Giveaways and Getaways: Semioticians are not only interested in what they see, but even more in what there is still to see. As the deer panteth for the waters, so longeth a semiotician for the signature giveaways.

As the proverb goes, "Nobody knows anything."[3] And yet, it's in the unknowns, the in-betweens, and the unspoken that we find the deepest truths. The poet Rosemarie Waldrop reminds us, "What matters is not things but what happens between them."[4] The gaps keep the questions in relation, inviting us to fill in the blanks and find our unique meanings.

Toys are never just toys; food is never just food. Commercials are never just commercials. Almost everything ("sometimes a cigar IS just a cigar") carries a hidden message, a secret code waiting to be deciphered. The best way to read the world is not through the lens of our expertise but through the fresh eyes of the amateur, or child, unencumbered by assumptions and expectations. A semiotician looks again at things we thought we had already seen.

… SEMIOTIC TELL #7

> *We look at the world once, in childhood.*
> *The rest is memory.*
>
> LYRICAL STORYTELLER AND FORMER POET LAUREATE LOUISE GLUCK[5]

As Ernest Hemingway wrote, failures happen "gradually and then suddenly."[6] The surface may appear calm, but beneath the waves, currents are shifting. The surface is the last thing to go. Regimes crumble from within. The edifice may remain, but it's only a facade. Semiotics teaches us to see the front from the back, the surface from the depth. Only then can we understand the hidden dynamics that shape our world.

The Way of the Child: Semiotics is the sacred art of seeing the unseen, of hearing the unheard. It's the alchemy of transforming noise into narrative, of finding the divine in the hum of the humdrum. Like a child, the semiotician is a wonderer, a questioner, a seeker of hidden treasures. They are detectives of the soul, sleuths of the spirit.

One way of seeing the world is as a text, a holy book written in the language of signs and symbols. Every object, every interaction, every silence is a chapter waiting to be read. The semiotician, like the child, approaches this text with fresh eyes, unburdened by the weight of expectation. They see the world not as it is, but as it could be, a canvas of infinite possibilities.

To be a semiotician is to recover the lost art of play.[7] It is to inhabit the world with the curiosity of a cat, with the wonder of a newborn. It is to dance with shadows, to sing with the wind, to find magic in the ordinary. The semiotician, like the child, lives in a world of enchantment, where anything is possible, and every corner holds a surprise.

The semiotician, like the child, is a conceiver of reality. They shape the world as much as the world shapes them.

"Quench not the Spirit"[8] is such an imposing warning that some theologians (e.g., John Calvin) associated it with the Unpardonable Sin and Blasphemy Against the Holy Spirit. One of the most dangerous spirits to quench is the child's spirit. To quench the child's spirit in a human yields an aborted human, since the divine pattern for humanity is based on "becoming like a child,"[9] and humans have been gifted with the very "power to become the children of God."[10]

To quench the spirit of a child is to extinguish the spark of divine creativity. It is to close the door to the sacred, to hasten away from the mystery that hazes us. Semioticians, in our quest to uncover hidden-in-plain-sight meanings, are devoted to keeping that spark alive. Semioticians are guardians of wonder, the FBI of creativity, the MI5 of the imagination, the Mossad of the Maker's Mark.

In the end, semiotics is not just about decoding signs; it's about releasing the genie (genius?)[11] of the child within, the one who knows that the universe is a playground, and every day is a sandbox adventure in taking risks. God is The Original Risk-taker: the greatest risk ever taken was the creation of human beings made in God's image. The way of the semiotician is the way of the child.

SEMIOTIC TELL #7

*If you manage to succeed don't boast of it.
What you have done is enough in itself.*

FRENCH HIGH-WIRE ARTIST PHILIPPE PETIT[12]

"What Things?" The Most Revealing Window into Jesus' Mind: No human systems of meaning (semiotics) can fully understand something that precedes and transcends human systems. Hence embracing humility is vital in semiotics. Signs can have multiple meanings and cultural significance, making it impossible for any individual, no matter how knowledgeable, to fully grasp their complexity. Recognizing this limitation ensures a deeper understanding. True humility sometimes means knowing when to withhold, even when you know the answer.

Imagine you've just pulled off the greatest victory in all of history. We're not talking Alexander the Great beating the Persians, William the Conqueror taking England, or even the Soviets turning the tide against Nazi Germany. No, you've just defeated the real axis of evil: the trifecta of Satan, death, and hell itself.

So what do you do next? If it were me, I'd be strutting back into town on a majestic stallion, sword raised high, ready to rub it in the faces of everyone who doubted me. I'd be unleashing a cannonade of accolades and a drumbeat of accomplishments. But Jesus? He takes a different approach.

Jesus, fresh from his cosmic triumph, casually strolls up to a couple of his followers on the road to Emmaus. Clopas and Mary are deep in conversation about the earth-shattering events of the past few days. When they realize this stranger doesn't seem to know what's happened, they're baffled. "Are you the only one in Jerusalem who doesn't know these things?" they ask.

And here's where Jesus drops the line that, to me, offers the deepest insight into his character:

"What things?"

Can you believe it? The guy who just flipped the entire universe on its head is playing dumb. No bragging, no victory lap—just two simple words that invite others to share their perspective.

It's this moment of profound humility that reveals the true essence of Jesus. He's not here to boast or dominate, but to listen and engage. It's so unexpected, so counterintuitive, that it's almost comical.

This "What things?" approach is so fascinating, so rich with meaning, that I'm considering devoting my next book to exploring just this phrase. It's a semiotic peephole that opens up a vast view into the heart, mind, and spirit of Jesus. The one who knew everything was humble enough not to show off that he knew everything. That's humility.

Humility is a word which means "groundedness." We all need to be "grounded" to grow, rooted in the ground. How firmly are you planted?

Semioticians are gardeners, constantly tending to their spiritual soil. They ask each other, "Are you still grounded?" It's a friendly reminder to stay humble, just like my mom, Mabel, used to say, "My job, Lenny, is to keep you humble." If we're not grounded in the Spirit, it's like a power outage. Our humility shows how well we're charged, and the quality

SEMIOTIC TELL #7

of our semiotics depends on that surge of connection and current.

Of course, some people think they're "rooted" and "grounded" when they're really stuck. There is a big difference between the two: rooted and stuck. We easily get stuck in blame-laden finger-pointings of what's wrong rather than the common ends and commonsense strategies to lead us forward. Paradoxically, the more your roots stretch down, the less stuck you are.

Imagine a tree reaching for the sun, its roots firmly planted in the earth. That's humility. Humility, like a strong root system, allows us to grow tall while staying grounded. It's acknowledging our strengths without arrogance and accepting our weaknesses without shame. True humility leads to self-acceptance. It allows us to appreciate our value without inflating our ego. We can be comfortable in our own skin, knowing we are loved and valued for who we are, not what we achieve. In essence, humility lets us stand tall with our roots firmly planted in reality.

Humility can go in two directions. One is humiliation, which is a negative experience of shame and disgrace. The other is "humilification," a positive experience of self-acceptance, where one is valued, comfortable in one's own skin, and "loved for who you are" precisely because of having true humility—a grounded, non-arrogant sense of one's authentic self that is neither inflated nor diminished. True humility allows one to appreciate one's worth while staying rooted in "what things?" reality and social harmony. Humilification is what happens to you when you are loved for who you are and not for what you did.

Tradition and Change: There is a new saying circulating in Catholic circles today: "Tradition is For the Young." This slogan carries multiple levels of meaning, hinting at a subterranean revival of ritual in the church; it conveys the preference of some young Catholics for the Latin mass (Extraordinary Form) or high liturgy in worship; it also channels the semiotic principle that tradition and change are intertwined.

Timeless Truth always surprises with its timeliness and timefulness. What keeps the timeless timely and timeful is change. You can't have tradition without adaptation. You can't have timeless truths without the ability to adapt. The concept of an unchanging God is paradoxically reinforced by the freshness of divine mercies every morning. This tension between stability and change is a fundamental aspect of semiotics.

The Danger of Ignoring Semiotic Signs: Institutions that fail to read the signs of the times and dive beneath the surface risk demise. The decline of General Electric serves as a cautionary tale of ignoring semiotic signs.

Once the mighty behemoth of American industry, GE was the Apple of its time, reigning supreme in 1993. Fast-forward twenty-five years, and it's a shadow of its former self, ousted from the Dow in 2018. Semioticians learn from failure.

I can already hear some of you, my students like the founder of Faith Inkubators, Rich Melheim, break into this conversation and demand more proof of the demise of those who ignore semiotics. So I'm pre-empting your questions with my own: What can we learn from the GE case study about the peril of ignoring semiotics?

SEMIOTIC TELL #7

GE Case Study: Here are some semiotic warning signs GE missed

1. Technological Disruption Signals
   - Rise of digital-first companies
   - Changing patterns of innovation and value creation
   - New symbols of corporate success in the digital age
2. Market Communication Patterns
   - Shifting investor preferences toward specialized companies
   - Growing market skepticism of diversified conglomerates
   - Emerging narratives about agile business models
3. Societal Value Shifts
   - Changed perception of corporate size and power
   - New environmental and social responsibility expectations
   - Evolution of workplace culture preferences

Lessons for Semioticians

1. Surface vs. Deep Structure
   - GE focused on surface-level market indicators while missing deeper structural changes

- GE failed to decode the changing semiotics of corporate success
- GE overlooked emerging signs of fundamental market transformation

2. Sign System Evolution
   - Markets evolved from industrial to digital sign systems
   - Traditional symbols of corporate success lost their meaning
   - New symbolic hierarchies emerged that GE failed to recognize
3. Interpretative Framework Failures
   - GE relied on outdated frameworks for reading market signs
   - GE failed to update semiotic interpretation methods
   - GE missed the emergence of new meaning-making systems in business

Contemporary Applications: The GE case demonstrates how semiotic blindness can lead to corporate decline. I hope students like my colleague Dr. Rich Melheim can be confident now in asserting that healthy organizations must:

1. Develop robust semiotic reading capabilities
2. Regularly update their interpretative frameworks

3. Look beyond surface-level signs to deeper structural changes
4. Maintain flexibility in response to changing sign systems
5. Foster cultural sensitivity to emerging symbolic meanings

Case Study of Cathedrals: The reason why cathedrals endured for 850+ years? Masons mixed a mortar and lime layer between the stones that enabled the structure to move so it could withstand extreme wind pressure. Cathedrals are stable and survive for millenia because they are constantly moving and accommodate motion.

Life is a Paradox. Life itself is change—a heart that beats, lungs that breathe, cells that divide and die and renew. The moment all change ceases, the curtain of death drops (and new life begins). Nature teaches us this supreme irony: to remain alive, we must never remain the same. Adapt or fade away—there is no middle ground.

Cathedrals have endured for centuries by incorporating change and flexibility into their structure. So theo-semioticians help the church to welcome change so it can remain stable. For the church to be the Pentecost church it was meant to be, it must welcome the new Breeze and Blaze, Fresh Wind and Fresh Fire.

Know nothing … is as it seems.

Source Code Interactives

1. Isaac Watts, the "father of English hymnody," wrote many magnificent hymn texts for children, such as "I Sing the Almighty Power of God," and also provided some moralistic admonitions for kids in his *Divine Songs in Easy Language for Use of Children* (1715). Here from the 1880 edition is Song XVI, "Against Quarreling and Fighting":

   > Let dogs delight to bark and bite,
   > For God has made them so:
   > Let bears and lions growl and fight,
   > For 'tis their nature, too.
   >
   > But children, you should never let
   > Such angry passions rise:
   > Your little hands were never made
   > To tear each other's eyes.

   Try that out in your local Sunday School.

2. What is the difference between a dead metaphor and a live metaphor?

3. How do you see that tradition and change are semiotically intertwined?

4. Give some more examples of how ignoring semiotic signs leads to institutional decline.

5. If adaptation is crucial for stability and survival, how can the church better welcome change to remain incarnational and thrive?

SEMIOTIC TELL #7

6. How many times have your digital devices flashed the words "Memory is Full." Using this phrase as a word metaphor, here are some semiotic-inspired discussion questions:

   a. The human brain's capacity for memory is impressive, but whether it's limitless is still debated among scientists. Are there practical boundaries we haven't yet discovered beyond capacity constraints like the research that suggests the brain's capacity for storing memories may be finite, estimated to be around 2.5 petabytes (1 petabyte = 1,000 terabytes)?

   b. How has the prevalence of digital memory storage affected our natural memory capabilities?

   c. Is forgetting a flaw in human memory, or a crucial feature for our mental well-being?

   d. To what extent do we consciously control what we remember and forget?

   e. In an age of information overload, how can we effectively manage our cognitive load without sacrificing important knowledge?

   f. Is there a point at which additional information becomes detrimental rather than beneficial to our understanding?

   g. Can emotional experiences "fill up" our capacity for empathy or compassion? If so, how might we "clear space"?

   h. How does being "full of" an emotion impact our ability to process and store new memories?

i. Can we truly be "over" a significant life event while retaining a vivid memory of it?

    j. How does the process of emotional detachment from a memory differ from forgetting?

7. The stethoscope was invented in 1816 by French physician Rene Laennac to avoid putting his ear directly to the chest of a particularly buxom patient. Laennec was also motivated by the need to better hear heart and lung sounds, especially in overweight patients. Stethoscopes had limited functional value, although they did allow physicians to hear heart rhythms, lung sounds, and other internal bodily functions. But more than anything, they were semiotic signals that the physician was listening to you and your body. The stethoscope did not convey all that much information. But it was comforting and confirmation of the physician's expertise.

    a. How do symbolic objects in healthcare (like stethoscopes or white coats) influence patient perception and trust in medical professionals?

    b. In what ways might ritual actions or symbolic gestures in various professions serve to reassure clients or customers, even if they're not strictly necessary?

    c. How does the placebo effect relate to our human need for tangible signs of care or treatment?

    d. What are the ethical considerations of using placebos or symbolic gestures in professional settings, particularly in healthcare?

    e. In an increasingly digital world, how are traditional

SEMIOTIC TELL #7

symbols of professionalism and care evolving? What new symbols are emerging?

Semiotic Tell #8

Cosmic Curveballs

―――――◇―――――

A man can control only what he comprehends, and comprehend only what he is able to put into words. The inexpressible therefore is unknowable. By examining future stages in the evolution of language we come to learn what discoveries, changes and social revolutions the language will be capable, some day, of reflecting.[1]

POLISH SCIENCE FICTION WRITER STANISLAW LEM (D. 2006)

―――――――――――――――

The Semiotics of Surprise: Surprise is the golden thread that catches the light, drawing our eyes to the unexpected beauty of life's design. Future semioticians, you stand as watchful guardians of the unforeseen, knowing with a wry smile that the future is a trickster, forever dodging your well-laid plans and neatly packaged predictions.

The most predictable thing about the future is that it seldom conforms to our predictions. It's as if the cosmos itself delights in confounding our forecasts, be they derived from tea leaves, horoscopes, chicken entrails, or the latest predictive algorithms. The thing most predicted is often the least likely to occur, a paradox that forms the core of what we might call the Predictable Unpredictability of it all.

Predictable Unpredictability: Robert Heinlein (1907–1988), one of the most self-reflective of science fiction writers, famously declared that "Science fiction is not prophecy." Instead, it's an exercise in "extrapolating" from the present, based on the direction of current trends.[2] This insight reveals a profound truth: science fiction, and indeed all our attempts to peer into the future, are less about what's to come than about our present moment's hopes, fears, and preoccupations.

As we navigate this labyrinth of potential futures, we must remember that history's march is characterized by its favorite literary device: the plot twist. The foreseen is seldom seen, while the unforeseen takes center stage. Wild cards and black swans aren't just lurking around corners; they're throwing surprise parties and inviting everyone. And when the divine enters this cosmic shindig? Hold onto your sandals, because anything can happen—and probably will.

The Serendipitous Symphony of Discovery: Science, for all its lab coats and clipboards, harbors a delightful secret: the greatest discoveries are often happy accidents. It's not the triumphant "Eureka!" that changes the world, but the puzzled "Hmmm, that's funny . . ." or the bewildered "Ahem, that's weird . . ." These moments of serendipity have given us everything from penicillin to post-it notes, from X-rays to vulcanized rubber.

Consider the story of Alexander Fleming, whose accidental contamination of a Petri dish led to the discovery of penicillin. Or ponder the tale of Percy Spencer, who noticed a chocolate bar melting in his pocket while working with radar equipment, leading to the invention of the microwave oven. These stories remind us that the universe often speaks to us

SEMIOTIC TELL #8

in whispers and winks, rewarding those attentive enough to notice the unexpected.

As semioticians, we must cultivate this spirit of curious observation. The next time you spill your coffee and it forms the shape of a new galaxy, pay attention. When your GPS takes you on an unintended detour, keep your eyes open for the hidden wonders along the way. In embracing these moments of serendipity, we open ourselves to a world of discovery that rigid expectations might otherwise obscure.

Our thoughts are seeds that we plant, and we eat the fruit. Every cell in your body is listening to your thoughts.

PASTOR AND PSYCHOTHERAPIST JO HARGREAVES

Theo-semiotics: God's Surprise Party: Theo-semiotics isn't just a fancy word to impress your friends at dinner parties. It's the art of praising a God who's the ultimate cosmic prankster, the divine disruptor of our too-small expectations. It's worship that doesn't just expect the unexpected—it dresses up and brings a potluck dish.

Where the Spirit of the Lord is, there's not just liberty—there's a liberation from the middling and mediocre. It's spontaneity with a holy twist, the wild unleashed in sacred spaces. Just as nature needs its wild places, so does the human spirit. Our faith should be a grand adventure, full of surprising twists and turns that leave us breathless with wonder and awe.

Consider the biblical narratives: A burning bush that isn't consumed. A donkey that speaks. Water gushing from a rock. Walls falling to the sound of trumpets. A virgin birth. An empty tomb. The story of God's interaction with humanity is a litany of the unexpected, a divine comedy that continually subverts our expectations and expands our understanding of what's possible.

In our theo-semiotic approach, we're called to embrace this divine unpredictability. Our worship should be infused with a sense of holy anticipation, our prayers filled with the expectation that God might answer in ways we never imagined. After all, as the prophet Isaiah reminds us, "For my thoughts are not your thoughts, neither are your ways my ways," declares the Lord.[3]

Protecting the Wild Within: Every child is born with a wild spirit, a free-ranging imagination that needs protecting, not pruning. We're not talking about letting your kids run amok in the supermarket (though that could be an interesting sociological experiment). We're talking about cherishing those wild dreams, those impossibly big hopes, those expectations that make adults nervously check their calendars.

This spiritual wilding needs gentling, not breaking. Sanctification is about channeling that holy wildness, not caging it. As we grow older, the weight of years can dim our spark of surprise and capacity for spontaneity, leaving us jaded and jejune. But Jesus' call to "become like little children" isn't a regression, but a revolution. It's an invitation to rediscover the world with wide eyes and open hearts. Semiotics sets the stage for letting the unexpected paint each day with its vibrant colors.

How do we protect this wild spirit within ourselves and others? Here are a few suggestions:

> Cultivate curiosity: Ask questions, especially

"what if" or "how come" or "who says" questions.

Embrace play: The first time we meet Yahweh Elohim in Genesis 2, God is at play, making mud pies. Engage in sandbox activities without a specific goal or outcome.

Practice wonder: Take time to marvel at the world around you, from the intricate design of a flower to the vastness of the night sky.

Encourage creativity: Express yourself through art, music, writing, stamp collecting, or any form of creation.

Welcome diversity: Expose yourself (I do this through my randomization rituals I introduced in my semiotics textbook on evangelism *Nudge*) to different ideas, cultures, and perspectives.

By nurturing this inner wildness, we remain open to the surprises God has in store for us, ready to rock'n'roll with the unexpected rhythms of life.

The Divine Drama: Suspense vs. Surprise: Alfred Hitchcock, that master of the macabre, knew a thing or two about keeping people on the edge of their seats. He taught us that suspense is knowing there's a bomb under the table, while surprise is when it unexpectedly goes "BOOM!"

In the grand narrative of faith, we're living in the delicious suspense of knowing God's up to something big. Every moment is pregnant with possibility, every ordinary day hiding out-of-this-world potential. We're not just waiting for the other shoe to drop; we're expecting it to sprout wings and fly.

This divine suspense calls us to live with a sense of holy anticipation. We wake up each morning with the expectation that today might be the day when God breaks into our routine in a spectacular way. It's about approaching each conversation, each task, each seemingly mundane moment with the awareness that it could be the stage for a divine encounter.

Surprise, on the other hand, is God's favorite party trick. It's the "plot twist" that makes you want to read the whole Book again, just to see how you missed it the first time. It's the resurrection that turns defeat into victory, the Pentecost that turns fearful disciples into bold apostles, the Damascus road experience that turns a persecutor into a preacher.

You are semioticians of the sacred. You are called to live in this tension between suspense and surprise. So cultivate expectancy without presumption, readiness without rigidity. Know that God is always at play, often in ways we can't see or understand. Remain open to the delightful surprises the divine has in store for us humans.

The Magic of Mystery: For some poor souls, mystery is misery. They want life predigested, predictable, and wrapped up with a neat little bow. Pity these packaged-life enthusiasts, forever missing the joy of living with the inexplicable and the thrill of unwrapping existence's glorious surprises.

But you're a semiotician. Mystery is where the magic happens. It's the space between the known and the unknown, the gap in the fence where wonder sneaks in.

Mystery invites us into a dance with the divine, a holy hide-and-seek where each discovery leads to new questions, each answer opens up new realms of exploration. It's in

SEMIOTIC TELL #8

embracing mystery that we find the freedom to grow, to change, to become more than we ever imagined possible.

Consider the mysteries that surround us every day:

> The miracle of consciousness emerging from the complex interplay of neurons.
>
> The vast, largely unexplored depths of our oceans.
>
> The quantum realm, where particles can be in two places at once.
>
> The origins of the universe and the nature of dark matter.
>
> The complexities of human relationships and the depths of love.
>
> The ineffable wonder of God's love, an infinite embrace that spans the cosmos yet touches each heart uniquely.

Each of these mysteries invites us to wonder, to explore, to remain open to new discoveries and revelations. They remind us that the world is far more complex and beautiful than our limited understanding can grasp.

As you navigate this wild, wonderful world, semiotics teaches a life lesson: expect the unexpected, cherish the surprise, and when in doubt, look for the divine fingerprints on the everyday extraordinary. After all, in the grand semiotics of life, the most profound sign might just be a wink from the divine, reminding us that the best is yet to come—and it's probably nothing like we imagined.

Parable of a Painter's Last Masterpiece: Renowned artist

Eliza Fontaine was nearing the end of her life. Her family gathered around her bed in her studio, surrounded by a lifetime of colorful canvases.

"I have one last painting in me," Eliza declared weakly. "But I need your help."

Her children exchanged worried glances. "Mother, you're too frail," her daughter Sophie protested.

Eliza waved her hand dismissively. "Nonsense. Art is my life force. Now, fetch me my brushes and set up a blank canvas."

Reluctantly, her family complied. They propped Eliza up in bed and arranged her paints within reach.

"What would you like us to do?" her son Thomas asked.

Eliza's eyes twinkled. "Each of you, choose a color and paint one brushstroke on the canvas. Don't tell me what you're doing. Just add your mark."

One by one, her children and grandchildren approached the canvas, each adding a single stroke of color.

When they finished, Eliza nodded satisfactorily. "Now, turn the canvas to face me and hand me a brush."

They did as she asked. Eliza studied the random assortment of lines and splotches, then dipped her brush in paint. With trembling hands, she began to work, connecting lines, blending colors, and adding new elements.

Her family watched in awe as a beautiful landscape emerged from the chaos. Rolling hills, a winding river, and a brilliant sunset took shape under Eliza's skilled hand.

As she put the final touches on the painting, Eliza smiled contentedly. "You see," she whispered, "life is full of

SEMIOTIC TELL #8

unexpected brushstrokes. The true art lies in how we connect them."

She set down her brush and leaned back, closing her eyes. "Now, my dears, when people ask about my final painting, tell them I said …"

Her family leaned in close to hear her last words.

Eliza's eyes flew open, sparkling with mischief. "Surprise me!"

And with that, the great artist took her final breath, leaving behind a masterpiece born from the unexpected and a legacy of embracing life's surprises.

Every day, where the Spirit of the Lord is, there is … "Surprise Me!"

We end this exploration of the unexpected with Eliza's final words ringing in our ears: "Surprise me!" Please, my semioticians in training, please, please, approach each day with the same spirit of openness and anticipation, ready to connect the unexpected brushstrokes of life into a masterpiece of faith, wonder, and joy.

Embrace divine plot twists. Expect the unexpected.

SOURCE CODE INTERACTIVES

Squire Rushnell, an American author and former television executive, coined the term "Godwink" in the late 1990s and popularized it through his series of books, the first of which was titled *When God Winks: How the Power of Coincidence Guides Your Life* (2001).

1. What does the term "Godwink" mean to you personally? How would you explain it to someone who's never heard of it?

2. Can you share an experience from your life that you would consider a "Godwink"? A moment where it seemed God was saying, "Hey, I'm here. I'm watching over you." What made this event stand out as more than just a coincidence?

3. How do you distinguish between random coincidences and potential "Godwinks"? Are there any specific criteria you use?

    Do you think the concept of "Godwinks" can be comforting during difficult times? Why or why not?

4. How might actively looking for "Godwinks" change one's perspective on daily life?

5. Are there any potential downsides to interpreting coincidences as divine interventions? How can we maintain a balanced view?

6. How do you think different faith traditions might view the concept of "Godwinks"?

7. Have you ever experienced a series of related "Godwinks" that seemed to be guiding you towards a particular decision or path?

8. Do you think "Godwinks" always have a clear message, or can they sometimes be mysterious or open to interpretation?

9. How might the concept of "Godwinks" relate to other spiritual ideas like prayer, meditation, or mindfulness?

10. Has learning about the concept of "Godwinks" changed how you view unexpected events in your life?

11. In examining the role of surprises in interpretation, how do we balance openness to unexpected meanings while maintaining appropriate theological and interpretive boundaries? Consider both the risks and potential benefits of allowing for interpretive surprises.

12. What are the implications of focusing on the "signs of the end of time" rather than the "signs of the times"? How does this impact our understanding of God's kingdom?

13. How do you think the idea of the kingdom of God being both "present" and "not yet" affects our daily lives and our faith?

    In what ways have we, as a faith community, ignored the work of God in the present moment? What are some examples of this?

14. How has the idea of escapism influenced our faith and our understanding of God's role in the world?

15. What are the potential consequences of emphasizing the second coming of Christ to the point where the significance of the first coming is diminished?

16. How can we integrate our hope for Christ's return with a sense of responsibility to engage with the world and participate in God's mission today?

17. What are some ways we can critically evaluate our own traditions and practices without rejecting them entirely?

18. How can we rediscover the power and significance of the first coming of Christ, and what implications might this have for our faith and our lives?

19. What does my statement "When the establishment wants you to look one way, look another" mean to you? Can you think of historical examples where significant changes or innovations came from unexpected directions?

20. How can we distinguish between "noise" and valuable signals when looking for emerging trends? What strategies can we use to filter out distractions and focus on meaningful developments?

21. Can you identify any current fringe movements or ideas that you believe might shape the future? What makes them stand out to you?

22. What are some potential risks or challenges in focusing

primarily on the margins while ignoring mainstream trends? How can we distribute attention between the two?

23. How might the semiotic concept of "the future forming on the fringes" apply to different fields such as technology, culture, spirituality, or politics? Can you give specific examples for each?

24. What does the phrase "Centers collapse as the margins gain momentum" suggest about the nature of change in society? Can you think of any examples where this has happened in recent history?

In your own life or work, how can you apply the principle of looking to the margins for new ideas or opportunities? What areas or sources might you explore that you've previously overlooked?

How does the idea of focusing on the fringes challenge our natural tendencies or biases? What psychological or social barriers might we need to overcome to effectively practice this approach?

Consider a field you're familiar with. What are its "fringes" or margins, and what interesting developments are happening there that the mainstream might be overlooking?

How might education systems change if they embraced the idea that "the future forms on the fringes"? What would a curriculum designed around this principle look like?

In the context of faith and spirituality, how might the concept of looking to the margins for the future align or conflict with traditional religious teachings? Can you think of examples where religious innovations came from the fringes?

How can we cultivate a mindset that's open to identifying and valuing fringe ideas without becoming overwhelmed by every new trend or losing touch with valuable established knowledge?

In an age of algorithms and personalized content, how can we ensure we're exposed to truly fringe ideas rather than just variations of what we already know or believe?

How might the principle of "the future forms on the fringes" inform our approach to problem-solving, both on a personal level and for larger societal issues?

25. What are some cosmic curveballs that have been thrown your way, and how did you handle them?

Semiotic Tell #9

The Cyclops' Gaze

EVER HEARD THE PHRASE "Good things come in threes"? It's more than just a charm; it's a fundamental pattern woven into the very fabric of reality. So hold onto your seats, because we're about to take that idea for a philosophical spin on a tilt-a-wheel that would make even Goldilocks' head turn.[1]

The Rule of Threes: The French have a saying: "*Jamais deux sans trois*" or "Never two without three." It's not just about winning streaks or celebrity deaths. This "rule of threes" reflects a deeper truth about reality itself. From fairy tales to philosophical concepts, it's a recurring theme.

The mark of the Trinity is everywhere: "*vestigia Trinitatis*" as the early church called it, or "footprints of the Trinity." The triunity of the universe is reflected in space: height, width, depth; in light: particle, wave, beam; in matter: energy, motion, phenomenon; in creativity: idea, execution, refinement. The Rule of Three is the Rule of Life.

The Rule of Three is the Rule of Creativity. Jasper Johns once said that the way to make art is to take something and to do something to it and then do something else to it.[2] All Creativity is a Three-Dog Night. Or as Sherlock Holmes would put it, that's a three-pipe problem.

But here's the kicker: it's not just about counting to three;

it's about the magic that happens when two paradoxical ideas collide and create something entirely new.

Humans are wired for three. The luminous and harmonious paradox seeks resolution in three:

> Faith, Hope, Love
>
> Yesterday, Today, Forever
>
> Old Testament, New Testament, Your Testament
>
> kenosis, plerosis, henosis (union)
>
> Maranatha: was, is, is to come.
>
> Henceforth: from now on (from=past, now=present, on=future).
>
> In ancient Greek philosophy, truth was a three-ring circus: dogma, doxa, pragma. (Dogma refers to established, often unquestioned beliefs or principles. Doxa refers to popular opinion or belief, not necessarily based on reason or proof. Pragma refers to practical action or deeds.)

Early Christian theologians, particularly those influenced by Greek thought, used these terms to discuss faith and practice. Dogma was the core Christian doctrines like the Trinity or Incarnation, seen as divinely revealed truths. Doxa was the popular Christian beliefs or practices that may not be formally defined doctrines, but widely held within a particular tradition. Pragma was putting faith into action through acts of love, service, or justice.[3]

Triadic Thinking*:* Enter Charles Sanders Peirce, the American Aristotle. We can't escape Peirce (pronounced "purse," in case

SEMIOTIC TELL #9

you want to impress your uninitiated friends). This guy wasn't working from an overtly Christian playbook, but did he love his triads. And so do we.

Peirce came up with three big ideas to explain, well, everything:

> Firstness: The realm of possibility. Think of it as the "once upon a time" of reality.
>
> Secondness: The realm of actuality. This is where things start bumping into each other and causing a ruckus.
>
> Thirdness: The realm of patterns and relationships. It's like the cosmos looked at Firstness and Secondness and said, "I'll give the universe its narrative."

Firstness is the cosmos doing the math.
Secondness is the universe connecting the dots.
Thirdness is reality getting its rhythm.

Welcome to Charles Sanders Peirce's magic world of triadic thinking, which he believed unraveled the mystery of signs and meaning. Let's approach Peirce's "triadic" by imagining you've just got done with a lecture and someone hands you a magic puzzle box. This box has three interconnected pieces that only work when they're all together, a box that symbolizes the profound underlying structure to reality that transcends religious beliefs but reflects divine reality.

Peirce's theory stars three essential performers, each with a crucial role in the magic of meaning:

The Sign: Meet "The Great Sigmund," our charismatic magician. Sigmund is the showman who catches your eye with flourishes and dramatic gestures. He could be waving a wand, showing a card, or uttering a mysterious incantation.

The Object: This is "The Enigmatic Orbo," the subject of Sigmund's trick. Orbo is the rabbit in the hat, the assistant in the box, or the coin that's about to vanish—the thing in the real world that Sigmund is trying to manipulate.

The Interpretant: Say hello to "The Mystified Izzy," our audience volunteer. Izzy represents the "Aha!" moment in your mind when you watch Sigmund's performance and try to figure out what's happening to Orbo.

Watch closely as our magical trio performs their astonishing feat of semiosis—the process by which meaning mysteriously appears.

The Great Sigmund starts the trick with a flourish, drawing all eyes to him.

The Enigmatic Orbo waits in plain sight, though perhaps disguised or hidden.

The Mystified Izzy observes intently, attempting to connect Sigmund's actions with what's happening to Orbo.

But here's where the real magic happens. Different audience members might interpret the trick differently. Your Izzy might gasp at a levitation, while your friend's Izzy applauds a metamorphosis. The meaning of the trick isn't just in Sigmund's performance or Orbo's changes. It's in the mysterious connection between them, like the invisible wire in a floating act.

Peirce's grand finale shows us that meaning isn't just about the magician's performance (Sigmund) or the props used (Orbo), but also about how the audience interprets and experiences the illusion (Izzy). Or to put it another way, Peirce is saying that meaning is like a three-way conversation at a really cool party. It's not just about what's said (Siggy) or what's being talked about (Orby), but also about how everyone understands it (Izzy).

So the next time you encounter a sign, remember: you're not just observing it, you're part of a magnificent magic show of meaning.

The Trinity Tango: Where Philosophy Meets Theology: Here's where things get really interesting. Some brilliant scholars noticed that Peirce's triadic thinking has an uncanny resemblance to Christian trinitarian theology.[4] It's like they're dancing the same dance, just with different partners.

Just as the Trinity is one God in three persons, Peirce's categories are three aspects of one reality.

Interrelatedness: The Father, Son, and Holy Spirit are in a constant group hug, and Peirce's categories are similarly inseparable.

Both systems emphasize that reality is all about relationships, not static entities.

When you bring the ends together you create a third, a tertium quid. Bring affirmation and negation together and a third position emerges. Two eyes give you a third perception—depth perception or The Third Eye.

Peirce took this relational idea and ran with it in his theory of signs. As we saw above, he said every sign has three parts: the sign itself, what it represents, and how we interpret it. It's like a cosmic game of telephone, where the message changes as it passes through these three stages.

Trialectic Theology: Let's take this "magic show" to the next level. It's the most mystical magic show ever conceived:

Trialectic Theology. This mind-bending presentation will take you on a journey through the very fabric of existence, from the singularity of oneness to the dance of duality, and finally to the grand finale of reunification. Are you ready?

<u>Act I</u>: The Mysterious Singularity: Our show opens with a single spotlight on an empty stage.

This is One, the chaotic original "number" that's not really a number at all. It's the magic hat from which all of reality will emerge. The One is like a magician's unopened prop box—full of potential, but not yet realized. It's the moment before the show starts, when anything is possible.

<u>Act II</u>: The Split and the Dance of Duality: With a dramatic gesture and a puff of smoke, our cosmic magician splits the One into Two. Creation comes out of separation, as we learn in Genesis 1:

> And God separated the light from the darkness.
>
> And God separated the day from the night.
>
> And God separated the waters above from the waters below.
>
> And God separated the sky from the earth.
>
> And God separated the land from the seas.
>
> And God separated the dry ground from the gathering of waters.
>
> And God separated the greater light to rule the day, from the lesser light to rule the night.
>
> And God separated the creatures of the water, from the creatures of the air.
>
> And God separated the beasts of the earth,

> from the creatures that creep upon the ground.
>
> And God separated humanity, setting it apart in God's own image.
>
> And God separated the seventh day, hallowing it as a day of rest.

Two volunteers are called from the audience, representing the duality that emerges from unity. They stand on opposite sides of the stage, sometimes in conflict, sometimes in harmony. This is the source of love and strife, attraction and repulsion. The audience feels terse and tense, desirous for these two to reunite, to become One again.

Act III: The Magical Reconciliation: But wait. Our magician isn't finished. With a wave of the wand, a third element appears—the Three. Three is the bridge, the numinous link between the two volunteers. It's the diaphanous rope in a spectacular levitation act, invisibly connecting the separated parts. Three is the magician's assistant, helping to bring the two volunteers back together.

A New Kind of Oneness: In a breathtaking finale, our magician uses the power of Three to reunite the Two, creating a new, more complex but complete One: The two volunteers and the assistant join hands, forming a circle. They begin to spin, faster and faster, until they blur into a single, shimmering entity called "*perichoresis*."

But this new One is different. It's not the simple, undifferentiated One we started with. It's a One made of many, a unity of diversity, a communion rather than a simple singularity.

As the curtain falls, we're left with a sense of wonder. We've witnessed the cosmic dance of unity, division, and reunification—all through the lens of a magical performance!

Remember, dear semioticians: in Trialectic Theology, as in magic, the whole is always greater than the sum of its parts. One becomes Two, Two needs Three to become One again, but this new Oneness is a mystical synthesis, a harmony of differences, a true shalom of cosmic proportions.

Did you notice the mind-bender here? Trinitarian thinking thrives on paradox. It's like trying to pat your head and rub your belly at the same time, but for your brain. This approach keeps the mystery alive while revealing the loving, relational nature of reality.

Parables are themselves paradoxical: they reveal at the same time they conceal. Baylor theologian Joshua Mobley talks about the joy of discovering things hidden in symbols: "Concealment gives rise to the desire for revelation and the delight of discovery."[5] When we give rules, platitudes, teachings we remove the wrestling. We remove the relationship and replace it with representation.

Now for the grand finale: the *tertium quid* (Latin for "a third something"). This is what happens when two opposing ideas have a baby. It's not a compromise or a mix—it's something entirely new and unexpected. Peirce called this the *tertium non datur* (Latin for "a third is not given"), which is a fancy way of saying, "Expect the unexpected."[6]

Embracing the Power of Three: So, there you have it. Trinitarian thinking isn't just about counting to three—it's about embracing paradox, finding unexpected connections, and dancing with mystery. Whether you're pondering the nature of God or trying to understand the world around you, remember this, semioticians: sometimes, the most profound truths come in threes, but the threes emerge from the relationship of reverse twos.

Next time someone tells you to "think outside the box," you can smile knowingly and say, "I prefer to think inside the triangle." Just be prepared for some confused looks—and maybe a spirited philosophical debate. But never forget that trialectics is built on dialectics, or more precisely, the ability to handle paradox.

The Nature of Paradox: G. K. Chesterton, the Prince of Paradox, is often credited with the best definition of paradox ever uttered: "Truth standing on its head to gain attention." While this quote's origin remains elusive,[7] the image perfectly showcases how paradox brings opposites together as one. In other words, paradox involves a third element uniting two opposites.

High-decibel dissonance lies at the heart of harmony. When discussing God, language falters, becoming entangled in paradox or reverently surrendering to the sundering silence that surrounds divine mysteries. Ampersands are at play in every theological statement.

Semiotics is a form of jazz. It runs toward and tames dissonance, turning noise into music. It dares us to find harmony in the chaos of a harsh, tragic world, opening our ears, minds, and lives to the unheard and unimagined.

The tribal instinct of humans is paradoxical: it embodies both the need to belong and the need to exclude. Even hermits and monks belong to orders.

Our imaginations struggle with Earth's scale: It feels vast, an endless horizon, making it hard to believe our actions could truly wound it.

Yet, compared to the cosmic canvas, Earth shrinks to a precious, fragile blue Fabergé egg levitating in the vastness and void.

Paradox presents a choice. You can break your head on paradox, or you can build your life on it. You can shatter your mind on the anvil of paradox, or you can forge your existence with it. Paradox is the labyrinth in which thoughts are lost or the adventure in which the trinitarian life thrives: *Jamais deux sans trois.*

The Third Eye: Uniting Insights and Outsights

In our twenty-first century world, many people experience faith in what we might call "2D"—a flat, simplistic understanding that lacks depth and dimension. Yet semiotics calls us to embrace a three-dimensional perspective that integrates multiple layers of meaning and experience.

The Three-Dimensional Vision: The concept of The Third Eye represents more than just another way of seeing—it embodies the semiotic integration of multiple forms of knowing:

- Insights: Our internal wisdom and spiritual discernment
- Outsights: Our empirical observations and experiential knowledge
- The synthesis: Where divine revelation meets human understanding

SEMIOTIC TELL #9

Bind us together Lord
Bind us together with cords
That cannot be broken
Bind us together Lord
Bind us together
Bind us together with love

BRITISH WORSHIP LEADER AND SONGWRITER BOB GILLMAN (1974)

The Holy Braid: A Theo-semiotic Grid

The principle of "a threefold cord is not easily broken" (Ecclesiastes 4:12), manifests in what you, my students, have heard me call many times The Holy Braid:

1. Jesus: The incarnate Story

2. Scripture: The written Story

3. Spirit: The living Story

This triadic structure creates not just a combination but a transformation—a "thirding" that transcends binary thinking and opens new possibilities for understanding. Dionysius the Areopagite, who coined the word "hierarchy" in the late fifth century and defined it as a sacred order approaching the divine, said that all hierarchies come in threes.[8]

The Three Liturgies in Practice: The early church's wisdom is revealed in their practice of three interconnected liturgies:

The Liturgy of Heaven
- The cosmic praise of Creation to Creator

- The eternal worship taking place in celestial realms
- The perfect pattern of divine harmony

The Liturgy of the Altar
- Celebrated on Earth in daily life
- Embodied in communal worship and sacramental practice
- Manifested through ordinary people in extraordinary ways

The Liturgy of the Heart
- The individual's internal response to divine love
- The personal transformation that bridges heaven and earth
- The point where vertical and horizontal dimensions meet

Trialectics: Beyond Binary Thinking.

This three-dimensional understanding moves us beyond simple either/or thinking into a more nuanced realm where:
- Mind, body, and spirit integrate
- Heaven, earth, and human heart align
- Divine truth, human experience, and spiritual insight converge

This three-dimensional faith has profound implications for:
- Personal spiritual practice
- Community worship

SEMIOTIC TELL #9

- Understanding of scripture
- Engagement with the world
- Interfaith dialogue
- Social justice work

The Third Eye perspective transfigures not just how we see, but how we live and move in the world. It offers a path to:
- Deeper spiritual understanding
- More authentic faith practice
- Greater integration of all aspects of life
- Enhanced ability to navigate complexity
- Richer engagement with divine mystery

It is easy to fall off the log at either end ... and hell doesn't care which side you fell off.

SEMIOTICIAN TIM VALENTINO

Elon Musk's Three-Word Tweet That Shook the Financial World

It's 20 December 2020. Elon Musk, the enigmatic tech mogul, fires off a three-word tweet. The result? A company's stock skyrockets 20 percent overnight. But before we reveal those game-changing words, let's take a quick dive into the fascinating world of Elon Musk.

Musk's journey is like something out of a movie. Born in South Africa, he hopscotched through universities in three countries before landing at the University of Pennsylvania.

Today, he holds triple citizenship and regularly trades places with Jeff Bezos for the title of "World's Richest Person."

Many compare Musk to Thomas Edison, and it's easy to see why. Both men were visionaries, pushing the boundaries of what's possible. Edison advocated for electric cars long before they were cool—a dream Musk is now bringing to life with Tesla. But if you ask me? Musk is more like Tony Stark from Iron Man—a brilliant mind with a flair for the dramatic.

Now, back to that earth-shaking tweet heard 'round the world. Are you ready? Here it is:

"One word: doge"

That's it. Three simple words that sent Dogecoin—Bitcoin's quirky competitor—soaring. In that three-word tweet, a meme becomes a cryptocurrency.

Dogecoin, named after the internet's favorite Shiba Inu meme, went from joke to serious player overnight. As a long-time Shiba Inu owner myself, I can't help but smile at how this playful breed took over the crypto world.

Just as Musk saw potential in Dogecoin, I see potential in you. While others focus on the present, I challenge you to "carpe mañana"—seize the future. Be like the tribe of Issachar in the Bible, known for understanding the times and knowing what to do. And here's my challenge to you, future semioticians. It's one word, not three.

Stereopsis.

In a world that's increasingly flat, you're called to bring depth. Stereopsis is about seeing in 3D, using both eyes to truly perceive the world around you with a Third Eye and finding that third way. It's a skill we're in danger of losing, but one that's crucial for understanding our complex reality.

Remember: Jesus comes in stereo. If you're not hearing two things from Jesus, you're not getting the whole gospel. You've heard me say many times, if you're not hearing Jesus come in surround sound, you're not hearing Jesus (or missing a big part of his message). In a world of black-and-white thinking, be the ones who see—and share—the full, vibrant picture. Are you ready to rock the world with your 3-D vision? Your Third Eye?

The Trinitarian Challenge: As we conclude this exploration of trinitarian thinking, I leave you with a challenge: For the next week, commit to seeking out the "third eye" in every situation you encounter. When faced with a dilemma, resist the urge to choose between two options and posit a trilemma. Instead, ask yourself:

What unexpected possibility might emerge if I hold these opposites in tension?

How might a "third eye" perspective reveal something I'm currently missing?

Where can I find unity in diversity, or diversity within unity?

Document your experiences. You may be surprised at how this simple shift in perspective begins to reshape your world.

In embracing trinitarian thinking, we're not just adopting a semiotic stance. We're tuning into the very rhythm of reality. From the subatomic dance of quarks to the cosmic waltz of galaxies, the universe seems to delight in threes. By cultivating our "double vision that grows a third eye," we're not just observers of this grand spectacle—we become active participants in the ongoing story of existence. We move from flat, monochromatic understanding to rich, stereoscopic wisdom.

So go forth, beloved semioticians, armed with your trinitarian perspective of third eyes and third ways. See the world not as it appears on the surface, but as it truly is: a magnificent tapestry of interconnected triads, each one inviting us deeper into the mystery of being.

Remember, in the words of the great William Blake: "If the doors of perception were cleansed, everything would appear to man as it is, Infinite."[9]

Develop your double vision, and grow a Third Eye.

SEMIOTIC TELL #9

source code interactives

T.S. Eliot discusses the poet's ability to create "new wholes" out of disparate elements in his essay "Tradition and the Individual Talent." In this influential piece, he argues that the poet's function is to "purify the dialect of the tribe" and to create a new language that transcends the limitations of personal emotion. By combining seemingly unrelated elements and experiences, the poet can create a new, unified whole that is greater than the sum of its parts.

1. How does Eliot's concept of creating "new wholes" from disparate elements relate to creativity in other art forms or fields beyond poetry?

2. What does Eliot mean by "purify the dialect of the tribe," and how might this idea apply to contemporary communication?

3. How desperate is this culture for someone (i.e., semioticians?) to make "new wholes" out of the most disparate?

4. In what ways might Eliot's ideas about combining unrelated elements to create something greater challenge or support current views on originality and innovation?

5. How relevant do you find Eliot's theories in today's creative landscape?

6. Discuss the potential benefits and drawbacks of poets striving to create a "new poetic language" as Eliot suggests. Does the church need a "new poetic language" for faith, hope, and love?

7. How might Eliot's ideas about poetry inform our understanding of the creative process in general?

8. The resonance between Peircean triadic thinking and Christian Trinitarian thinking lies in the shared insight that reality is fundamentally relational, consisting of interconnected and interdependent aspects that are necessary for understanding the complexity and unity of existence.

   How does viewing reality as inherently relational, rather than as a collection of independent entities, change our understanding of causation, agency, and meaning-making in both philosophical and theological contexts?

   What are the implications of understanding unity not as uniformity or singularity, but as emerging from the dynamic interplay of distinct but interdependent elements, as suggested by both Peirce's triadic semiotics and Trinitarian theology?

9. Trinitarian thinking is a form of paradoxical reasoning that preserves the mystery of God's nature while revealing its relational and self-giving character. The Trinity is a paradox that generates a tertium quid, revealing the relational and loving nature of God. In fact, paradox is the hermeneutic key that unlocks the meaning of the divine, revealing a God who is both human and divine, Father and Son, and yet beyond both. Most importantly, paradox preserves mystery. By acknowledging the limitations of human understanding and the impossibility of fully grasping the divine, Trinitarian thinking maintains a sense of awe and reverence for the mystery of God.

SEMIOTIC TELL #9

How does paradox function differently from contradiction, and why might paradox be particularly suited for understanding divine reality?

What is gained, and what might be lost, when we try to resolve theological paradoxes into more logically consistent formulations?

How does the preservation of mystery through paradoxical thinking relate to our modern scientific impulse to explain and demystify everything?

What is the relationship between mystery and meaning? Does maintaining mystery enhance or detract from our ability to find religious meaning?

How might the idea of paradox as a 'hermeneutic key' change our approach to interpreting other religious and philosophical texts?

10. This makes paradox the generator of the tertium quid: The combination of two opposing aspects (human and divine, Alpha and Omega, Lion and Lamb) creates a tension that gives rise to a third aspect, the tertium quid, which is distinct from the original two. This tertium quid is not a synthesis or compromise between the opposites but rather a novel entity that emerges from their interaction.

How does the concept of tertium quid differ from Hegelian dialectic (thesis-antithesis-synthesis), and what might this difference tell us about the nature of religious understanding versus philosophical resolution? Consider specific examples of religious paradoxes where the 'third thing' that emerges is neither a compromise nor a synthesis?

11. Is this a paradox, or a contradiction?

> "Beat your swords into plowshares, and your spears into pruning-hooks; nation shall not lift up sword against nation, neither shall they learn war any more" (Isaiah 2:4).

> "Beat your plowshares into swords, and your pruning-hooks into spears: let the weak say, I am strong" (Joel 3:10).

Or how about another one? Paradox or Contradiction?

"He that is not against us is for us." (Mark 9:40).

"He that is not with me is against me." (Matthew 12:30).[10]

12. Ancient and medieval Christians had many theories about how to read the Scripture. Most of those theories were based upon the belief that the Scripture could be understood in multiple ways because it contained levels of meaning. Origen (185–253) maintained that there were three levels of meaning corresponding to the body, soul, and spirit.[11] The belief was that through these levels of meaning "God enables the Christian to progress from the visible to the invisible, from the material to the intelligible."[12]

How might our modern preference for singular, definitive textual meanings limit our engagement with sacred texts? Consider what could be gained or lost by adopting a multilayered approach to reading scripture like Origen's body-soul-spirit framework?

What are the implications of viewing faith formation as a movement from "visible to invisible" and "material to intelligible?" How does this compare with contemporary approaches to spiritual development that might emphasize different kinds of progression?

13. Yahweh is "The Great I Am." But Jen Pollock Michel defines incarnation as "The Great I And."[13]

    What are the implications of understanding God's incarnation as "The Great I And" for Christian theology and practice?

14. How does this "The Great I And" impact our understanding of the Trinity, particularly the relationship between the divine and human natures of Jesus Christ?

15. Does this "I And" perspective offer new insights into the role of the Church as the body of Christ, or the significance of human participation in God's redemptive work?

16. How does the shift from "I Am" to "I And" in the concept of incarnation reflect the nature of God's relationship with humanity?

17. Does this shift imply a change in God's essence or merely a revelation of a previously unseen aspect of God's nature?

18. A Triquetra is made by the interlacing of three portions of circles—used in Christian art as a symbol of the Trinity—frequently found on Celtic crosses.

How does the visual symbolism of the Triquetra—with its interlaced circles that cannot be separated without destroying the whole—offer unique insights into Trinitarian theology that verbal explanations cannot capture? Consider particularly how Celtic Christian art used visual paradox to express theological truth.

19. Stereopsis is the ability to see in depth. The ability to see in 3D which means you are using both your eyes and looking at the world as God designed you to see it: with binocular vision, and with depth perception. Those stereograms or "Magic Eye" book images were first created to see whether people were using both their eyes or had lost their stereopsis.

   a. How does stereopsis differ from monocular vision?

   b. Have you ever played with stereograms that utilize binocular vision to create 3D images? What challenges do they pose to viewers?

   c. What are some common conditions that can affect stereopsis (e.g., astigmatism)? How can these conditions that prevent seeing in depth be diagnosed and treated?

   d. How does stereopsis contribute to our sense of self and our perception of reality?

   e. Are there ethical considerations related to the manipulation of depth perception, such as in virtual reality or augmented reality?

Semiotic Tell #10

Storms of Signs

THE WORD OF GOD IS more than words. The Word of God did not become more words or wordiness. The Word of God is not a disembodied doctrine or principled position or concept to be grasped. The Word of God is a person, The Divine DNA, birthing life-as-we-don't-know-it and vitality through the nurturing womb of the bride of Christ. The Word of God is a living relationship to be encountered, a divine presence to be experienced. The Word of God is not something, but someone. Theo-semioticians don't worship a Word made words. We worship God made flesh.

The church's one foundation
is Jesus Christ, her Lord;
she is His new creation,
by water and the word.

ANGLICAN HYMNWRITER S. J. STONE (1866)

What is the foundation of the church?

Paul, who first explicitly used the phrase "body of Christ" (σμα Χριστο, *soma Christou*) for the church, clearly states: "For no one can lay any foundation other than the one already laid, which is Jesus Christ."[1] This foundation isn't merely conceptual—it's the living, active presence of Christ within his body, the church.

The church as the "body of Christ" is more than a metaphor; it represents the real, dynamic presence of Christ among his people. This "Real Presence"—Christ living and active within the community of believers—is what truly establishes and sustains the church. As Paul writes, "Christ in you, the hope of glory."[2]

Therefore, the foundation of the church is not primarily physical structures, human institutions, or even doctrinal propositions. Rather, it's the Real Presence of Jesus Christ, embodied in and through his people. The church only comes alive and fulfills its purpose when it recognizes and lives out this reality.

Christ is the foundation, the church is his body, but the body comes to life through the power of the Spirit in his Real Presence. In other words, the foundation of the church is a Presence, and we are called not merely to represent or present that Presence but to presence that Presence. The master key to decoding the divine is to "sense" the presence.

Anything that makes our walk with Jesus more a routine than a romance, something that puts furrows on the forehead rather than reveals a sparkle in the eye and a radiance on the face, something that leads to an obligatory checklist rather than an enchanting journey, something that is more onerous than pleasant, more dutiful than delightful—is not of the Spirit.

SEMIOTIC TELL #10

All sign-making is the action of hope, the hope that this world may become other and that its experienced fragmentariness can be worked into sense. He makes the world, in Christ, to be his 'sign,' a form of living and acting that embodies his nature and purpose. Christian sign-making—in the whole of the community's discipleship as in normal acts—is a working in and with that creative energy.

WELSH ANGLICAN THEOLOGIAN AND POET ROWAN WILLIAMS[3]

My dear students, while 1 Peter 2:21 NIV states, "Christ suffered for you, leaving you an example, that you should follow in his steps," the Greek word Peter uses—πογραμμός, *hupogrammos*—conveys a far more profound meaning. It doesn't merely suggest imitation; rather, it calls us to trace His pattern, follow His direction, and track His trail.[4]

The English idiom "to follow in someone's footsteps" fails to capture the vivid, active nature of Peter's original Greek. Instead, envision "Following His Tracks"—a dynamic image of pursuing Christ's fresh footprints, aligning ourselves with His ongoing journey and purpose.

Reducing Jesus to a mere "example" grossly understates the transformative power of the Incarnation. Jesus is Emmanuel, "God With Us"—a present, active force in our lives, not a static model to replicate. The danger in viewing Christ as merely an example echoes the heresy of Arianism, which reduced salvation to simply imitating Jesus (*imitatio Christi*).[5]

As the late British sociologist David Martin eloquently summarized the New Testament's essence: "It is about God's presence with us as flesh of our flesh, about the proclamation of an invisible kingdom and a banquet to which we are all invited, as well as about the signs of that kingdom and that banquet."[6]

Jesus transcends the role of exemplar. He is the living, breathing manifestation of God's presence, inviting us into an active, ongoing relationship that shapes our very being. To follow Christ is not to mimic a historical figure, but to participate in the unfolding narrative of God's kingdom.

Let others preach success, or preach prosperity, or preach social justice, or preach leadership, or preach apps. Let us preach Jesus—crucified, risen, rising, reigning, returning. For when you preach Jesus and his story, you preach everything else. God's mission is a Person.

The mission is not a "what," but a "who."

SWISS CATHOLIC THEOLOGIAN HANS URS VON BALTHASAR[7]

One of the greatest compliments I ever received came as an insult. An invitation to deliver a lecture series at a seminary was rescinded when the head of the faculty committee overseeing the student's selection said disparagingly, "When you get Sweet, all you get is one thing: Jesus." Yep, that's me, all right. A one-trick pony—no, a one-trick donkey:

> Issachar is a strong donkey, crouching between the sheepfolds. He saw that a resting place was good, and that the land was pleasant, so he bowed his shoulder to bear, and became a servant at forced labor.[8]

SEMIOTIC TELL #10

For a theo-semiotician, all the dots connect to form one thing: Jesus. It is the only epitaph I want on the tree that grows from my decomposed remains: "Give Me Jesus."

Semiotics is not virtue signaling, moral posturing, righteousness flagging but truth signaling or Jesus signaling. Yet signaling can take many forms, beyond winks, whistles, nudges.

Lee Kwan Yew in Singapore and Paul Kagame in Rwanda both tried to break systemic corruption in their countries by adopting the same strategy: they jailed not only corrupt enemies but corrupt friends. Anyone can jail his enemies for corruption. But jailing your corrupt friends "signals" seriousness and integrity. Such "signaling" conveys a clear story and confirms the importance of integrity for other public officials.

Semioticians help others discover their true self in Christ. Life without knowing your essence and divine presence is hollow. As Paul said, "To live is Christ."[9] Paradoxically, the more Christ fills us, the more authentically ourselves we become. This mirrors artistic influence: The Beatles, Beach Boys, and Bob Dylan's mid-sixties work shows how creative cross-pollination of essence and presence can refine unique voices. Embrace divine inspiration to uncover your genuine identity.

◇

It's life, Jim, but not as we know it.

BONES (VOICED BY DEFOREST KELLEY)
IN THE SONG "STAR TREKKIN" (NOT THE SERIES)

"The kingdom of heaven is like a merchant in search of fine pearls" Matthew 13:45 NIV, reads. "When he found one very precious pearl, he went and sold all that he owned and bought it." That "Pearl of Great Price" is Christ—presencing Jesus by knowing Christ and making Christ known.

How many times can the Jesus story be told before it loses its power to enchant and edify, convict and convince? A thousand tellings, and a thousand more, the story told anew, yet ever old, still stirs the soul, still strikes the core, its timeless truths forever shine forth bright to heal and deliver that balm in Gilead. The story will never lose its power.

Jesus is God incarnate (God WITH us).

The Church is Christ embodied and empowered (Christ with us).

You are the Church embedded and expressed (Christ through us).

The Holy Spirit is the Ultimate App.

You are the penultimate app.

But the Ultimate Sign is Jesus.

SEMIOTIC TELL #10

source code interactives

1. Listen to Matt Redman's "The Heart of Worship" and go over the lyrics line by line. What does it mean "I'll bring you more than a song?" How do you respond to the affirmation: "It's all about you, Jesus. It's all about you."

2. Discuss the thesis: The point of philosophy is to change one's point of view. The point of theology is to change how one lives.

3. How many chairs will you have helped pull out for people at the Great Supper of the Lamb?

4. The parents can be "read" in the child even after generations. Can Jesus be "read" in us like that? How is Jesus "read" in us at all?

5. Is our culture getting more "secular," or is it sacralizing everything it touches? I have argued other places that secularization theory is a zombie concept that is wrong but refuses to die. When you look at sports, politics, food, entertainment, you name it, are these becoming more "secular" or are these our new religions?

6. Here is a call for the return of the sacred, which Ludwig Wittgenstein defines this way: "It is the experience of seeing the world as a miracle."[10] Do you agree with this definition? Would you add anything to it? Do you think people are tired of living life scared, not sacred lives?

7. What are you doing to make the commonplace become special? How are you turning ordinary living into sacred living?

8. "What is religion?" Robert N. Bellah, in *Religion in Human Evolution: From the Paleolithic to the Axial Age* (2012) defines it this way: "Not as beliefs in gods or God, but as the symbolic representation and apprehension of the sacred, or non-ordinary reality." Do you agree with that definition, and what follows?

> "Few today see religion as a set of propositions. It makes better sense to fuse the experiential/expressive approach where innate human potentials manifest themselves in varied religious forms with the cultural/linguistic approach where inchoate potentials are shaped by cultural and symbolic forms.... From the very beginning religion had some association with the intrinsic, the playful and the unitive."[11]

semiotic tell #11

The Fog of Meaning

The Semiotic Landscape of Uncertainty: In the realm of semiotics, we often find ourselves venturing into uncharted, uncertain territories. Whatever way we turn, whichever direction we look, we see looming on the horizon wars, nuclear war, climate change, unraveling nation states, pestilence, and a Titanic-like tryst with an iceberg of time and technology unlike the world has ever seen.

This unexpected journey into an uncertain future mirrors a profound truth about life, especially the life of faith: the sign of God's presence is often revealed when our feet tread paths we never anticipated. Semioticians often "go in directions you do not wish to go."[1]

What is it you plan to do with your one wild and precious life?

POET MARY OLIVER[2]

Our world is shaped by signs and symbols that speak of unpredictability:
> Wild Cards and Black Swans: Unforeseen events that dramatically alter our reality.[3]

White Elephants and Gray Rhinos: Obvious yet ignored threats that loom on the horizon.[4]

Red Heifers and 900 Pound Gorillas: Symbols of potential paradigm shifts in religious and secular realms.

Dropping Dinosaurs and Runaway Trains: Metaphors for sudden, unstoppable changes.

Carrington Events and Houses of Cards: Reminders of our systems' vulnerabilities.[5]

In this semiotic landscape of unpredictability, our ability to adapt becomes paramount. The future favors not those who plan meticulously, but those who prepare wisely.

Consider the future as a plate of fugu, the Japanese puffer fish delicacy. If not properly prepared, it contains a lethal poison. Yet, in skilled hands, it becomes a coveted dish. Similarly, the uncertain future holds both peril and promise. Semioticians are called to be the master chefs of fugu, skillfully navigating the fine line between danger and delight in our uncertain world.

The Semiotics of the Spirit-Driven Life: Jesus didn't operate on strategic plans, set agendas, or to-do lists. His mission unfolded organically, with His most impactful teachings and miracles occurring "as He passed by."[6] This spontaneity reflects a profound hermeneutic about Spirit-led semiotics, beautifully captured in one of the most famous passages of Scripture not known for this insight.

John 3:16 is known as "The Gospel in a Nutshell." But the shell needs to be cracked to get to the nut. The verse is part of a larger Nick-by-Nite story ("Nicodemus ... came to

Jesus by night" [John 3:1–2 NIV]) that highlights how the Eternal enters the Earthly. It insists that humans carry within us, as finite creatures, the infinite, and continues (vs. 8):

> The wind blows wherever it pleases. You hear its sound, but you cannot tell where it comes from or where it is going. So it is with everyone born of the Spirit.[7]

This passage is less about wind than about those who live Spirit-driven, wind-swept lives—the "pneumanauts" or "sailors of the Spirit." Weathervanes are not prophets. Semioticians chart the currents that the future will sail by, and lay down some buoys that guard through dangerous waters.

Signs of Spirit-Led Living: How do Jesus-followers know if we're truly living in the Spirit? Consider these semiotic questions:

> Are we predictable, or do we surprise even ourselves?
>
> Do we startle others with unexpected wisdom or compassion?
>
> Are we open to heavenly hijacks in our daily routines?
>
> Can we bridge life's in-betweens with imagination, patience, and grace?

If we find ourselves too predictable, it may be time to reassess who's truly in charge of our lives.

Even Jesus' enemies were startled, surprised, and stunned by his powers and authority. The only question for them was whether such surprising power came from the devil or the

Spirit, which is the context for Jesus' contentious quote about blaspheming the Spirit and the "unpardonable sin."

Spirit-led living isn't about having all the answers, but about being willing to ask the right questions. It's about being open to divine detours, cosmic curveballs, and holy happenstance. It's about living with a sense of holy anticipation, ready for God to show up in unexpected ways and unlikely places.

Cultivating Semiotic Agility: To thrive in a world marked by constant change, semioticians must develop a unique set of skills. These are not merely tools for academic inquiry but practical strategies for navigating life's unexpected turns.

1. Semiotic Flexibility: The ability to shift perspectives and adapt to new realities is paramount. This requires a readiness to "repair and reposition," much like adjusting one's stance in response to a changing environment. Practice looking at situations from multiple angles, considering alternative interpretations, and being willing to change your mind when presented with new information.

2. Lifelong Learning: Semiotic agility is rooted in a commitment to continuous learning. It's about embracing life as a rich palette of experiences from which to gain knowledge, rather than solely focusing on material acquisition. Cultivate curiosity,

SEMIOTIC TELL #11

read widely, engage in diverse experiences, and never stop asking questions.

3. Futures Thinking: Semioticians must be adept at envisioning multiple potential futures. "Scenario thinking" allows us to anticipate a range of possibilities, from the most optimistic to the most challenging. Practice creating multiple scenarios for any given situation, considering both likely and unlikely outcomes.

4. Building Semiotic Networks: Strong relationships are essential for understanding the world around us. By cultivating a diverse network, semioticians can access a wealth of perspectives and information. Engage with people from different backgrounds, disciplines, and worldviews to broaden your understanding of the world.

5. Prophetic Imagination: Semiotics is inherently linked to the ability to discern patterns, anticipate future trends, terrains, and trajectories, and prophesy your way forward. This "prophetic imagination" involves more than prediction; it's about creating alternative realities through ritual and symbolic action. Ritual is subjunctive, not subjective. In fact, ritual may be another name for prophesying your way

forward, acting as if something were true, and in so doing, making it so.[8]

By mastering these five dimensions, semioticians become agents of change, capable of interpreting the signs of the times and shaping the future.

The Nature of True Prophecy: True prophecy in the context of semiotics is not about predicting the future with certainty, but rather about discerning patterns, understanding the present, and imagining possible futures. Here are some key aspects of true prophetic practice for semioticians:

> Humility in Uncertainty: Recognize that our understanding is always limited. Use language that reflects this, such as "it seems" or "it appears" rather than definitive statements.
>
> Collective Wisdom: Engage with a community of thinkers and believers. As 2 Peter 1:20–21 suggests, prophecy is not a solo act but a communal discernment.
>
> Continuous Recalibration: Be ready to adjust your understanding as new information emerges. True prophets are not afraid to say, "I was mistaken" or "I see things differently now."
>
> Ethical Responsibility: Use your insights to benefit others and promote justice, not for personal gain or to manipulate.
>
> Symbolic Literacy: Develop the ability to read the "signs of the times" in culture, technology, and social movements.

SEMIOTIC TELL #11

Remember, the goal is not to be a fortune-teller, but a wise interpreter of the present with an eye toward possible futures that keep people moving in a forward direction.

Life is movement. Life moves whether you're moving or not. In fact, even when you think you're not moving, you're moving. In 2025 you will have traveled 584 million miles ... and that's if you don't move a muscle. Just standing still you travel in one hour 64,000 miles around the sun. The only question is: which direction are you moving?

The true successors to Moses are not kings, but prophets (Joshua, Deborah, Gideon, Samson, Saul, David, Solomon, etc.). Kings are permitted but only when they submit to God's laws and listen to the prophets (Samuel, Nathan, Elijah, Isaiah). Semioticians are the vanguard voyagers that keep life moving, keep people moving with Jesus, and make sure the church's moves are steps not stunts.

Some of the semiotic skills necessary to do this?

End sentences with ellipses, not exclamations.

Avoid absolute terms like "will" and "will not."

Imagine, discern, and listen rather than predict.

Auto-correct, course correct, improvise, and think on your feet.

Operate out of a prophetic community.

This last one is important. 2 Peter 1:20–21 reads, "No prophecy of scripture is of private interpretation" but is best translated "no prophecy can be understood through one's own powers."

Dancing with Divine Detours: In a world where AI's algorithms threaten to overtake human ingenuity, our capacity for Spirit-led living becomes not just crucial, but revolutionary.

As we navigate the labyrinth of an uncertain future, semioticians should embrace these passages as our motto, mantra, and meme:

> We may chart our course, but it is the LORD who authors our journey.[9]

> Trust in the LORD with all your heart and lean not on your own understanding; in all your ways acknowledge Him, and He shall direct your paths.[10]

To embrace divine detours is to waltz with wonder, to tangle with transcendence, to wrestle with angels. It's in these unexpected encounters that we shed our everyday chrysalis and emerge, butterfly-like, into the fullness of our human potential.

Practical steps for dancing with divine detours include:

> Cultivate Flexibility: Hold your to-do-lists loosely, ready to adjust when unexpected opportunities arise.

> Practice Mindfulness: Stay present and aware, ready to notice subtle signs and synchronicities.

> Embrace Discomfort: Growth often happens outside our comfort zones. Welcome challenges as opportunities.

> Maintain a Sense of Wonder: Approach each day with curiosity and openness to the unexpected, finding humor in strange places.

> Journal Your Journey: Record your experiences,

SEMIOTIC TELL #11

looking for patterns of divine guidance over time.

Practice Resilience: Develop the ability to bounce back from setbacks and adapt to change. Set-backs are set-ups for come-backs.

Cultivate Hope: Maintain a positive outlook, grounded in faith and the belief that good can emerge from uncertainty. Every great story started with a single sentence: "Once upon a time ..."

Trust the Process: Even when it feels like you're walking through fog—you'll find your way, or at least a good excuse for being late.

Stay Curious: Approach uncertainty with a learner's mindset, always ready to discover something new. And remember, curiosity is contagious—so go ahead, infect someone with your enthusiasm for learning.

As we yield to these holy disruptions, we metamorphose from passive observers into active participants in God's grand narrative of redemption and renewal. We become living epistles—not of a static, predictable faith, but of a dynamic, ever-unfolding revelation of God's story. We embody the vibrant, surprising work of God who delights in turning our "why?" into "why not?" and our "how?" into "behold!"

In this dance of detours, semioticians don't merely adapt to the future—we become its sub-creators. In embracing uncertainty, we don't just witness miracles—we become them. We transform into living testaments of a faith that thrives in the face of the unknown, demonstrating that with God, the uncertain path often leads to the most extraordinary destination. Each step off our planned path is an invitation to partake in the divine improvisation, to harmonize with the cosmic rhythm of the Spirit that pulses through creation.

The important thing is not to stop questioning. Curiosity has its own reason for existence.

ALBERT EINSTEIN[11]

It is in losing our carefully crafted maps that we truly find our way, becoming beacons of hope in an uncertain world.

SEMIOTIC TELL #11

source code interactives

1. I'm really bad at something in my preaching: repetition and redundancy. I want to keep moving. But repetition and redundancy are necessary to make sure the audience is following you and keeping up.

    How important do you think repetition and redundancy are to great communication?

2. Warren Buffet is known as the "Oracle of Omaha." But he himself claims not to be a seer, or visionary with keen foresight, only a great investor in value. He once joked that any firm which hires an economist has one employee too many, and boasts that he has never made an investment decision at Berkshire Hathaway based on an economic prediction. Only on sound principles of picking high value stocks at low cost openings.[12]

    What does Warren Buffet's approach to investing reveal about his values and priorities? How can we apply this to our own decision-making processes?

3. Buffet's success is not based on predicting the future, but on sound principles. What are some "sound principles" that guide your own life and decisions? How can you rely on these principles more consistently?

4. Buffet's comment about economists suggests that he values practical wisdom over theoretical knowledge. What is the difference between these two approaches? When is it more important to focus on practical wisdom?

5. How can we distinguish between "high value" opportunities and those that are merely attractive or promising? What criteria can we use to evaluate opportunities and make wise decisions?

   Buffet's approach to investing is long-term and focused on value, rather than short-term gains. How can we apply this mindset to other areas of our lives, such as relationships, personal growth, or community involvement?

6. What are some ways that we can simplify our decision-making processes and focus on what is truly important? How can we avoid getting caught up in unnecessary complexity or analysis paralysis?

7. How can we balance the need for planning and preparation with the uncertainty and unpredictability of the future? What role can faith and trust play in our decision-making processes?

8. When you read that experts predict that eighty to ninety percent of all the current jobs in the world will be augmented by AI, and many will even become completely obsolete, there are two proper responses.

   First, we must think about how to prepare for this shift and be able to change gears to do the work that only humans are capable of doing.[13] Second, we can be sure that the future will not unfold the way the experts predict and that we must deal with detours, delays, and disruptions.

   a. What are some jobs or tasks that you think will be most impacted by AI? How will this affect our society and economy?

What are some skills or abilities that are unique to humans and cannot be replicated by AI? How can we develop and emphasize these skills in our own lives and work?

b. How can we prepare for a future where many jobs are augmented or replaced by AI? What steps can we take to adapt and stay relevant?

c. What are some potential benefits and drawbacks of AI augmentation in the workforce? How can we ensure that the benefits are shared equitably and the drawbacks are mitigated?

The paragraph suggests that the future is uncertain and will likely involve detours, delays, and disruptions. How can we cultivate a mindset of flexibility and resilience in the face of uncertainty?

9. What role can faith and trust play in navigating the challenges and uncertainties of the future? How can we position preparation and planning with trust in a higher power?

10. How can we prioritize human connections and relationships in a world where AI is increasingly prevalent? What are some ways to foster empathy, creativity, and other uniquely human qualities?

semiotic Tell #12

The Symphony of Differences

SEMIOTICIANS BRING OPPOSITES TOGETHER INTO a tension that vibrates in harmonious difference. It is not about a dialectic that resolves. It is about a dynamic that harmonizes.

Mentors pass on many things to their students. I hope you will let me pass on to you one of my stronger allergies. I am temperamentally allergic to the language and metaphor of "balance." Life is not a balancing act. Life is a dance floor: a dance in the park, dance in the dark, and dance in the rain—and all dances are tipsy, dizzying, lopsided. Don't think scales. Think salsa … or spinning top.

The biblical story introduces an even stronger semiotic framework for understanding the themes of harmony, opposites, and the sacred dance of life as one finds in Charles Sanders Peirce's triadic model (icon, index, symbol) or Ferdinand de Saussure's dyadic model (signifier and signified).

In the beginning, God entrusted humanity with a two-word Prime Directive for life in the Garden: Avad and Shamar.[1] Till and Tend. Cultivate and Care For. Conceive and Conserve.

This ancient wisdom holds the secret to a life of wholeness, where opposites harmonize in a sacred couplet. In other words, "avad and shamar" function as a signifier of a divine mandate for truth and trusteeship.

Mastery of this rhythm of resonance requires embracing the harmonious interplay between:

    Innovation and Consolidation

    Stability and Motion

    Settling down and Stirring up

    Roots and Wings

    Being and Becoming

    Rest and Renewal

    Vocation and Vacation

    Tradition and Transfiguration

In the Garden of Eden, The Pillar or Tree of Knowledge represents the upright, masculine energy, while the Tree of Life embodies the circular, feminine energy. Together, they form a harmonious union, reflecting the interplay between opposites in the natural world.

From the very beginning, The Story of God flies on two wings—constancy and change, reverie and revolution. In this beautiful paradox, we find the mystery of a life of harmony that flourishes—where health, hope, and happiness entwine like the tender shoots of a garden, nurtured by the harmony of opposing forces. Semioticians have an oppositional consciousness because opposites function as signs or symbols in a broader semiotic system.[2]

Jesus is The Truth: the ultimate harmony of the human and the divine.

The sacred dance of life is a rich and intricate melody, a symphony of contrasts that blend together in a beautiful harmony. This enigmatic ballet can be distilled into a singular

SEMIOTIC TELL #12

essence: DNA, or Dance N' Attune, Dare N' Abide—the sublime union of the linear and the loop.

The Majestic Curve: Where the Spirit of the Lord is, where abundant life resides, lies the Majestic Curve. In the grand design of nature, straight lines are a rarity. The serpentine path of a river meanders, ambles, and rambles, occasionally reversing course before forging ahead (the oxbow's gentle reminder). Even landscape designers eschew straight lines, opting instead for winding pathways that transport us on a journey, crafting an experience that awakens the senses. The shortest distance between two points may be a straight line, but it's also the ugliest and most boring. The best stretch is not straight home.

The shortest distance between two points is a relationship.

MASTER NETWORKER JAMES O. DAVIS

The whimsical wisdom of nature reveals that even the Divine Architect doesn't think straight. The sole exception, the man-made cross, ironically underscores this suspicion, as two straight lines intersect, canceling each other out. This paradox resonates with the timeless Portuguese proverb, *"Deus escreve direito por linhas tortas"*—"God writes straight with crooked lines."

Indeed, whose life story unfolds in a straight, unbroken trajectory? Every journey is a winding mélange of twists and turns, detours and dead ends, with its own unique rhythms and crescendos. We meander through life's labyrinth, navigating unexpected swerves and bends. No one traverses the path from birth to death without encountering setbacks, surprises, and serendipity.

Our faith practices reflect this winding path. We shun the linear "prayer line" for the contemplative "prayer labyrinth" or the communal "prayer circle." In embracing these symbolic spirals, we acknowledge the beauty of life's unpredictable journey, where every curve and crook writes its own unique story.

You might point to Proverbs 3:5–6, which says, "Trust in the Lord … and He will make your crooked paths straight." Or perhaps Isaiah 45:2–3 KJV, which promises: "I will go before you and make the crooked places straight; I will break in pieces the gates of brass and cut in sunder the bars of iron … that you may know that I, the Lord … am the God of Israel."

These verses do speak of straightening crooked paths. But if we delve deeper, what are they truly celebrating? Is it the virtue of straightness itself, or rather God's liberating power? These passages rejoice in God's ability to clear our path, open up new possibilities, shatter barriers, and free us from the shackles of fear, bad habits, and limitations. They highlight God's transfigurative power to guide us toward new horizons, empowering us to form good habits and discover hidden riches in the secret places of our lives.

We vaporize myth into the ethereal realms at our peril. My students, you already know I consider myth a Möbius strip of truth—it appears to have two sides (fact and fiction) but follow its path and you'll find it has only one surface. Like paradox, myth lives in the space where opposites meet and merge. When we say a myth "never was but always is,"

SEMIOTIC TELL #12

we're tracing that same circular path that anthropologist Mary Douglas identifies in ritual thinking: the eternal return that somehow moves both nowhere and everywhere at once.[3]

The paradox itself is mythic in structure—it loops back on itself like Ouroboros, the serpent swallowing its tail. And mythic thinking is inherently paradoxical, embracing contradictions that linear logic cannot hold: heroes who must die to live, gods who are both one and many, truths that can only be spoken in lies.

Myths function as semiotic systems where symbols and signs convey truths, and semioticians interpret these myths to uncover underlying cultural or spiritual meanings. Hence semioticians are not afraid of the word "myth" and are always on the prowl for the truths, not the facts, in myth. Myth is often misunderstood as simply "not-real" or a relic of ancient superstition. The myth-busting mission of the modern world, long defunct, refuses to submit to a decent burial as the demolition job continues in both the worlds of science and religion. But in the ancient world, myths were revered as vessels of profound truth, revealing the workings of ultimate reality. These stories, often featuring divine characters, were not merely fanciful tales but rather attempts to convey the deepest essence of existence.

Myths offered explanations for how the world functioned, and the ancients considered them historically actual, not factual but not fictional either. Iain McGilchrist calls one legend from Iroquois mythology "one of the most remarkable intuitions of the structure of the mind and its influence on human destiny ever brought forth from the depth of the human imagination."[4] Myths die hard and do not rest easy for a reason.

In the truest sense, myth is "something that never was but always is"—a window into the timeless, underlying fabric of reality. The theme of myth is not the essence of the divine or of science, but the essence of reality itself. Myths transcend empirical verification, speaking to the truth of what truly matters. By embracing myth in this way, semioticians unlock its potency as a source of wisdom, guidance, and connection to the deepest truths of human experience.

> *Myth ... is the imaginative use of symbol and parable, of the poetic and pictorial, to express the inexpressible. Far from false, it is the only way to come close to what is ultimately true.*
>
> "HOLY SATURDAY" THEOLOGIAN ALAN EDMOND LEWIS[5]

A semiotician is always saying, "these are the facts, but this is the truth," moving people from mythos to ethos. This is why theo-semiotics is a form of dialectical theology, which I think is better framed as trinitarian thinking called trialectics not dialectics (but that's another conversation).[6] In his famous 1927 Eisenach address, German theologian and biblical scholar Rudolph Bultmann (d. 1976) asks:

> What, then, is meant by *dialectic*? Undeniably it is a specific way of speaking which recognizes that there exists no ultimate knowledge which can be encompassed and preserved in a single statement.... The dialectical method in philosophy depends on the conviction that every

SEMIOTIC TELL #12

truth expressed is a partial truth and that the whole truth which is its basis can best be found by first setting beside it the contrary statement. For the contrary statement ... must also contain a portion of the truth. By setting the two partial truths against each other and combining them, it may be possible to grasp the underlying principle.[7]

When he was eight-years-old, our son Luke was asked what "my truth" means when people say it. He responded, "'My truth' is *the* truth [... pause ...] with a little tiny twist [... pause ...] that makes it better for me."

No matter what anyone says, even an eight-year old, the truth is out there. In life's dance of opposites, affirmation hides within negation. Negatives nest positives. Critiques cradle celebrations. Condemnations conceal affirmations. Atheism anchors to theism. Post-truth presumes pre-truth. My truth murmurs universal truth. Even every denial dances with truth.

Learn the score of harmonious difference.

source code interactives

1. Discuss how the Cross, as a symbol, signifies the intersection of divine and human, life and death, and what other opposites?

2. If life is a sacred dance, do you think training in semiotics might be well-served to include dance lessons? It was said of the greatest dance team in history, Fred Astaire and Ginger Rogers, that Ginger had the harder task because she did everything Fred did but backwards, in high heels, and in a long flowing skirt. What dance form might be best to learn to become adept at the union of opposites—forward motion and backward reflection, the structured and the spontaneous, strength and softness, leading and vulnerability?

   Here are some suggestions to prime the pump:

   Tango, a dance of intense connection and contrast, requires partners to be deeply attuned to each other, moving in perfect harmony while also maintaining a strong sense of individuality. The push and pull, the moments of tension and release, and the intricate footwork mirror the dance of opposites in life.

   Ballroom Dancing, like the Waltz or Foxtrot, emphasizes grace, poise, and the seamless blending of two individuals moving as one. The lead and follow roles in ballroom dance represent the dynamic between action and reaction,

SEMIOTIC TELL #12

initiative and response, reflecting how we must sometimes lead and other times follow in life's dance, symbolizing the balance between stability and motion, tradition and innovation.

Swing Dance (Lindy Hop, East Coast Swing, etc.), with its playful, energetic style, embraces improvisation within a structured framework. Partners must be quick to adapt to changes in rhythm and direction, much like the way life throws unexpected challenges our way. The interaction between the grounded, rhythmic footwork and the light, airy lifts and spins represents the balance between being rooted in reality and reaching for new heights.

Contemporary Dance often explores themes of conflict, contrast, and resolution through movement. It allows for a high degree of emotional expression and often plays with the tension between opposing forces, such as stillness and motion, strength and vulnerability. Contemporary dance can be a powerful medium for exploring the union of opposites, as it encourages dancers to find harmony in the midst of discord.

Capoeira is a Brazilian martial art that incorporates dance, acrobatics, and music. It is rooted in the idea of balance between opposing forces, and requires practitioners to be both strong and graceful, strategic and spontaneous. The "game" of Capoeira, played between two participants, involves a continuous flow of movements, where attacks and defenses blend seamlessly, embodying the idea of harmony within conflict.

Ballet is the juxtaposition of rigidity and fluidity, a metaphor for navigating the rigid structures of society while finding personal freedom and expression within them.

To become adept at the union of opposites, discuss how one must learn to navigate life's complexities with grace, resilience, and an openness to the unexpected—just as one would in dance.

3. How might the *"Acriter et Fideliter"* ("Courageously and Faithfully") Latin motto of the Swiss Guards, the military corps responsible for the safety of the Pope and the Vatican City, embody the essence of God's Prime Directive to humanity: conserve ("faithfully") and conceive ("courageously")?

4. Evaluate the role of the interpreter (or sign reader) in creating meaning. Semiotic theory holds that meaning is not inherent in signs themselves but is generated through interpretation.

Do you agree with that theory?

How might semioticians be more careful about bringing their own experiences and contexts to their understanding of symbols, stories, and scriptural texts?

But if there is such a thing as absolute truth, isn't there

such a thing as absolute meaning? Or is the only meaning things have the meaning we give them?

5. Talk about the intersemiotic translations of this chapter, including how the concepts being discussed translate across different sign systems (e.g., from verbal to visual, or from one cultural context to another).

6. Discuss what some scholars call intertextuality. How do different texts and cultural contexts interact to create new meanings? How do biblical narratives, philosophical ideas, and contemporary culture intersect in the formation of the chapter's arguments?

7. The meaning of a sign is influenced by its context. How does the cultural, historical, and religious context shape the interpretation of biblical passages and other examples?

8. Would you agree with my thesis that a harmonious people is a humorous people?

9. I personally find this one of the most depressing and scandalous things any artist has written. It is nestled in the midst of Matisse's *Notes on Painting* (1908): "What I dream of is an art of balance, of purity and serenity, devoid of troubling or depressing subject matter, an art which could be for every metal worker, for the businessman as well as the man of letters, for example, a soothing, calming influence on the mind, something like a good armchair which provides relaxation from physical fatigue."

Do you find this as problematic as I do? Or do I need to

consider the context of a global community of artists, in which each contributes to the body of the whole?

10. Thomas Jefferson said that the debates during the Constitutional Convention contained "opposition enough to do good and not enough to do harm."[8]

   a. What does Jefferson mean by "opposition enough to do good" and "not enough to do harm"? Provide examples.

   b. How does Jefferson's quote relate to the concept of harmonious difference?

   c. What benefits arise from having opposition or diverse perspectives in decision-making processes?

   d. Think of a personal experience where constructive opposition led to a better outcome. Share the story.

   e. How can you apply Jefferson's principle to your own relationships, team, or community?

   f. What strategies can be used to foster harmonious difference in discussions and debates?

   g. Can too little opposition lead to poor decisions? Provide historical or personal examples.

   h. How can groups harmonize the need for consensus with the value of opposition?

   i. What role do active listening, empathy, and respect play in maintaining harmonious differences?

   j. Is harmonious difference essential for democratic societies? Why or why not?

SEMIOTIC TELL #12

k. How does Jefferson's quote relate to the principles of dissent, free speech, and minority rights?

l. Can harmonious difference be maintained in the face of deeply divisive issues?

m. Role-play scenarios demonstrating harmonious difference in action.

semi̲o̲tic tell #13

Tick Bites

Dancing with Dawn in a Dusk-Obsessed World: Clicks bring bricks—that should be a meme on social media. But semioticians get hit with bricks more than their share for a bunch of reasons.

First, the bane of semiotics is seeing the dawn before the rest of the world, which often mistakes it for dusk. The curse of clear vision can be pictured thus: You're at a party, and someone offers you a pair of glasses that let you see tomorrow. Imagine putting them on, and everyone thinks you've gone mad. That's the daily life of a semiotician.

In the well-known words of celebrated British science fiction writer, inventor, and futurist Arthur C. Clarke: "If by some miracle, a prophet could describe the future exactly as it was going to take place, his predictions would sound so far-fetched, so absurd, that everyone would laugh him to scorn."[1] Or in the words of another science fiction writer, in a slogan written for Paul Masson Vineyards in 1978, and spoken by Orson Welles himself in several commercials: "We will sell no wine before its time."

Semioticians are always violating this slogan. The mission statement of the semiotic business might be precisely this: We sell wine before its time. We're not just selling wine before its time; we're fermenting grapes that haven't even been planted yet. It's no wonder the granddaddy of sci-fi, H. G. Wells (d. 1946), who profoundly influenced both Clarke and Welles, wanted his tombstone to read:

> I told you so. You damned fools.[2]

Second, nothing neuters a prophet (or semiotician) faster than popularity. That's why when the prophetic voice becomes the politically correct one, or the conventional, establishment voice, the role of the prophet is subverted and scuppered.

To be sure, a semiotician's or prophet's role isn't to alienate through bluntness or brusqueness, but to inspire through compassion and encouragement. True prophetic voices balance challenging truths with empathy and support.

Prophetic voices typically speak from beyond the horizon of their own time—their words find their fullest resonance not in the immediate echo of their speaking, but in the deeper listening of future generations.

Outliers are oracles. The margins birth tomorrow while the mainstream mummifies. This is no mere metaphor, but an iron law of culture: what throbs with life always begins at the edge. The center is a cemetery of yesterday's revelations. Watch the periphery—there you'll find the first whispers of what's to come. The most vital voices speak from the wilderness, not from the temple. Their very rejection by the mainstream marks them as harbingers. The more the established order turns its back, the more likely these voices are to be naming the future.

The potency of a semiotic message—whether prophet or cultural critic—is inversely proportional to their mainstream acceptance. When revolutionary ideas become commonplace or institutionalized, they lose their power. The moment a prophetic voice aligns with the status quo or becomes the prevailing narrative, its ability to challenge, provoke, and instigate change is severely diminished. This paradox of influence versus impact often results in the dilution of once-radical concepts, rendering them palatable but ultimately ineffective in driving substantive societal shifts.

Martin Luther King Jr.'s message provides an excellent example of this paradox. His now-popular "I Have a Dream" speech has become so mainstream and institutionalized that it's often reduced to comfortable soundbites about racial harmony, while his more challenging and less-cited works like "Letter from Birmingham Jail" or his speeches against the ravages of capitalism and the Vietnam War remain potent and disruptive because they continue to challenge the status quo. The sanitized, widely-accepted version of King that appears on posters and in elementary school lessons has lost much of its revolutionary force, while his more radical critiques of militarism, economic inequality, and white moderate complicity retain their full prophetic power precisely because they remain uncomfortable and less widely embraced.

The meaning and impact of signs and symbols associated with prophetic or revolutionary ideas can shift dramatically as they move from the margins to the center of cultural discourse. The challenge for modern prophets and semioticians alike is to continually evolve their language and symbols to maintain their disruptive and metamorphic potential in the face of mainstream co-option.

Third, semioticians routinely buck the system, hold back the storm, and critique the conventional, with attendant kickback and blowback and pushback. Some of these punches can connect and lead to fallback. But be thankful. Not too long ago, authors were maimed if people didn't like what they said. Ears were cropped, noses nubbed, fingers cut off by critics.[3] So the next time you're at a party and treated like a booger in the punchbowl, count your blessings by pulling your ears, counting your fingers, and touching your nose.

But here's the kicker: Sometimes, when you toss out the rulebook, you're not being a rebel—you're being a purist. You're not embracing heresy; you're hugging heritage so tightly it squeaks.

The Orthodoxy Jig and Jib: Two Steps Forward, One Step Silenced.

George Orwell, who knew a thing or two about swimming against the tide, wrote in his original introduction to *Animal Farm* (1945), never published in his lifetime:

> At any given moment there is an orthodoxy, a body of ideas which it is assumed that all right-thinking people will accept without question. It is not exactly forbidden to say this, that or the other, but it is 'not done' to say it, just as in mid-Victorian times it was 'not done' to mention trousers in the presence of a lady. Anyone who challenges the prevailing orthodoxy finds himself silenced with surprising effectiveness.[4]

Sometimes when you discard received notions you aren't being "heretical," but being orthodox. You aren't embracing "heresy" but you are embracing heritage, a deeper and older heritage than the received notions express.

Come close, huddle together, circle the wagons, keep your

SEMIOTIC TELL #13

heads down. Now picture this: You're at a church potluck, and someone whispers, "Psst! Wanna hear a secret?" You lean in, expecting juicy gossip about who put raisins in the potato salad. After all, the church is a Mirandized Ministry: You have the right to remain silent because what you say CAN be and WILL be used against you. But no. It's something far more scandalous—the church's dirtiest big secret–one that I keep learning the hard way.

You think shouting "The earth is flat!" at a NASA convention would ruffle feathers? Child's play. Try standing up to or going against a church bureaucracy—that's when the real fireworks start. A bureaucracy: born to serve a cause, destined to become one.

Remember playing "The Floor is Lava" as a kid? Well, in church politics, it's "The Floor is Heresy," and whoa, can church bureaucrats be trigger-happy with that label. Anyone who dares deny the doctrine of the immaculate perception of the Holy Order of Red Tape are dealt with mercilessly, and can face swift excommunication from the Church of Conformity. Anyone who dares decline the honors of the establishment will be shunned and shamed.

The Great Methodist Tick Caper: Once upon a time in a galaxy far, far away (okay, it was just the United Methodist Church), yours truly was invited to a Cabinet retreat. The mission? Church revitalization—because nothing says "hip and happening" like a committee meeting extended to a retreat. Am I right?

There I was, talking about reframing "the system." My brilliant idea? Make "Trust the Spirit" as important as "Trust the Process." Revolutionary stuff, de-sainting St. Roberts and de-platforming his Rules of Order.

But wait! Plot twist. After lunch (probably those suspicious potato salad raisins), the bishop decided to channel his inner Picasso. He squiggled what looked like a mosquito on the whiteboard and proclaimed: "Sweet wants us to think in images. Here's my image for him. See the tic? See the hairs all over the tic? He's a hairy-tic. A heretic."

And there you have it, my beloved students. I went from "church revitalizer" to "hairy heretic" faster than you can say "Amen." Who knew challenging church bureaucracy was more dangerous than suggesting we replace communion wine with Mountain Dew? The loudest cries of heresy that will ever be hurled at you in your life will not come when you challenge established orthodoxy, but when you stand up to the establishment ecclesiocracy—the church bureaucrats who rule by procedures and policies and protocols. Online hate sites and O.D.M. attacks (Online Discernment Ministries) are nothing—every platform speaker has them—compared to the "off-with-his-head" outcries when you buck the bureaucracy.

Now when the establishment calls me a heretic, I just smile and say to myself, "At least I'm not as hairy as that whiteboard tick—or the long-bearded bishop who drew it."

The Prophet's task is to speak from the heart of the tradition, to criticize and warn those who, claiming to represent the tradition, are in fact abandoning it.

N. T WRIGHT[5]

SEMIOTIC TELL #13

Timothy Garton Ash, historian at Oxford University, one of the best political writers of our day, says that there are three serious challenges to free speech and the frank expression of views today. There are really four. But let's look at his three. You need to know all four, my students, because you will experience all of them as you exercise your semiotic muscles.

He calls one "the heckler's veto" which attempts to shout down the opposition. He calls another the "offensiveness veto" by which a minority group or someone representing a minority group takes a collective affront and squelches any use of language that it finds offensive. The third is the "assassin's veto" which is when a person or group is prepared to kill those with whom they disagree or deem wrong.[6] The one Ash forgets (besides the fact that not everything we think is worthy of being said aloud) is probably the most choking of free speech: the "fear of giving offense veto," the self-imposed censorship of not saying what one thinks or believes because of the fear that others will jump on you for saying it.

The Rebel's Rumba: Dancing Against the Current: Being a semiotician is like being a salmon at a bear convention. We swim upstream, buck the system, and hold back storms with nothing but our bare hands and wild ideas. It's a miracle we still have all our fingers, considering that not too long ago, critics expressed their displeasure by turning authors into human jigsaw puzzles.

In the grand ballroom of ideas, semioticians are the ones doing the Charleston while everyone else is still learning the waltz. We're not just thinking outside the box; we're using the box as a soapbox, a beat box, and occasionally, a time machine. And building a better box.

My own ministry and mission has evolved because of this. I once believed my semiotic task was to decipher the world's complexities to better explain Jesus to it. Now, I understand that our calling is more profound:

> To stand as a loving if perplexing presence in a world that has lost its bearings.
>
> To embody the gospel's transfigurative power amidst a society that resists fundamental change.
>
> To be an incarnational witness: simultaneously compassionate and defiant, mirroring God's love for a world that may take offense at this radical love.
>
> To trust in God's providence beyond our understanding, knowing that our role is to faithfully live out the gospel's teachings.

The gospel will inevitably confound a world adrift from its true purpose. Our mission is not to make this message palatable, but to live it out authentically, aesthetically, trusting that its inherent power will resonate with those seeking genuine change.

So the next time you get pelted with metaphorical (or literal) tomatoes, remember: We're not just seeing things differently—we're tasting the marrow of tomorrow. And tomorrow is always worth a few bruises today.

Those who offend the most should take the least offense. Christian theology is deeply offensive. Is there any greater offense than "the offense of the cross"—a cosmic reversal where up is down, in is out, losing is finding, emptying is

SEMIOTIC TELL #13

filling, defeat is victory, a cheek greets a smack, brokenness births wholeness, and Truth wears sandals and eats with sinners. Jesus praised those who "take no offense in me,"[7] but he knew they would since his own flesh and blood and hometown "took offense at him"[8] and tripped over his stumbling block of grace.[9] So worst offenders? Be least offended.

A divine finger dance gives us a case-study of what happens when Jesus rewrites the rules. Jesus stopped a stoning and gets "stoned" in return for his trouble.

The Hot Potato Story: You know the story: A dusty Jerusalem street. A woman, trembling. A mob, stones in hand. And there, in the midst of it all, Jesus—about to turn the world upside down with nothing more than his finger.

Ever played hot potato with a live grenade? That's what handling John 8 feels like. "Some ancient manuscripts treat it like a nomad, never quite sure where it belongs. Early church fathers give it the silent treatment. Modern translations slap on more warnings than a pack of cigarettes.[10]

Why all the fuss? Because this story isn't just radical—it's revolutionary.

Imagine the scene: Jesus, faced with a mob ready for blood, decides it's the perfect time for … doodling? But this isn't your average sidewalk chalk art. This is cosmic graffiti, and the canvas is the Temple floor itself.

What did Jesus write? Maybe a heavenly "Naughty List"?[11] The accusers' browser history? Or perhaps he was sketching out a new commandment, right there on the sacred stone?[12] That's called a hard reset.[13]

Remember when God got all finger-painty with those stone tablets? Jesus is pulling the same move, but with a twist.

He's not just writing law; he's rewriting it. Overwriting it. Upgrading it from stone 1.0 to flesh 2.0.

What irony. The same finger that once etched "Thou shalt not commit adultery" is now tracing grace in the dust for an adulteress. If that doesn't make your theology do backflips, check your pulse.

God likes to write with the finger. Jeremiah's mouth was touched by the Lord's hand. Isaiah's lips were touched by a fiery charcoal from God's hand. God wrote on two stone tablets with the finger.[14] God wrote on the wall of Balthasaar's palace with the divine finger.[15] Jesus wrote in the stone tablets of the Temple floor with the finger …

But wait, there's more. In this cosmic drama, Jesus doesn't just save the woman—he takes her place. When the Pharisees start throwing verbal stones about his parentage, Jesus doesn't dodge. He catches them and throws back love bombs.

"Where's your daddy, Jesus?" they sneer.[16]

"Right here," he replies, "and He's your Father too, if you'd only open your eyes."

It's the ultimate identity swap. The judge becomes the judged. The legitimate become illegitimate. And in the middle of it all, Jesus stands with the outcasts, echoing Hagar's wilderness cry: "I know where I've come from, and I know where I'm going."

In this divine street theater, Jesus isn't just telling a story—he's becoming one. His fingers trace more than words; they etch a new covenant. His body becomes the new tablet, his blood the new ink.

The Story isn't just something we read anymore. It's something we wear. It's on our lips, in our mouths, written on our faces, embedded in our flesh. The next time you feel the sting of stones for speaking truth, remember: You're in good company. The Semiotician of semioticians took those hits too. And He turned them into the cornerstones of a revolution. So when you're drowning in a veritable mud-slide of slimy algae and dirty water, cling to Christ as a drowning person to a boat hook. The cross will pull you out of the mud, snag your tormentors, and draw you closer to Christ.[17]

Welcome to the Jesus Graffiti Crew, my sister and brother semioticians. Time to make some divine mischief.

But brace for backlash and pushback.

Source Code Interactives

1. One of the biggest public backlashes I ever had is when early in August 2016 I called the Trump election in his favor. My students came at me harder than anyone. Just because you see something forming on the horizon doesn't mean you approve or disapprove. You just see it happening as clear as day.

   Tell some stories from your own life of when you got there ahead of the pack, or saw something before anyone else, and paid for it in some way(s).

2. Nine sins lead to automatic excommunication from the Catholic church. Murder? No. Rape? No. Sexual exploitation of minor? No. Slavery? No.

   Are you ready for the nine? Apostasy, heresy, schism, violating the sacred species (i.e., eucharistic sacrament), physically attacking the Pope, sacramentally absolving an accomplice in a sexual sin, consecrating a bishop without authorization, abortion, and violating the seal of confession.

   What does this say about the importance (or unimportance) of church polity?

3. Some say that universities are now bastions of unfree speech, filled with students as fragile as snowflakes who can't allow anyone into their space who might upset them with differing views. It is now a badge of distinction for being vetoed for speaking on campus or no-platformed because they might offend someone. This is a generation

SEMIOTIC TELL #13

who grew up on FB and twitter where you can report speech that offends you ("report spam or abuse") and you are social-media trained to silence speech you disagree with rather than debate it.

The most recent stat is that 47 percent of Brits eighteen to twenty-nine think the government should prevent someone from saying things that will offend someone else's religion. Do you think there is a global trend toward muzzling speech that some would find offensive?

Why?

4. When you defy reigning views of both God and Caesar, you are inviting double trouble. Throughout history, individuals who have challenged both religious and political authorities simultaneously have often faced the severest consequences, yet many of these figures are now remembered as pivotal agents of social change.

   Choose a historical figure who defied both religious and political establishments of their time. Analyze the immediate consequences they faced, how their ideas ultimately influenced society, and whether the personal cost they bore was instrumental to achieving lasting change. Here are some prompts:

   - Galileo Galilei, who challenged both Catholic doctrine and political power structures
   - Martin Luther King Jr., who confronted both segregationist politicians and segregationist religious leaders

- Baruch Spinoza, who questioned both religious orthodoxy and political absolutism
- Joan of Arc, who defied traditional gender roles in both church and state

Semiotic Tell #14

Nets Cast Forward

SEMIOTICIANS ARE A HIGH-HOPE PEOPLE. We hoist high the chalice of hope, even when the signs around us seem indecipherable, when the text of our times appears written in an unknowable cipher. Your commitment to hope persists even when the future looks dismal and dark, murky, and messy. In these moments of uncertainty and gloom, we hold our chalice of hope even higher, using it as a torch to illuminate the obscured meanings and hidden potentials in the world around us. This unwavering hope isn't Pollyanna optimism. Rather, it's a disciplined practice of seeking meaning and possibility in every sign, no matter how bleak. When others see only chaos, we look for patterns. When the narrative seems to lead only to despair, we search for alternative readings, unexplored subplots, and potential plot twists that could reframe and re-sign the story.

Our hope is the lens through which we read the world, even when that world seems to resist deciphering. It's the quill with which we write meaning into existence, even when the ink seems to fade on the page. In the bleakest times, when people are on the ropes or at the end of their ropes, the rope of hope becomes both our tool of analysis and our object of study—a sign itself of human resilience and the endless capacity for meaning-making.

Thus, we semioticians don't just maintain hope in difficult times; we elevate it. We study it, we practice it, and we propagate it. Because we understand that hope itself is a powerful sign—one that points not just to better futures, but to our present capacity to imagine, interpret, and create meaning in even the most challenging circumstances.

This vivid image encapsulates the reverence and importance that semiotics places on hope as a crucial element in understanding and creating meaning. In the realm of semiotics, hope emerges not merely as an emotion, but as a powerful interpretive lens through which we read and create signs. Semioticians elevate hope to a position of paramount importance, recognizing its role in shaping our understanding of the world and our place within it.

Hope: A Semiotic Perspective: The etymology of hope across languages reveals its profound nature. In Hebrew, words for hope such as "tikvah" connote expectation and steadfast reliance on divine promises. Greek terms like "elpis" suggest an anticipation of a sure outcome. These linguistic roots paint hope not as a vague wish for positive outcomes, but as a stance of confident expectation.

From a biblical perspective, hope transcends optimism. It's not about "hoping for the best," but about maintaining an open posture towards the future, regardless of immediate circumstances. The Apostle Paul's declaration, "I know whom I have believed and am persuaded that He is able to keep that which I've committed unto Him against that day,"[1] encapsulates this view. In this light, Christ is seen not just as the foundation of hope, but as Hope personified.

Semioticians interpret hope as a crucial element in the

SEMIOTIC TELL #14

process of meaning-making. Hope influences how we perceive and interpret signs around us, and in turn, how we create and project signs into the world. It's a dynamic force that shapes our semiotic landscape, influencing our interpretation of past signs and our anticipation of future ones.

Hope in Sign-Reading and Sign-Making: The acts of sign-reading and sign-making are inherently hopeful endeavors. When we interpret signs, we hope to uncover meaning and truth. When we create signs, we hope to communicate effectively and impact our world. This perspective transforms everyday semiotic activities into expressions of hope, imbuing them with deeper significance.

In semiotic terms, Issacharians are those who excel in reading the signs of their era and responding encouragingly. They embody a hope-filled approach to interpretation, maintaining high expectations for uncovering meaning and purpose in the signs around them.[2]

This Issacharian semiotic understanding of hope aligns closely with William MacAskill's concept of "longtermism."[3] Both perspectives emphasize the importance of considering the deep future in our present actions and interpretations. Hope, in this context, becomes a tool for engaging the future, motivating us to read and create signs that benefit not just ourselves, but generations to come, as we leave behind a vapor trail of hope that keeps humans moving and without which we lie down and die.

Embracing this view of hope has profound practical implications. It encourages us to:

> Approach sign-reading with expectancy, looking for deeper meanings and connections.

Engage in sign-making with intentionality, considering the long-term impact of our communications.

Maintain an open and positive stance towards the future, even in challenging circumstances.

Consider the implications of our interpretations and actions for future generations.

In the semiotic worldview, hope is not a passive sentiment but an active force that shapes our interpretation and creation of meaning. By embracing this robust understanding of hope, we equip ourselves to read the signs of our times more effectively and to create signs that resonate with enduring significance.

The Rope of Hope: The best way to change the present is not railing and flailing against the status quo or dismantling its decaying structures but to showcase and body forth a mesmerizing and enchanting alternative future that makes the current realities outdated, outlandish and outrageous. Like Jesus did.

> People swear by someone greater than themselves, and the oath confirms what is said and puts an end to all argument. Because God wanted to make the unchanging nature of his purpose very clear to the heirs of what was promised, he confirmed it with an oath. God did this so that, by two unchangeable things in which it is impossible for God to lie, we who have fled to ***take hold of the hope set before us may be greatly encouraged. We***

SEMIOTIC TELL #14

have this hope as an anchor for the soul, firm and secure. It enters the inner sanctuary behind the curtain, where our forerunner, Jesus, has entered on our behalf. He has become a high priest forever, in the order of Melchizedek.[4]

Semioticians throw from the future the rope of hope to people thrashing and drowning in the present. The writer of the Hebrews portrays an anchor that doesn't hold firm in the depths of the sea, but it is cast forward into the future, or even cast upward to the heights of the heavens, and there we are lifted up to the heights in the hope that has been fulfilled in Jesus.[5]

Best man/in the wedding of the sailor/to the sea ...

ENGLISH POET SAM WILLETTS ON THE ANCHOR[6]

This kind of anchor referred to in Hebrews 6 is known as a kedging anchor. Using anchors to assist in ship maneuvering dates back to the earliest days of seafaring. Ancient civilizations like the Egyptians, Phoenicians, and Greeks were advanced sailors and probably used similar techniques. While we don't have explicit records of kedging from the first century, it's highly probable that Roman ships used this or similar techniques since the Romans were accomplished maritime engineers and traders, operating large ships in the Mediterranean and beyond. Kedging was a well-known technique used historically for moving ships in confined areas or when there was little wind.[7] The procedure involved:

a. Using smaller anchors (kedge anchors) to move a ship

b. Employing longboats to carry the anchor out

c. Dropping the anchor at a distance from the ship

d. Using a capstan to pull the ship toward the anchor

This method was particularly useful for large sailing ships in harbors, rivers, or other tight spots where maneuverability was limited.

The Royal Navy's seamanship manual from 1904 describes kedging as a means for maneuvering large engineless ships in and out of tight harbors and tidal river entrances. Strapping young lads would take to the longboats and row out one of the ship's smaller anchors in the direction they wanted to move the ship. They would then drop anchor when they ran out of cable, return to the ship and take up on the capstan to pull the ship up to the anchor, usually 600 feet or so at a time. It was a slow, hard process.

This image of the anchor of hope was a favorite of early Christian artists, especially the fossors (Latin *fossores*). On the catacomb walls fossores painted the ship, one of the earliest metaphors for the church. But these artists-priests-gravediggers also painted the anchor, the symbol of "the faith once for all delivered to the saints" (tradition). If you're sailing with Jesus today on his "old ship of Zion," look carefully at your ticket: Jesus permits no passengers. All are members of the crew.

In a world often consumed by present struggles and past regrets, Jesus offers us a revolutionary perspective: He comes to us from the future, pulling us forward into God's grand design. To study Jesus is to study the future itself, for His teachings and actions were not mere points of discussion but turning points that reorient our lives and our world towards God and the future God promises.

While the academic discipline of futurology typically projects from the present to the future, semiotic futurology works in reverse: from future to present. It starts with the vision of the New Jerusalem in Revelation and works backwards to inform our present reality. This approach is less about predicting the end times (eschatology) and more about understanding God's purposes (teleology) for our world today.[8]

The promise that Christ is "seated at the right hand of the Father" is not about celestial seating arrangements but a powerful affirmation of who holds the future—and thus, who should shape our present.

The Gospel of Transfiguration: The essence of the gospel lies not in static points but in dynamic turnings. Jesus invites us to experience metanoia—a profound turning about of our hearts and minds. This transfiguration is the core of biblical futurism, calling us to re-turn our present towards the future God envisions.

In this light, we are all called to be prophets—not foretellers, but forth-tellers—speaking for the future that God is bringing into being. It's time for the prophethood of all believers, where each of us plays a role in shaping a hope-filled future.

Living Abundantly in Three Dimensions: Jesus teaches us to live abundantly by embracing a three-dimensional existence:

> Living OUT OF the past, learning from it without being bound by it.
>
> Living IN the present, fully engaging with the world around us.
>
> Living INTO the future, allowing God's promises to shape our actions today.

This forward-looking perspective echoes Immanuel Kant's 1798 insight: Remembering "occurs only with the intention of making it possible to foresee the future."[9] Our memories should serve not as moorings but as launchpads into God's future.

In a world often paralyzed by futility, we need hearts "full of futurity," as William Blake beautifully expressed.[10] This echoes Jesus' promise of more to come,[11] inviting us to live with anticipation and hope. Our challenge is to nurture this sense of hopeful expectation in ourselves and others, countering despair with visions of God's promised future.

To live an inspired life is to live an in-Spirited life—one breathed into by God Himself. The Holy Spirit gives us a foretaste of the future God has in store, described in Scripture as the "first fruits,"[12] "down payment,"[13] and "seal" of what is to come.[14] This Spirit-led life is inherently dangerous because its presencing of Jesus challenges the status quo, subverting rather than supporting the systems that often stand against God's purposes.

In embracing this biblical futurism, we find a wellspring of hope. Our lives are not determined by the limitations of the present or the mistakes of the past. Instead, we are continually drawn forward by a God who is already in the future, calling us to participate in God's mission of rebirth and restoration.

This perspective infuses our present with purpose and our actions with eternal significance. It challenges us to live not just for today, but for the tomorrow God is bringing. In doing so, we become agents of hope, embodying the future in our present and inviting others into this grand, unfolding story of God's redemption and reign.

As we align ourselves with God's future, we find that hope is not just a feeling but a force—a divine energy that propels us forward, empowering us to face today's challenges with the confidence that comes from knowing the end of the story. In Christ, the future is not just a distant promise but a present reality, continually breaking into our world and transforming it from glory to glory.

Concluding Litany for *The Issacharian Mission*:
> L: Let us be beacons of hope, standing tall
> P: Like lighthouses on the shores of despair
> L: Our spirits, prisms that fracture the dark
> P: Into rainbows of infinite possibility
>
> L: We are the torchbearers, the dream-casters
> P: Crafting tomorrow from the threads of today
> L: Who but us can rekindle the flames of faith?
> P: In our hands, we hold the embers of change.
>
> L: So let us rise, radiant with mission
> P: Our hearts, constellations guiding the lost

L: For in this twilight of uncertainty
P: We are the dawn that breaks, unfailing

L: Together, we'll paint the sky with divine designs
P: A masterpiece of resilience and grace
L: For hope is not found, but forged in our souls
P: And we are its guardians, its voice, its home.

Throw from the future the Rope of Hope.

SEMIOTIC TELL #14

Source Code Interactives

1. Holy Saturday stands as the great silence between death and rebirth—a liminal space where time itself seems to pause. While Christ's work continues unseen, breaking open the gates of death below, we who remain above wait in the tension of the "already but not yet," a state of Inbetweenness. On this nameless day, when words fail and metaphors fall short, the earth holds its breath. Below, the first seeds of resurrection stir in preparation for the cosmic renewal promised by scripture - the new heaven and new earth yet to come. Above, we can only wait in reverent silence, suspended between the cross of Good Friday and the empty tomb of Easter morning.

   Perhaps it's fitting that this day defies our attempts to define it. Holy Saturday may well be Christianity's truest "Earth Day," when the ground itself was first infused with the power of resurrection. But that's a mystery that deserves its own contemplation.

   In what ways do we experience "Holy Saturday moments" in our own lives—times of waiting and uncertainty between profound loss and hoped-for renewal? How do you navigate these in-between spaces?

   If Holy Saturday is potentially Christianity's real Earth Day, how might we understand the connection between Christ's redemptive work and the physical renewal of creation itself?

   Holy Saturday is a time when "words fail and metaphors fall short." When have you encountered experiences in your life that transcend our ability to express them? How do you respond to such moments?

Consider the image of the earth itself "holding its breath" on Holy Saturday. How does this perspective change your understanding of the relationship between the natural world and sacred history?

2. How do these ancient Christian symbols of hope (dove, sparrow, anchor, ostrich egg) differ from modern representations of hope (solar panels, signal bars, software updates, system reboots, cloud storage, open source, etc.) and what might this reveal about cultural shifts in the concept of hope?

   a. What specific qualities of each symbol (dove, sparrow, anchor, ostrich egg) might have led to their association with hope in early Christian contexts?

   b. How do these symbols relate to or differ from hope symbols in other religious or cultural traditions?

   c. In what ways might the natural elements (birds, sea, reproduction) represented in these symbols reflect early Christian understandings of hope's role in the world?

   d. How might the material properties of these symbols (e.g., the strength of an anchor, the fragility of an egg) inform our understanding of how hope was conceptualized?

   e. What biblical or early Christian texts might have influenced the adoption of these particular symbols for hope?

SEMIOTIC TELL #14

    f. How do these symbols interact with other important Christian symbols, and what might this reveal about the relationship between hope and other theological concepts?

    g. In what ways might these symbols have functioned differently for literate versus illiterate early Christians?

    h. How has the semiotic meaning of these symbols evolved over time within Christian tradition?

    i. What might the inclusion of both common (sparrow) and exotic (ostrich) elements in these symbols suggest about the early Christian view of hope's universality or particularity?

    j. How might these ancient symbols of hope be reinterpreted or repurposed for contemporary Christian practice or wider cultural contexts?

    k. What semiotic analysis can be applied to the use of inanimate objects (anchor, egg) versus living creatures (dove, sparrow) as symbols of hope?

3. Joan Chittister has written in *Scarred by Struggle, Transformed by Hope* (2005) that "memory is the seedbed of hope." Hope is not "in spite of" struggle and pain. Hope is born in the midst of struggle and pain from the memory of goodness and beauty and truth. "Biblical hope sees the present circumstance with the eyes of memory."[15]

    a. How does Chittister's concept of hope differ from more common or popular understandings of hope?

    b. Can you recall a personal experience where memory

served as a "seedbed of hope" for you during a difficult time?

c. How might the idea that hope is born "in the midst of struggle and pain" change our approach to dealing with hardships?

d. What role do you think "goodness, beauty, and truth" play in fostering hope? Can you give examples of each?

e. How does the concept of "Biblical hope" as described here compare to other religious or philosophical perspectives on hope?

f. In what ways might our current culture's focus on the present moment and instant gratification affect our ability to cultivate hope as Chittister describes it?

g. How can we actively use our memories of stories and songs to build hope in challenging situations?

h. What are the potential dangers of relying too heavily on memory as a source of hope? Could this approach ever be limiting?

i. How might this understanding of hope influence the way we support others who are going through difficult times?

j. In what ways could institutions (educational, religious, or governmental) apply this concept of hope in their practices or policies?

k. How does Chittister's idea of hope relate to concepts of resilience and post-traumatic growth?

SEMIOTIC TELL #14

1. Can hope exist without memory? If so, how would it differ from the type of hope Chittister describes?

4. Pope Francis' second encyclical "Saved by Hope" came out before Christmas 2007, based on Romans 8:24: "In hope we were saved." His first encyclical was on love. This one is called "Spe Salvi" (Saved by Hope).

   In this he says that "hope" is the distinguishing mark of the Christian, and hope is almost indistinguishable from faith. He calls the gospel "performative," that is, it is good news "that makes things happen and is life changing."

   a. How does Pope Francis' linking of hope and faith challenge traditional theological distinctions between these concepts?

   b. In what ways might the idea of hope as a "distinguishing mark of the Christian" influence interfaith dialogues and relationships?

   c. How does the concept of the gospel as "performative" relate to semiotic theories about language and action? Do you like "performative" or "participative" (my phrase) better?

   d. What semiotic implications arise from describing hope as something that "makes things happen and is life changing"?

   e. How does Pope Francis' emphasis on hope in this encyclical build upon or differ from his first encyclical on love?

   f. In what ways might the sequence of Pope Francis'

encyclicals (love, then hope) reflect a particular theological or pastoral strategy?

g. How might the characterization of hope as "almost indistinguishable from faith" impact the way Christians understand and practice their faith?

h. What semiotic analysis can be applied to the use of the Latin title "Spe Salvi" alongside its translation "Saved by Hope"?

i. How does Pope Francis' interpretation of Romans 8:24 reflect broader trends in contemporary Catholic biblical hermeneutics?

j. In what ways might the emphasis on hope as transformative and action-oriented challenge or complement other religious traditions' concepts of hope?

k. How might this encyclical's teachings on hope inform approaches to addressing global challenges like climate change or social inequality from a Christian perspective?

l. What semiotic shifts in the understanding of "salvation" are suggested by the phrase "Saved by Hope"?

Semiotic Tell #15

The Truth in the Maze

SEMIOTICIANS KNOW THAT EVERY AGE, every epoch, has its trends. The question is: which trends tend toward truth, and which trends tend toward falsehood and evil?

Theo-semiotics specializes in truth-tracking, not trends-tracking. Scientisim is an idolatrous religious system which believes that scientific and technological progress is human progress. Theo-semioticians are the refs that see the ball and make the call whether the trend is in the strike zone of truth.

Some trendlines turn into trajectories, some of which turn into tornadoes that reshape the cultural landscape.[1] But every trend has a trigger, and the challenge is to spot the triggers, which lead to trends, which lead to tipping points,[2] which lead to trajectories, which lead to tornadoes. Pay attention to the little things, because the little things can become big things very quickly and trigger trends that become trajectories that become tornadoes.

Trends have a lifespan.[3] They are born, they grow, mature, reach old age, and die or become passe. Plus not all trends follow a linear progression. Facts about nonlinear trends include:

* Some trends may decline, only to experience revival by new technologies or cultural values.
* Others may undergo forking or branching,

splitting into multiple sub-trends or evolve into new, related trends.

* Merging or convergence happens when trends combine to spring forth a new trend. Plateaus or stagnation, periods of slow growth, may interrupt a life cycle.

* Disruption or shock are outcomes of external events, such as technological breakthroughs, economic shifts, or global crises, all of which can accelerate, decelerate, or completely alter a trend's trajectory.

* Trends can also exist within larger, longer-term trends, creating nested cycles, or cycles within cycles.

* Feedback loops can shape trajectories through feedback mechanisms, such as social media amplification or self-reinforcing behaviors.

In short, nonlinear factors can lead to trend life cycles that are: S-shaped (slow growth, rapid acceleration, slow growth); Bell-curve (gradual growth, peak, gradual decline); Wave-like (repeated cycles of growth and decline); or Spiral (evolving, iterative cycles).

In the grand tapestry of history, theo-semioticians must discern which threads lead towards truth and which unravel into falsehood and malevolence. Trends (like social media trends that seem meaningful but may be ephemeral, or political movements that claim to represent eternal truths, or technological advances that promise utopian futures) are not immutable laws to be revered, but rather signs to be interpreted through the lens of truth. Our foundation must be truth itself, from which we can then evaluate the trajectory and consequences of societal trends.

Consider the fate of the Ten Lost Tribes of Israel. Their story serves as a cautionary tale of cultural dissolution. Rather than adapting to their new environment while maintaining their core identity, they allowed themselves to be wholly absorbed by the dominant Assyrian culture. This process was not one of selective integration or cultural exchange, but a complete surrender of their unique heritage. The Ten Lost Tribes of Israel acculturated themselves into oblivion.

The tribes' approach to cultural interface was fundamentally flawed:

They adopted rather than adapted.

They integrated rather than incarnated.

In other words, part of semiotics is reading the "signs" of heaven: "Thy will be done on earth, AS IT IS IN HEAVEN." God's will, The Truth, is being done now in heaven. Semioticians are looking for the things that are in heaven, seeing and signaling the "as-it-is-in-heavens" and then making heaven here on earth, bringing reality to the truth of heaven on earth, not taking the trends on earth to heaven.

Theo-semioticians look for the wintering trends and trajectories where creativity has chilled into compliance and the air is becoming frozen. Whenever cliches harden into conventions, pet phrases are stroked into iconic mantras, consensus frosts into icy orthodoxy, and sentiments coagulate into canons with all the attendant cants and chants, it is time to chip away at the frozen surface of the lake. We bow and kowtow to our sacred cows at the price of seizing tomorrow.

In doing so, we clip the wings of our message, when it should be free to soar over generational fences and scout out fresh territory in young hearts.

"He Gets Us" is a multimillion-dollar advertising campaign that presents Jesus Christ and his teachings in a contemporary, relatable context. The campaign launched in 2022 and gained significant attention during Super Bowl LVII (2023) and LVIII (2024), where they aired some of their most high-profile commercials. The "He Gets Us" campaign is primarily funded by the Servant Foundation (also known as The Signatry), and developed by marketing agency Haven.

Yes, "He Gets Us." But do we "Get Him?" If we truly "get" that "He Gets Us," then "He Changes Us" and we "Get Over Ourselves" and "Get A Hold" of a new life that isn't afraid of trends but holds fast to Truth.

Stalk the Zeitgeist as Truth-trackers, not just trend-trackers.

SEMIOTIC TELL #15

Source Code Interactives

1. Various developments in my life interrupted and disrupted my relation to the zeitgeist in the eighties, to the point where I didn't know what was "in," or "out," or if truth be told, what was really going on in popular culture.

   Are there segments of your life where you were unplugged to what was going on around you?

   What major cultural or technological shifts have you missed due to personal circumstances, and how did you eventually catch up?

   How has being "unplugged" from popular culture at certain times in your life affected your perspective on current trends?

   Can you recall a moment when you realized you were "out of it," namely, out of touch with current events or popular culture? How did it make you feel?

   In today's hyper-connected world, is it still possible to be truly "unplugged" from the zeitgeist? Is it desirable?

   How do you think being disconnected from popular culture for a period might impact one's personal growth or worldview?

   Have you ever deliberately chosen to disconnect from popular culture or current events? If so, why? What are the potential benefits and drawbacks of being "out of the loop" when it comes to popular culture?

   How do you integrate staying informed about current

events and popular culture with maintaining focus on your personal life and goals?

In what ways might being disconnected from the zeitgeist actually provide unique insights or perspectives?

How has the concept of being "plugged in" to popular culture changed with the advent of social media and constant connectivity?

2. Semioticians grow uneasy when we observe unquestioning consensus on matters of truth and faith.

   a. What are the potential dangers of widespread, unexamined agreement on important issues?

   b. How can we distinguish between genuine consensus and groupthink?

   c. In what situations might quick agreement be beneficial, and when is it potentially harmful?

   d. What role does critical thinking play in forming one's views on truth and morality?

   e. How can we encourage healthy skepticism without promoting cynicism or contrarianism?

   f. How do social media and echo chambers affect our ability to question prevailing views?

   g. What strategies can individuals use to challenge their own beliefs and assumptions?

3. What does it mean that the gospel is able to perform reconnaissance missions behind the lines of each new generation?

Semiotic Tell #16

The Reimagined Box

THEO-SEMIOTICIANS DON'T HELP people read different things in the Bible and culture but read the same things differently.

Jesus didn't reject the past or reject the law, but reframed our reading of the past and how we are to read the Scriptures.[1] Like a master of ostranenie,[2] Jesus didn't introduce novel rituals to his followers. Instead, he took the familiar covenant between Jehovah and Israel and transformed their perception of it. Through his stories and metaphors, he invited people to see this ancient bond not as something different, but to see it differently—with new depth, meaning, and significance. He didn't abolish the Torah or abandon the Temple, he himself became embodied Torah and embedded Temple.

Jesus, the ultimate paradigm-shifter, dropped truth bombs left and right. His catchphrase? "You've heard it said, but I say ..." Bingo! That's reframing, re-coding, re-signing—pick your flavor, but I'm partial to reframing. It's like Jesus is handing out cosmic glasses, letting us see the world through God's eyes—*sub specie aeternitatis*.

Jesus wasn't about PowerPoint presentations or listicle lectures. For example, when the religious bigwigs tried to trap him with tricky questions, he flipped the script. He answered hermeneutic questions with semiotic stories. Take the whole Caesar's taxes, coin debacle. After the Gotcha! moment of being caught hiding graven images in their pockets when Jesus said, "Empty them!" Jesus highlights Caesar's mug but grins and drops the mic: "Give Caesar his face back, but give God what's got God's own image on it—that's you, buddies!"

Or how about when the disciples begged for a faith upgrade? Jesus, who had nicknames for everyone (Rocky, Sons of Thunder, Didymus, Magdalene, you name it),[3] called them collectively his "little faiths," a phrase which resonated with his favorite designation of children: "little ones." But when the "little faiths" asked for the secret to leveling up, did he whip out a self-help book? No. He served up a mustard seed story with a side of mulberry tree-moving action. The message? Trust God more, and watch the impossible become your new normal.

But for the pièce de résistance, feast your semiotic eyes on Luke 10:25–37. A lawyer tries to outsmart Jesus with a legal curveball, but Jesus knocks it out of the park with the Good Samaritan story. He doesn't just answer the question; he reframes the whole game. It's like Jesus is saying, "Scripture is less a book to read than a mirror to reveal your true self."

And let's not forget the trilogy of "lost" stories—the coin, the sheep, and the prodigal son (a.k.a. the greatest short story ever told). Each one is Jesus' way of turning our world upside down and inside out. In Jesus' hands, the same old scriptures become a fresh revelation. He's not changing the words; he's changing how we see them. It's like he's got a divine Instagram filter, making the familiar look fabulous and the ordinary extraordinary.

So next time you crack open that Bible, remember the semiotics of Jesus' pedagogy. Jesus isn't just teaching—he's

SEMIOTIC TELL #16

inviting us to see the world through his semiotic eyes. He isn't downloading content, he's rebooting our perspecting and installing an old/new paradigm. Brace yourself, students. It's a lens of life that'll rock your world as it rocked the world of John Wesley in his day.

Seeing Through Jesus' Eyes: Semiotic Spectacles or Spectacle?
Imagine slipping on a pair of Jesus-tinted glasses. Bam! The world explodes into new colors and connections. That's semiotics in action—not just reading the "Good Book," but living the story in technicolor.

The metaphor of glasses and hearing aids places the emphasis on helping people see/hear God's activity. That is the point—helping people see the moving of God all around them, then respond as individuals and as communities.

But here's the kicker: Clarity isn't always king. Sometimes, we need to embrace the fuzz to find the flash. Think about it—when do your brightest ideas pop? In the shower. Why? Because you're marinating in morning mist, you're groping your way in the grogginess and cloudiness, you're letting your mind wander in the wonderful world of "what if?" and "where am I?"

Arthur Fry wasn't seeking enlightenment in that Minnesota Presbyterian church in 1973. He was dozing and daydreaming through a snoozer of a sermon. But in that drowsy haze, the Post-it Note was born, sticking 3M with a billion-dollar brand idea.

When you're trying to see through Jesus' eyes, dance in the shadows, play in the fog, and let the Holy Spirit paint your world with divine doodles. Sometimes the most spectacular spectacles are born in the spectacular spectacle of an unspectacular moment.

John Wesley, the OG Methodist, got this. Wesley understood that Scripture wasn't meant to be collected like information, or learned like lessons, but absorbed like rain into dry soil—it changed him from the inside out. Here's his secret sauce, as outlined in his preface to his *Explanatory Notes upon the Old Testament* (1765). Wesley details how he read the Bible with "earnest prayer" and attended to its overarching narrative, which he calls its "analogy of faith:"

1. Set aside Bible time (morning and night, if you can swing it)
2. Read with purpose (like you're on a treasure hunt for God's presence)
3. Connect the dots (Original Sin, Faith, New Birth, Holiness—it's all linked in the story)
4. Pray before, during, and after (give up control to the Spirit, since "scripture can only be understood through the same Spirit whereby it was given")
5. Pause, mull, and apply (how does this apply to my life?)[4]

Spectacle Seekers and Spectacle Wearers: C.S. Lewis contended that there are two types of readers.[5]

The "Spectacle Seekers": They're in it for the show. Reading is like watching TV—passive and popcorn-worthy.

The "Spectacle Wearers": These folks don't just read from a distance or tip-toe in; they dive in headfirst. Books aren't

SEMIOTIC TELL #16

just entertainment; they're a whole new way of seeing the world.

Lewis put it brilliantly to explain the difference between a non-semiotic reading and a semiotic one: "The many use art, and the few receive it."[6] It's the difference between watching a sunset and actually feeling the warmth on your face. As one of my mentors likes to say (again and again), it's the difference between reading the Bible, and letting the Bible read you.

Semioticians channel their inner Wesley and Lewis when "reading" anything. When you put on those semiotic spectacles of reading the same things differently, you are preparing for a mind-bending, soul-stirring adventure that sees the whole world in a whole new light.

This act of imaginative engagement is what allows us truly to experience and understand a story, rather than just passively consuming it. And to see the same things differently.

I believe in Christianity as I believe that the sun has risen: not only because I see it, but because by it I see everything else.

NARNIA'S INKSMITH C. S. LEWIS[7]

Semiotic Angling: Whatever word or phrase you see, look at it from an angle. The Semiotic Angle. How might I reframe this word? How might its root metaphor or back story or under story be a re-signing or re-coding of the word that make it fresh again?

For example, I read the words "human nature" this morning. I've always thought of them as describing basic characteristics of our species. But this time I paused and pondered them afresh in standard semiotic practice.

"Human nature." Hmm. Say each word slowly. Isn't this the same as saying "wet water?" Genesis paints us as earth-sculpted, breath-infused beings. We're not nature's tenants; we're its heartbeat. So is there any separation between "human" and "nature?" I'm not a pantheist (or panenthiest), but doesn't our story portray humans as a part of nature, and nature a part of us?

British author Gareth E. Rees, known for his "Weird" series, has captured this in his mind-bending *Sunken Lands: A Journey through Flooded Kingdoms and Lost Worlds* (2024): "There is no such thing as 'nature.'" When I read that, my mental fireworks and thunderclaps joined in unison and I couldn't stop playing with images of nature. We're Russian dolls of creation—galaxies, ecosystems, and gut bacteria, all nested within each other.

In this light, the phrase "human nature" becomes both a pleonasm (redundant words) and a tautology (repeating the same idea). We're not separate from nature; we're part of nature itself, in all its complexity and beauty. To harm the earth is to harm ourselves; to heal the earth is to heal our own humanity.

Harming Mother Earth? That's self-sabotage. Healing her? That's the ultimate self-care. So next time you hear "human nature," remember: It's not us vs. them. It's all us—in glorious, messy, beautiful harmony. To attack nature is a personal attack.

Semiotics embraces this symbiosis, and to find a language that reflects the harmony we seek with the natural world.

SEMIOTIC TELL #16

I'm impressed. You're impressive: Here's one more semiotic "angling." Have you ever said about someone "They're impressive." What if we re-signed and re-framed that word "impressive" by exploring its original meaning: "to impress." Impressment is a process of being "pressed" by a more powerful force. Like a glob of wax is "impressed" by the Maker's Mark?

"Impressive" isn't about you—it's about who's pressing into you.

We're all clay in the Potter's hands, bearing God's fingerprints, the divine impressment. We are God's selfie stamped on every human. The first "impressment" was when the Divine Creator "impressed" on the first human the divine image. Each human is "impressed" with the divine. Jesus the Perfect Human is the ultimate impression of the invisible God.

So maybe it's time to make "You're impressive" not about the person themselves, but about the person's reflection of the image of Christ that is "pressed" on them.

When we say "You're impressive," semiotics invites us to mean "I see Jesus in you." Less human accomplishment, more divine imprint. Less "Look at me," more "Look who's looking through me." You're not the masterpiece. You're the canvas.

I'm impressed.

And you can do this with every word or phrase you see. As I've warned you, my students, over and over again, semiotics is like crack.

Don't see different things so much as see the same things differently.

source code interactives

1. Can you provide examples of art or literature that primarily function as a "spectacle" versus those that invite a more active, "spectacles" approach? How do these different modes of engagement affect our appreciation and understanding of the work?

2. Lewis emphasizes the importance of imagination for understanding truth. How does imagination interact with critical analysis? Can excessive imagination hinder or enhance our interpretation of a work?

3. In an age of rapidly consumed media, how can we cultivate a more active and engaged approach to art and literature? What role do education and cultural institutions play in fostering this shift?

4. Lewis suggests that a "spectacles" more than a "spectacle" approach to art involves a semiotic engagement. How does understanding the underlying symbols and meanings of a work contribute to a deeper appreciation? Can you provide examples of how semiotic analysis can enrich our understanding of a specific piece of art or literature?

Semiotic Tell #17

Symbolic Truffles

No one escapes living in a time-capsule.

Jesus time-travels with each one of us. Or as Crystal Downey contends, "Semiotics ... is as much about a sign's context as it is about its content."[1] You can't understand a sign's meaning just by analyzing the sign itself (its content). You must also consider the context in which the sign appears. The meaning of a sign is not fixed or inherent but depends on the interplay between content and context. Semiotics, therefore, must consider both aspects to fully understand how signs create meaning.

What brings both content and context together is the harness of "condensed symbols." I call them "symbolic truffles."

Anything can be anywhere.

EVERY COLLECTOR'S MOTTO

In her concept of "condensed symbols," anthropologist Mary Douglas refers to everyday practices and beliefs that become a shorthand for an entire worldview.[2] She illustrates this with the example of the Bog Irish, a largely working-class Irish Catholic community in England, who persisted in the tradition of fasting on Fridays despite the advice of their more educated, upper-class clergy to engage in acts of charity or other practices more beneficial to humanity. Douglas argues that the Bog Irish continued this practice not out of blind traditionalism or a misguided belief in the magical efficacy of fasting, but because it served as a "condensed symbol"—a concise marker connecting them to their Irish heritage, their past, and a less culturally compliant vision of religious practice. Fasting gained a disproportionate significance because it linked various systems of meaning.

For me, the book is one of my condensed symbols. My wife Tia aptly describes me as a "booktrovert," a term that encapsulates my love for books. Every room in my house features a unique architectural form: stacks or shelves of books, serving as another kind of windows to the world. If I could choose my manner of death, I would opt to be crushed by a collapsing tower of books. While I have never understood the desire to be buried with one's favorite possessions, I make an exception for books.

I harbor an unholy envy towards Houdini, a fellow bibliophile who employed a full-time librarian to manage his collection of 10,000 autographed books and pamphlets. Upon his death in 1927, nearly 4,000 volumes from his collection were bequeathed to the Library of Congress. Umberto Eco, a semiotician renowned for his encyclopedic knowledge, insight, and engaging style, owned a personal library of thirty thousand books. He divided his visitors into two categories: those who marveled at the size of his library and inquired about the number of books he had read, and the rare few who understood that a private library is not a mere ego-boosting appendage but a valuable research tool. Unread books hold

SEMIOTIC TELL #17

far more value than read ones, as a library should contain as much of what one does not know as their financial means allow. As one ages and accumulates more knowledge, the number of unread books on the shelves grows, beckoning seductively. The more one knows, the larger the collection of unread books becomes. Some refer to this extensive collection of unread books as an "anti-library," but I prefer to think of them as my emotional support system.

My addiction to books is deeply rooted in my upbringing. Despite living on the poorest street ("Hungry Hill") in a town initially called "Stump City," the Sweet family's daily life was enriched by books, music, and the arts, regardless of financial constraints. We never dined out or indulged in candy, instead saving our modest means for books, music, and the arts.

However, the book is merely an artifactual delivery system. While I cherish the tactile qualities of books, particularly those bound in leather, my addiction lies not in the artifact itself but in the knowledge it imparts. The book is a condensed symbol, not of my love for books per se, but of my passion for learning, scholarship, and lifelong growth. I cherish great ideas as if they were dear friends, and the book symbolizes my love for learning and sharing that knowledge with others.

In essence, each book in my library serves as a condensed symbol, a microcosm encapsulating the myriad thoughts, themes, and intellectual journeys that have shaped and defined my life. The entirety of my library, then, stands as a powerful representation of my personal history, with every volume acting as a symbolic vessel carrying within its pages the distilled essence of my experiences, passions, and the profound ideas that have captivated me throughout my existence.

Study should always be in beautiful and pleasant books, containing harmonious script, written on fine vellum, with luxurious bindings, and in pleasant buildings ... since the behold and study of beautiful forms pleases the soul, urges and strengthens its power.

FROM *SEFER HA-PARDES* BY JEWISH AUSTRIAN THINKER AND WRITER ISAAC BEN MOSES OF VIENNA (ISAAC HA-LEVI) WHO LIVED IN THE LATE THIRTEENTH/EARLY FOURTEENTH CENTURY[3]

Every symbol is in some degree condensed, but some condensations are so deep they deserve the category "condensed symbols." Everyday life is filled with such condensed symbols, where a simple object or image carries a complex web of meaning. Here are some examples:

> Wedding Rings: A simple band of metal becomes a condensed symbol of commitment, love, and partnership in many cultures.

> Handshake: This physical gesture condenses ideas of greeting, respect, and potentially reaching an agreement.

> National Flags: A flag condenses a nation's history, values, and identity into a piece of cloth that takes on an almost sacramental status.

> Brand Logos: Companies like Apple or Nike

SEMIOTIC TELL #17

use logos as condensed symbols, instantly conveying brand identity, values, and quality.

Emojis: These digital icons condense emotions and ideas into small pictures, facilitating communication in the digital age.

Body language: Gestures, facial expressions, and posture can act as condensed symbols, conveying emotions, attitudes, and intentions without the need for words.

Condensed symbols are all around us, simplifying communication and conveying complex ideas through a single image or object. Once you identify a "condensed symbol," handle it with tact and caution. When you treat concepts and practices with concentrated meaning, you are entering a hyper-sensitive realm of assumptions, umbrage and anger which can ambush you when you least expect it, and take you on magic carpet rides that resist folding and can trip you up. Red flag a condensed symbol.

For example, ritual issues like vestments, ad orientem, and the availability of the cup to the laity provide symbolic carriers for profound subjects like authority, equality and participation.

Food, much like a nation's flag or anthem, serves as a potent and emotionally charged symbol that encapsulates the very essence of a country's identity. As a condensed symbol, food has the unique ability to evoke a deep sense of belonging, pride, and connection to one's roots, playing a crucial role in the construction and perpetuation of national and cultural identity. Through its capacity to embody the cherished traditions, stories, and flavors passed down through generations, food becomes an integral part of the invented traditions that nations rely upon to assert their legitimacy and claim a timeless, unbroken connection to their past.[4]

A condensed symbol can be hidden in plain sight. For example, the use of Roman numerals to enumerate Super Bowl games carries several semiotic meanings:

> Tradition and prestige: Roman numerals are often associated with classical antiquity, evoking a sense of history, tradition, and importance. By using this numbering system, the NFL suggests that the Super Bowl is a historical, heroic, time-honored event.
>
> Uniqueness: The use of Roman numerals sets the Super Bowl apart from other sporting events, which typically use Arabic numerals. This distinctive numbering system emphasizes the game's special status.
>
> Timelessness: Roman numerals can convey a sense of timelessness, as they have been in use for centuries. This implies that the Super Bowl is not just a fleeting event but a lasting institution.
>
> Grandeur and spectacle: The use of Roman numerals aligns with the grand, gladiatorial nature of the Super Bowl, which is known for its elaborate halftime shows, celebrity appearances, and coliseum extravagance.
>
> Marketing and branding: The distinctive use

of Roman numerals helps to create a strong, recognizable brand identity for the Super Bowl, making the event easily distinguishable and memorable.

Continuity: The consistent use of Roman numerals for each Super Bowl creates a sense of continuity and connects each game to the larger narrative of the event's history.

Overall, the use of Roman numerals for the Super Bowl contributes to the event's image as a significant, prestigious, and enduring cultural phenomenon, setting it apart from other sporting events and reinforcing its unique brand identity.

A keen eye for condensed symbols is alert to the cultural follies and excesses of our moment. For example, Ben Lerner, a young American poet, novelist, and critic who criss-crosses many literary genres, picks up and mocks the quirks and quandaries of our arts culture in his title litany to *Angle of Yaw* (2006):

IF IT HANGS FROM THE WALL, it's a painting.

If it rests on the floor, it's a sculpture.

If it's very big or very small, it's conceptual.

If it forms part of the wall, or it forms part of the floor, it's architecture.

If you have to buy a ticket, it's modern.

If you are already inside it and you have to pay to get out of it, it's more modern.

If you can be inside it without paying, it's a trap.

If it moves, it's outmoded.

If you have to look up, it's religious.

If you have to look down, it's realistic.

If it's been sold, it's site-specific.

If, in order to see it, you have to pass through a metal detector, it's public.[5]

Every condensed symbol is wrapped in a hidden ribbon that warns "Handle with Care." Handle all condensed symbols with kid gloves if you don't want others to put on the gloves. Failing to heed this warning can lead to misinterpretation, offense, and even conflict. Different groups may have strongly divergent reactions to the same symbol based on their cultural, historical, or personal experiences.

As we navigate a world filled with condensed symbols, it behooves us to remember to handle them with care. By putting on the right kind of gloves—kid gloves, rubber gloves, surgical gloves, gardening gloves, winter gloves, driving gloves, oven mitts—we can evade the boxing gloves and foster greater understanding, respect, and harmony in our diverse communities.

During pivotal moments in history, condensed symbolic markers become particularly influential, demarcating the lines between different groups and solidifying their sense of identity. This can be especially true in the world of sounds. In Norse mythology, the Vikings were said to have swords that "sang" or "rang" when used in battle. They were "swords that sing." Songs that are condensed symbols are knives that

SEMIOTIC TELL #17

sing, where the same music can make your blood tingle, boil, run cold, or curdle. For example, the last line of our national anthem: "The land of the free and the home of the brave." There is one song, our global anthem for planet Earth, that seems to make everyone's blood flow faster: "Amazing Grace, How Sweet the Sound."

Look for the "Condensed Symbols" in their Context.

source code interactives

1. Think of an object that has become deeply meaningful in your family. What stories, values, or memories has it come to symbolize?

2. What everyday gestures in your culture carry the most symbolic weight? How might these same gestures mean something completely different in other cultures?

3. When does a regular object transform into a condensed symbol?

4. What's the process by which something ordinary becomes extraordinary?

5. Are there personal condensed symbols in your life that would seem meaningless to others? What's their story?

6. How do condensed symbols lose their power? Can you think of symbols that used to be meaningful but have lost their significance?

7. What role do condensed symbols play in building community identity?

8. How do shared symbols unite or divide people?

9. In our digital age, what new condensed symbols are emerging? Think about emojis, logos, or viral images.

10. Consider religious symbols like the cross or crescent. How do these differ from secular condensed symbols?

SEMIOTIC TELL #17

11. What happens when different groups interpret the same condensed symbol in conflicting ways?

12. If you had to choose one object to represent your entire life story, what would it be and why?

Semiotic Tell #18

Semiotic Fool's Gold

IN THE REALM OF SEMIOTICS, it's easy to get dazzled by shiny objects—bling, beads, baubles, banalities, and salt licks—which flourish in the ether air of social media and distract us from the horizons.

The Devil's Bling #1: Politics: Politics, with its theatrical spectacle, is a prime offender. Talk about some shiny, shady, seductive, soul-stealing. Politics is a bubble bath of power that prunes the spirit.

Like a mesmerizing Beltway soap opera, it can hijack our attention, leading us astray from the heart of the matter. We must listen to the hopes, fears, and concerns of the people, without getting seduced by the fleeting allure of political power or the 24/7 news cycle. Semioticians can see the hot air on both sides.

In 2024, delegates of a Christian organization convened in Derbyshire, England, under the theme "Just Politics."[1] One could argue that this slogan might fit almost any Christian assembly. Yet how rarely do we see gatherings rallied around the simpler, more profound theme: "Just Jesus."

But for the church to see itself in the business of politics is as bad as for the church to see itself in the business of charity. Our mission is different from politics and charity. Do we really think politics will save us? At its best, politics is the art of solving nothing rather well.

―◇―

> *Paul's revolution is not at the level of the Roman Empire but at the level of the household, not at the level of the polis [city] but at the level of the ekklesia [church].*
>
> SCOT MCKNIGHT[2]

Politics can be a treacherous bauble, a bubble that traps and encases us. It's a temporary, tangible way to change the world, but it's also a breeding ground for spiritual seductions and fleshly pleasures. Religions can provide a unifying narrative for a society, shaping ideas about good vs. evil, authority, and even social order. This narrative can then be used to maintain the status quo or justify political agendas.

But the power of truth is not in politics, but in narrative. Politics leads to identity deformation, as humans aren't being "formed" into the image of Christ, but deformed into political slogans and party platforms. Politics doesn't image Christ; it images campaign posters.

God's kingdom? Eternal.

Political kingdoms? Sandcastles at high tide. Storybooks that use The Story for a hostile takeover.

When it comes to politics, Jesus doesn't have a party. Jesus is the party, and it's not a political one. It's a kingdom one.

Jesus didn't run for office. He ran toward the cross. Are we chasing bling or embracing the King?

The world looks left and right. The church looks forward—peers ahead—guided by a rearview mirror of tradition and a peripheral awareness that snaps into focus at the precipice of decision. At the crossroads, caution whispers: Look Both Ways.

The cross points upward, its vertical directionality piercing the sky. The humble, horizontal beam that each of us bears defines our journey. Unique to our own path, shaped by our own struggles, we carry this burden with a beauty and a brokenness that is ours alone.

The Devil's Bling #2: Breaking NEWS Another "bauble" can be news itself, especially "breaking news" that never takes a break. Not to mention that breaking news is not always/hardly/ever good news.

The first newspaper published in the US, *Publick Occurrences Both Forreign and Domestick*, appeared in Boston in 1690. It promised news just once a month.[3] Now news is most often what historian Daniel J. Boorstin called in 1961 a distracting and relentless flood of "pseudo-events," that is drowning us in their artificiality, ephemerality, and hyperbole.

Celebrity culture is the ultimate "human pseudo-event," fabricated to feed our inflated expectations. In Boorstin's words, a celebrity has been "fabricated on purpose to satisfy our exaggerated expectations of human greatness."[4] A celebrity is someone who rises from obscurity on their way to oblivion.

To take on a Jesus identity is to reorient the world through contextualizing, not politicizing, the gospel. God does not endorse candidates, but encourages us to engage in respectful dialogue and seek common ground with those who may hold different views. God does not endorse candidates, but through Jesus, reminds us to seek the common good, and to work for the flourishing of all people.

We must beware the siren song of politics and pseudo-events, lest we forget our true mission. Let's focus on the simple, profound theme: "Just Jesus." Only then can we hear the hearts of the people and share their concerns, without getting lost in the bling and baubles of our times. The kingdom of God is not a restoration of some political entity but the reigning presence of Jesus.

The Devil's Bling #3: Business Blueprints and Corporate Culture For the last fifty years the church has been inundated by a fury and flurry of slurry management speak. It has been invasive, intrusive, and pervasive. There has been too much rubbernecking of leadership and too little rubber-hits-the-road, rolled-up-sleeves followership. In fact, the bling of a leadership fetish in which the value of leading overtakes other values has been a toxic addiction and an ideological tyranny from which it has been almost impossible to extricate.[5] That's because leadership is the ultimate seduction. "Seduce" originally derives from Latin "sub" (below or under) and "ducere (to lead). To seduce is to draw away, to draw someone to a place "under" or "below" their best. We're at our "best" when we're living a "Follow-the-Leader" life and the "Leader" is Jesus.

Forget the old blueprints of power structures and corporate cultures. The church isn't meant to be a concrete jungle of bureaucracy or a walled garden of monarchy or a cult community around a leader. It is up to semioticians to point to more fertile and faithful metaphors, like a lush, interconnected rainforest of relationships.

SEMIOTIC TELL #18

In this divine ecosystem, every disciple is a unique species, vital to the whole. Business bling doesn't work because we're not about top-down control, but about symbiosis—a holy web of give-and-take that mirrors the interconnected rhythms of creation.

Imagine roots intertwining beneath the soil, branches reaching out in mutual support. That's the church living out its truest nature. We're not competing for sunlight, but basking together in the radiance of Christ's love.

What if we saw each congregation as a microhabitat of grace? A place where diversity thrives, where the strong support the weak, and where every member contributes to the spiritual oxygen we all breathe?

This isn't about maintaining command-and-control order. Or making Jesus CEO. It's a whole different metaphorical universe. It's about embracing the beautiful complexity of God's design. I have learned from you, my students, that if you asked any church what they thought about this, they'd say, "But that's exactly what we do!" because they believe they are. But when they really do, watch how quickly the fruits of the Spirit blossom and spread their seeds.

It is time to trade in our organizational charts for a field guide to spiritual ecology. It is time to stop pruning people into shapes that fit our plans and start nurturing the wild, wonderful growth God intended. It's not in job descriptions, but spirit descriptions where true human flourishing begins—in the rich soil of mutual love and creative interdependence.

Forget the Church as a Fortune 500 company or a political party or a celebrity show. God's not looking for CEOs or senators or celebrities. The Bible paints the church as a love story—a cosmic romance between Christ and His bride. It's less boardroom and more ballroom.

The church isn't marching to a military drumbeat or following a corporate flowchart or adhering to a political platform. It's slow-dancing with the divine, cheek-to-cheek with the Creator. This holy swaying and swinging isn't about power plays or hostile takeovers. It's about two hearts beating as one, a rhythm of give-and-take, listen-and-speak, being-and-doing.

In this heavenly hootenanny, there's no room for control freaks or micromanagers or power-mongers. It's all about tuning your ear to your partner's whispers, feeling the gentle pressure of their hand guiding you across the dance floor of faith. Like any good dance partner, the church needs to be responsive, flexible, and yeah, maybe even a little bit sexy (in a holy way, of course).[6] This isn't your grandma's square dance—it's a fluid, freestyle fusion of human and divine. It's the Trinitarian tango, where Father, Son, and Holy Spirit invite us into their eternal dance party.

And when the Church really gets its groove on, moving in sync with the Divine DJ? That's when the real magic happens. That's when we start seeing some holy fruit punch being served up, and everyone's invited to the feast-bowl.

The Devil's Bling #4: Materialism/Consumerism

'He that's Prodigall, is a prey to the Diuell' [Devil]

SAYING IN RENAISSANCE ENGLAND
NAMING SATAN AS BEHIND MATERIALISM[7]

SEMIOTIC TELL #18

Christianity, at its core, is a deeply materialistic religion—not in the consumerist sense, but in its profound reverence for the physical world. Matter is one of God's prime languages; God created it and continues to create with it. Through the incarnation, God not only speaks through matter but sanctifies it, showing how ordinary human flesh can convey divine self-communication.

Paul did not say "your brain is the temple of the Holy Spirit." He did not say "your spirit is the temple of the Holy Spirit." He did not say "your soul is the temple of the Holy Spirit." He said: "Your body is the temple of the Holy Spirit."

Spirit matters. God matters. And God loves mattering.

You matter.

No.

You. Freaking. Matter.

God speaks through the raw, tangible stuff of existence. Matter isn't an afterthought—it's God's canvas, God's clay, God's very language. God chose Jerusalem to be the spiritual hub of the world: "I have chosen Jerusalem that my name would abide there."[8] God sent Jesus to be "God-made-flesh." When Jesus "slapped on a meat suit" and walked among us, He didn't merely tolerate flesh—He elevated it, made it holy.

Your body, with all its aches, pains, and imperfections? It's a human vessel fit for the divinity that makes it human. Don't dare think your physical self is worthless. Your spirit, mind, flesh, and bones—it all matters. God isn't some distant force but is here in the grit and grime, the blood and sweat, the meat and meet.

God doesn't love you despite your material nature but because of it—it's how God made you. You're not a soul trapped in a body but a unified being, and every atom of you matters to your Maker.

Semioticians must remember daily: God matters. God loves mattering. And we, in all our messy, material glory, matter to God. This truth echoes in Jewish tradition, where ceremonies often conclude with the materialistic prayer: "Next Year in Jerusalem" or better yet, "New Year in the New Jerusalem."

However, when materialism becomes a worldview, and its cousin consumerism rears its head, problems arise. Materialism, as a philosophical stance, posits that physical matter is the fundamental reality, prioritizing material possessions and physical comfort over spiritual or intellectual values. Consumerism, on the other hand, is the incessant acquisition of goods and services in ever-increasing amounts.

In materialism, satisfaction is sought from owning valuable items. In consumerism, it's derived from the act of purchasing itself, with a constant craving for the next new thing. Both can become dangerous diversions, leading semioticians astray from their true mission.

Particulars are indeed important, but they need to be the right particulars. Some are mere diversions and detours. Materialism and consumerism, when they become all-consuming worldviews, are precisely that—distractions from the profound truth that while matter matters, it's not all that matters.

SEMIOTIC TELL #18

*One single solar system equals
multiple
realities.*

ONE OF NELLY SACHS FINAL POEMS "COSMIC EMBRACE"[9]

The Devil's Bling #5: Nationalism: Nationalism is a constellation of ideas and themes whose time has come and largely gone. While nation-states still matter—as evidenced by the enduring emotional power of nationalism in places like Ukraine or Israel—the concept of nation-state building has proven problematic, as seen in Vietnam, Afghanistan, and Iraq. Even established nations are facing internal strife, exemplified by the dis-uniting states of America.[10]

Ernest Gellner aptly describes nationalism as "a response of harassed and bewildered people to the pressures of modernization."[11] The rapid social, economic, and political changes brought by industrialization left people feeling overwhelmed and disoriented, with traditional structures and identities eroding. Nationalism emerged as a coping mechanism, offering a new form of identity and social organization to replace older, fragmented loyalties. It created a sense of belonging in a rapidly changing world, unifying diverse populations within the nation-state framework. However, this was often a top-down imposition by elites rather than a spontaneous grassroots movement, promoting cultural homogenization at the expense of local or minority cultures.

German sociologist Max Weber described the nation-state as a "human community that [successfully] claims the monopoly of the legitimate use of physical force."[12] This form of state monopoly on violence, which began in the seventeenth century, marched through history alongside its insidious birth-mates: denominationalism and the nuclear family. Denominational became as demonological as nationalist became nativist.

When patriotism requires hatred of the other side as a moral duty, something is wrong.

When class, gender, politics, or nationality is more influential than the gospel, something is wrong.

When the closing lines of the Benedictus are missing from our liturgies—"the day-spring from on high shall visit us, to shine upon them that sit in darkness and the shadow of death; to guide our feet into the way of peace"—something is wrong.

Because of nationalism, American Christianity* comes now with an asterisk—

> Christianity in America can be more American than Christian,
>
> More jingoistic than Jesus-focused,
>
> More patriotic fervor than prophetic witness,
>
> More flag-waving than cross-bearing,
>
> More Pledge-led than Beatitudes-blessed,
>
> More stars and stripes than bread and wine,
>
> More red, white, and blue than Calvary's hue,
>
> More Capitol Hill than Golgotha's hill.

As a patriot who loves their country deeply, who cries when singing anthems like "America the Beautiful," I stand in tension. My allegiance to Jesus and His kingdom reigns supreme, yet I navigate the narrow path between civil religion and faith religion, between being a citizen of a republic and a disciple of a King.

In this age of resurgent nationalism and divisive politics, we as theo-semioticians are called to a higher purpose. We must recognize the "bling" and "baubles" of nationalism for what they are—distractions from our true mission. Our task is to interpret the signs of our times through the lens of the gospel, not through the distorting prism of national identity.

We are challenged to embody a faith that transcends borders, that sees the image of God in every human being regardless of their nationality. This doesn't mean abandoning our love for our countries, but rather holding that love in proper perspective—subordinate to our love for God and all of humanity.

As we navigate this tension, we must be vigilant against the seductive pull of nationalistic fervor that can blind us to injustice and suffering beyond our borders. We are called to be peacemakers, bridge-builders, and reconcilers in a world too often torn apart by national rivalries and xenophobia.

Let us, as theo-semioticians, strive to read the signs of our times with clarity, interpreting them not through the narrow lens of nationalism, but through the expansive vision of God's kingdom—a kingdom that knows no borders and embraces all of humanity in its infinite love.

Semioticians as Inspectors and Prospectors: If Jesus is your identity, your semiotics will exude an ethos of Introspection and Prospection.

Introspection is looking inward and being honest about who you are.

Prospection is looking outward and thinking about future possibilities.

Introspection isn't just navel-gazing—it's soul-excavation. It's about:

> Courageous Honesty: Dare to look at the good, the bad, and the ugly within. What if we approached self-examination with the same grace Jesus showed to those He encountered?
>
> Divine DNA Detection: Seek out the imago dei within. How are you uniquely reflecting God's creativity, compassion, and character?
>
> Holy Disruption: Allow the Spirit to challenge your assumptions. What if your greatest weaknesses are the cracks where God's light shines brightest?
>
> Authentic Vulnerability: Embrace your scars as story-tellers. How can your journey of healing become a map for others?

Prospection isn't fortune-telling—it's holy imagination. It involves:

> 1. Jubilee Possibilities: View the world through God's "what if" lens. What if every challenge is an invitation to continue God's creativity?
>
> 2. Prophetic Dreaming: Dare to envision a

future shaped by God's promises. How can you be a living trailer of "Thy Kingdom Come"?

3. Holy Restlessness: Cultivate a divine discontent with the status quo. What if your biggest frustrations are actually birth pangs of God's new creation?

4. Collaborative Visioning: Join in God's redemptive storyline. How can your unique gifts contribute to the unfolding cosmic drama?

The Introspection-Prospection Dance Here's where it gets exciting. These four prospections aren't isolated activities—they're partners in a divine circle dance (perichoresis). Your honest self-assessment (Introspection) fuels bold vision-casting (Prospection). Your dreams for the future (Prospection) reshape how you see yourself now (Introspection).

Living It Out: From Semiotics to Symphonics: When Introspection and Prospection harmonize, life becomes a vivid sign pointing to Jesus. You're no longer just reading the signs—you become a living, breathing semiotic symphony.

What if your workplace became a laboratory for incarnating God's future?

How might your family dinner table transform into a staging ground for kingdom values, virtues, and ventures?

What if your art/music/writing became a prophetic declaration of what's possible with God?

Remember, students, in God's economy, the deepest look inward often catalyzes the boldest leap forward. So, my novice semioticians, grab those Jesus-lenses and start exploring. The adventure of a lifetime—both inward and outward—awaits.

Beware the Semiotic Sirens: The Baubles, Beads, Bling, and Banalities.

SEMIOTIC TELL #18

Source Code Interactives

1. If you lived through the Trumpocene Era, you encountered two kinds of people: those suffering from Trump derangement syndrome (TDS), and those suffering from Trump enthrallment (deification?) syndrome (TES). Trump combined the roles of a chairman, a showman, a hitman, a mad man, and a shaman. Each feature that was loved or hated is bling.

    How well did your church survive the Trumpian Times? Did it become a one-party church of either TDS or TES? Or did it find semiotic ways to find unity in the midst of disunity?

2. One of the greatest rabbis of the twentieth century, a theologian, philosopher, and civil rights activist named Abraham Heschel (1907–1972), said this: "The supreme issue today is not the *halakha* for the Jew or the Church for the Christian but the premise underlying both religions, namely, whether there is a *pathos*, a divine reality concerned with the destiny of humanity which mysteriously impinges upon history; … The misery and fear of alienation from God make Jew and Christian cry together."[13]

    How does Heschel's emphasis on "divine reality concerned with the destiny of humanity" contrast with the distractions of contemporary culture (politics, breaking news, celebrity culture, etc.)?

3. In what ways might focusing on "baubles, bling, and

beads" prevent us from recognizing the "pathos" or divine concern that Heschel describes?

4. How can we cultivate an awareness of the "supreme issue" Heschel mentions while living in a world full of constant distractions?

5. Heschel suggests that the "misery and fear of alienation from God" unites people across different faiths. How might this shared experience serve as an antidote to divisive elements like nationalism?

6. In the context of semiotics, how do the signs and symbols of modern life (e.g., social media, consumer culture) potentially obscure our perception of deeper spiritual realities?

7. How can we distinguish between genuine religious practice and the "halakha for the Jew or the Church for the Christian" when these institutions themselves can sometimes become distractions?

8. In what ways does Heschel's perspective challenge us to reevaluate our priorities and what we consider important in life?

9. How might recognizing a "divine reality concerned with the destiny of humanity" change our approach to current global challenges?

10. Can you identify modern "semiotic sirens" in your own life that distract you from contemplating the "supreme issue" Heschel describes?

11. How can we integrate engagement with the world (including politics and current events) while maintaining focus on deeper spiritual truths?

12. In what ways might the shared experience of "crying together" that Heschel mentions foster unity and understanding across different belief systems?

13. How can we cultivate a sensitivity to the "pathos" or divine concern that "impinges upon history" in our daily lives?

Semiotic Tell #19

Signs Under Pressure

SEMIOTICS CAN BE A FASCINATING yet treacherous pursuit. Like a theological equivalent of crack, it can lead to an all-consuming obsession, leaving us unable to stop analyzing and interpreting everything around us. This phenomenon is akin to "hermeneutic vertigo," but with a more intense, dopamine-fueled high.

The Junkie's Guide to Semiotics: "Listen up" (to borrow a favorite Jesus phrase), you bright-eyed, bushy-tailed semiotics addicts in training. Buckle up. We're about to take a joyride through the twisted alleyways of your future obsession.

Fair warning: this isn't your grandma's textbook chapter. We're diving headfirst into the deep end of the semiotic ocean with unsafe places to swim, but I promise you'll come out the other side either enlightened or committed. Maybe both.

So loosen your defenses, unbutton that top button of clerical propriety, and prepare to have your mind twisted into a Möbius strip of meaning. We're going to dance on the razor's edge between the judicious and the jejune. Trust me, it's going to be one mind-bending salsa bachata.

By the time we're done, you'll either be seeing signs in your alphabet soup or checking yourself into rehab for chronic overthinking. Either way, you're in for a wild ride.

Ready to turn your brain inside out? Let's dive into

the five telltale signs that you're not just studying semiotics—you're mainlining it straight into your cerebral cortex. You've succumbed to what I call Narci-Narco Semiotics (Narci-ssistic/Narco-tic).

Welcome to the dark side of deconstruction, colleagues. Hope you brought your sense of humor—you're going to need it.

Five Telltale Signs of Addiction: From Substances to Symbols

1) *Control Slips Through Your Fingers*: Like anyone with a substance addiction (like drugs or alcohol) or behavioral addictions (like gambling or internet use), a semiotics addict dangles from the strings of the obsession. The Oscars cease to be a celebration of cinematic art; instead, it morphs into Hollywood's grandiose circle jerk. That golden statuette? Nothing but a gilded phallus, thrusting its way into your psyche.

Freud, that cigar-chomping maestro of the subconscious, couldn't resist seeing sex in everything. Yet even he had to admit, "Sometimes a cigar is just a cigar"—a rare moment of clarity in his smoke-filled world of symbolic intercourse. But let's face it: in the labyrinth of the mind, even the most commonplace object can be a minefield of meaning. Or can it? The line between profound insight and paranoid delusion is as thin as a cigarette paper, and twice as flammable.

2) *Death By Decoding—The Confessions of a Meaning Addict:* You're a kamikaze pilot of semiotics, crashing and burning in every social situation. Golf becomes a Freudian nightmare—every hole a honey pot, every club a phallus, every swing a stroke. Your friends' eye-rolls could power a

SEMIOTIC TELL #19

windmill, but you can't stop. You're not just reading between the lines; you're snorting them like cocaine. Congratulations, you've unlocked the superpower of instant social suicide. Semioticians are such good magicians—I can make an ass of myself in the snap of a finger. Abracadabra!

3) *The Hunger that Devours*: Your brain is a rabid beast, slavering for signs and symbols. Money isn't just cash; it's a crusty loaf of cultural anthropology. "Dough" rises like capitalism's bloated corpse, while "bread" lies flat like a communist's empty promises. You're not broke; you're a "temporarily embarrassed millionaire" in a world where even your empty wallet screams with semiotic significance. Sacred stories? They're your drug paraphernalia, and you're always jonesing for another hit of hidden meaning. You'd sell your soul for a fresh interpretation of the Bible, if you hadn't already traded it for a dog-eared copy of Barthes' "*Mythologies*."

4) *Chasing the Dragon's Tail*: Your synapses are fried, burnt out on pedestrian symbols. You need the hard stuff now—Baudrillard's hyperreality cut with a dash of Eco's semiotic cocaine. You're mainlining postmodern theory, your veins bulging with intertextuality. Rehab? It's a semiotic straitjacket, forcing you to go cold turkey on your beloved signs. You promise to stop fondling every Freudian slip. But let's face it, you'll be back on the streets soon, trading favors for hardcover copies of Foucault.

5) *The Shakes of Signification*: Try to quit, and the world becomes a terrifying blank slate. Every stop sign screams for deconstruction; every cloud formation begs for Rorschach analysis. You're not living; you're drowning in a sea of signs, gasping for the sweet air of simple reality. But here's the kicker: your addiction isn't an escape—it's an all-consuming engagement with existence. You're not running from life; you're sprinting towards it at breakneck speed, leaving a trail of overwrought interpretations in your wake.

Congratulations, you pretentious junkie—you've achieved the ultimate high of seeing everything and nothing simultaneously. Welcome to the eternal cerebral labyrinth that is semiotic addiction.

Is There a Sweet Spot? Semiotics is a double-edged sword sharp enough to slice through the veil of reality, but just as likely to sever your last social ties. One moment you're unraveling the fabric of existence, the next you're that wild-eyed lunatic at parties, foaming at the mouth about the subtexts of cocktail umbrellas.

Sure, you might unlock the secrets of the universe, but at what cost? Your sanity? Your relationships? Your ability to watch a movie without turning it into a Foucauldian discourse on power dynamics?

So here we are, strung out on signs, mainlining meaning, and overdosing on overthinking. We're the junkies of jargon, the addicts of allusion, teetering on the razor's edge between profound insight and inane insanity.

But perhaps there's hope. Maybe, just maybe, we can find that Sweet Spot—where we dance with symbols without letting them drag us into the abyss. Where we can appreciate both the depth of meaning and the simple joy of splashing in surface-level existence.

The Sweet Spot lies in the gentle art of knowing when to dive deep and when to float. It's about developing what we might call a "semiotic sensitivity" rather than a semiotic

SEMIOTIC TELL #19

obsession. Like a musician who knows precisely when to let a note ring and when to let silence speak, we must learn to recognize when meaning-making enriches our understanding and when it begins to obscure the very thing we're trying to see.

Remember, there is always one oddness too many. That's our warning sign—when we find ourselves hunting for significance in every shadow, every coincidence, every casual gesture. The moment we start seeing conspiracy in our morning coffee's foam patterns, we've strayed too far from shore.

The Sweet Spot reveals itself in moments of harmony: when we can appreciate the rich symbolic weight of a wedding ring while still delighting in its simple golden gleam. When we can analyze the cultural implications of a handshake while still feeling its basic human warmth. When we can read the semiotics of a sunset without forgetting to simply watch it paint the sky.

Perhaps the secret lies in approaching symbols like we approach old friends—with curiosity and affection, but without the need to dissect every word they say. We can acknowledge the deeper currents without drowning in them, dance with meaning without becoming its slave.

After all, isn't the richest kind of understanding one that knows both when to probe and when to pause? One that can shift seamlessly between depth and surface, between analysis and appreciation, between the search for meaning and the simple act of being?

In this Sweet Spot, semiotics becomes not an addiction, but a gift—a lens we can look through when it serves us, and set aside when it doesn't. A tool for enriching our experience of the world, rather than a compulsion that diminishes it.

So the next time you feel the itch to deconstruct, take a deep breath. Remember: sometimes an Oscar is just a golden paperweight for those drugged on the fumes of their obscenely high egos. Remember too: you're a Jesus junkie above all.

And if all else fails, there's always rehab for the chronically semiotic. Just don't expect the "Exit" sign to be free from analysis.

Caveat Emptor: Semiotics Can Be Addictive.

SEMIOTIC TELL #19

source code interactives

1. This chapter compares semiotics to an addictive substance, particularly crack cocaine. How effective is this extended metaphor in conveying both the allure and potential dangers of excessive semiotic analysis? What are the strengths and limitations of this comparison?

2. Sometimes a cigar is just a cigar"—How does this famous Freud quote serve as a central tension in the chapter? In what ways does it challenge the tendency toward over-interpretation in semiotic analysis?

3. The chapter suggests there's a "Sweet Spot" between profound insight and obsessive over-analysis. What practical strategies might help scholars and students find this balance in their own work with semiotics?

4. The chapter uses humor extensively to critique academic tendencies toward over-interpretation. How does this humorous approach strengthen (or potentially undermine) the serious underlying message about moderation in semiotic analysis?

5. Consider the portrayal of the "semiotics junkie" who sees meaning in everything from cocktail umbrellas to coffee foam patterns. At what point does interpretation become paranoia? How can we distinguish between legitimate semiotic analysis and excessive meaning-making?

6. The chapter references "Narci-Narco Semiotics." How does narcissism intersect with the addictive qualities of semiotic analysis? What role might ego play in over-interpretation?

7. The text suggests that semiotic addiction isn't an escape but rather "an all-consuming engagement with existence." How does this perspective challenge traditional notions of addiction as purely destructive or avoidant behavior?

8. The chapter mentions "hermeneutic vertigo." How does this concept relate to the broader theme of semiotic addiction? What are the symptoms and potential consequences of such intellectual dizziness?

9. Sweet uses the metaphor of "dancing with symbols without letting them drag us into the abyss." How might this image help us understand the relationship between the analyst and their subject matter in semiotic studies?

10. The chapter ends with a reminder that the reader is "a Jesus junkie above all." How does this religious reference complicate or enhance the chapter's exploration of addiction and meaning-making?

11. Sweet compares approaching symbols to approaching old friends—"with curiosity and affection, but without the need to dissect every word they say." How might this perspective transform our relationship with semiotic analysis in academic and personal contexts?

Semiotic Tell #20

The Navel's Pull

*Still a man [Everyone] hears what he wants to hear.
And disregards the rest.*

SIMON AND GARFUNKEL, "THE BOXER" (1970)

The Semiotician's Challenge: Simon and Garfunkel encapsulate a fundamental human tendency: we often perceive and interpret the world through the lens of our own experiences, desires, and biases. This autobiographical bias, while natural, poses a significant challenge for those engaged in semiotic analysis. Semiotics requires us to step outside our own personal narratives and enter others. Viewing the world through the lens of your profession or preferences or politics leaves you shortsighted to the possibilities.

Why can't we see five years beyond our lifetimes, or five feet beyond ourselves? It is not easy. As left-handed Dutch graphic artist M. C. Escher (d. 1972) pointed out in his classic lithograph *Drawing Hands* (1948), which depicts two hands drawing each other into existence. This visual paradox reflects Escher's belief that "Every artist draws himself,"[1] highlighting our tendency to project our own experiences and biases onto our interpretations of the world.

It is not just artists who draw themselves into existence through their work. It is remarkably difficult to detach oneself from personal experiences, as the autobiographical region of the brain is often the last to succumb. In that final, intense moment of life review, our entire existence is unveiled not as a linear sequence but as a comprehensive, self-centered panorama.[2]

It is not easy to leave yourself behind so you can reimagine yourself as others. Overcoming our instinct to retreat into the familiar is a constant challenge. But if autobiography keeps popping up, you can't do semiotics.

Semiotics, like faith, is exodus. It calls you to go out of yourselves and get outside yourself. Openness to life is an openness to others and strangers, another way of talking about the leap of faith. But it's easier to make a fist than shake a hand.

Semioticians must learn to suspend self in a hypothetical atheism, shedding biases and desires to confront reality unvarnished, while paradoxically remaining aware of their own perspective. A semiotician must learn to practice a form of atheism: political atheism, social atheism, cultural atheism, even religious atheism. In other words, you approach something not from the standpoint of what you believe, or what you like, or what you want, or what you dream. You approach something from the standpoint of what will be, whether you like it or not. At the same time you are being yourself, you have to learn not being yourself.

It's a paradoxical posture: maintaining self-awareness while simultaneously transcending the self's biases in entertaining false hypotheticals. This dual requirement creates a productive tension, pushing the semiotician to constantly question their own assumptions while striving for a more objective analysis.

A Proust-Sized Challenge: Just because I can't understand something, doesn't mean it isn't worth understanding. Just because a piece of music or art or literature doesn't communicate to me or resonate with me, doesn't mean that it isn't a great work of art or music or literature. Some things are too difficult for me, or too off-putting to me, or too distasteful to my palate.

I am told Marcel Proust is one of the greatest writers of the twentieth century. But let's be real: Who hasn't tried to tackle one of the seven volumes *In Search of Lost Time* (1913–1927) and thought, "This guy's either a genius or a masochist?" Just because a book is like a dense fog on a rainy day, doesn't mean it's not beautiful. It's like trying to understand a symphony when you're only used to pop music. It's a stretch, but it's worth the effort. Just because something only has a small audience doesn't mean it isn't as significant or meaningful as something that attracts a crowd. And vice versa.

Getting the self out of the way shouldn't be so hard for a Jesus human, since Christian theology is based on the need to crucify our egos. In Christian theology it's called cruciformity. This theological imperative underscores the universal challenge of moving beyond self-centered perspectives, whether in spiritual practice or academic analysis. Cruciformity is like saying, "I'm gonna die to myself so that something bigger can live."

And that's exactly what good semiotics is about. It's not

just about understanding signs and symbols; it's about stepping outside of our own little worlds and seeing the bigger picture. It's like climbing a mountain and realizing that the view from the top is way better than the one from the bottom.

Rising above autobiography is an ongoing process, not a destination. It requires constant vigilance, self-reflection, and a willingness to challenge one's own assumptions. If you don't find yourself reading around and beyond your own comfort zone, outside your own convictions even, you'll be stuck in the self. By cultivating this ability to self-transcend, semioticians can strive for more objective and insightful analyses, contributing to a deeper understanding of signs and meaning in our complex world.

So, the next time you're faced with a Proust-sized challenge, remember: it's not about proving yourself right or wrong. It's about expanding your horizons, transcending the self, and discovering the beauty in the unexpected.

Here are some summarial How-To Pointers for rising above autobiographical bias:

1. Practice "Semiotic Atheism"
   - Approach subjects without preconceived beliefs or preferences
   - Analyze what "will be" rather than what you want or believe
   - Suspend your political, social, cultural, and religious biases when analyzing
2. Challenge Your Comfort Zone
   - Read materials outside your usual interests

- Engage with art/literature you find difficult (like the Proust example)
- Don't dismiss something just because you don't immediately understand it

3. Develop Dual Awareness
   - Maintain self-awareness while transcending personal biases
   - Learn to "be yourself" while simultaneously "not being yourself"
   - Stay conscious of your perspective while considering others'

4. Expand Your Interpretive Range
   - Look beyond professional/political lenses
   - Try to see five years beyond your lifetime
   - Consider perspectives five feet beyond yourself

5. Practice Active Self-Transcendence
   - Treat it as an ongoing process, not a destination
   - Regular self-reflection and assumption-challenging
   - Approach difficult material as an opportunity for growth

6. Embrace the "Exodus" Mindset
   - Be willing to leave familiar territory
   - Stay open to strangers and others

- Choose to "shake hands" rather than "make fists"

Follow these tips, and you will rise above autobiography.

SEMIOTIC TELL #20

Source Code Interactives

1. "It still strikes me as strange," Sigmund Freud told his friend Wilhelm Fleiss, "that the case histories I write should read like short stories." Is it so strange? Isn't the "talking cure" the telling of stories? Freud's observation that case histories resemble short stories points to the storytelling nature of therapy, where both the act of telling and the act of listening are essential for healing.

   How do you think the process of sharing one's story, whether in therapy or in life, leads to healing? Additionally, how does the role of the listener contribute to this process?

   Can true healing happen without being genuinely heard by someone outside of ourselves?

2. Freud suggests that stories transform in the telling, which raises the question of how much of our own interpretation shapes what we hear. How might stepping outside our own stories allow us to better hear and understand the stories of others? In what ways could this practice not only enrich our lives but also serve as a means of healing—both for ourselves and for those we listen to?

3. After the Nuclear Holocaust in 1945, a school was built in Nagasaki. At the time of its inauguration the children of the school sang a song affirming their commitment to the basic pillars of religious faith for the survival of the future humanity. Excerpts (transl.) are quoted below:

> Let us build the northern side with love to block the wind of Fate
>
> Let us build the southern side with patience to destroy hatred
>
> Let us build the eastern side with daily rising of the ray of faith
>
> Let us build the western side with the beautiful enchanting hope
>
> Let its roof be eternity and its floor be humility.

The quote emphasizes the importance of hope and faith for the future.

    a. How do these qualities contribute to the rebuilding process after a disaster?

    b. Can you discuss the role of hope in human resilience and survival?

    c. How can individuals and communities cultivate hope and optimism in the face of adversity?

    d. How does the story serve as a reminder of the dangers of nuclear weapons?

4. Simon & Garfunkel note that "everyone hears what they want to hear." How have you experienced this in your own life or observed it in academic/professional discussions?

5. Escher's *Drawing Hands* shows hands drawing each other into existence. In what ways do you see this self-referential paradox playing out in modern communication or media?

SEMIOTIC TELL #20

6. The chapter suggests that "it's easier to make a fist than shake a hand." What makes it more challenging to be open to others' perspectives than to remain closed off in our own viewpoints?

7. How does the concept of "semiotic atheism" (suspending all beliefs to analyze something objectively) compare to scientific objectivity? Are they similar approaches?

8. The text uses Proust as an example of challenging material that may be worthwhile despite its difficulty. What has been your "Proust"—something initially impenetrable that proved valuable upon deeper engagement?

9. How does the Christian concept of "cruciformity" (dying to self) parallel or differ from the semiotic requirement to transcend autobiographical bias?

10. The chapter suggests that our autobiographical region is "often the last to succumb." Why do you think personal narrative is so persistent, even in academic or analytical work?

11. What role does self-awareness play in overcoming autobiographical bias? Is it possible to be too self-aware?

12. The text asks why we can't see "five years beyond our lifetimes, or five feet beyond ourselves." What are the practical implications of this limitation for research and analysis?

13. How might social media and our current information

ecosystem affect our ability to "rise above autobiography"? Does technology help or hinder this goal?

14. The chapter suggests that "just because something only has a small audience doesn't mean it isn't as significant." How does this challenge contemporary metrics of value based on popularity or reach?

Semiotic Tell #21

The Waltz of Memory and Pirouette of Imagination

―――――◇―――――

Curiosity killed the cat, but not the Christian.

FAITH-FILLED THERAPIST JO HARGREAVES

―――――――――――――

SEMIOTICS IS THE DYNAMIC INTERPLAY of memory and imagination. A Jesus human has a memory fashioned by a biblical imagination, one that has been sanctified through being captured by Christ. Theo-semioticians practice the discipline of historical context while using a sacred imagination to unlock new depths of understanding and meaning.

It's not just the brain where memory is located. Memory resides in the whole body: nerve connections, cells of immune system, five senses (especially smell), etc.[1] But brain science has now discovered that remembering the past and visualizing the future use the same neural mechanisms. Memory and prophesy are flip sides of the same mental coin. Human memory works forward, and the very skills that enable you to remember your past enable you to envision your future. In many ways, cognitive science is providing empirical verification for what our godfather Peirce proposed: that logic is the living connection between reasoning, imaginative action and habits that govern intellectual pursuits.

There is no pure relationship with a past moment. Or as one scientist puts it, "Memory constructs, stimulates, and predicts possible future events in an ever-changing environment."[2] To walk down memory lane is to prophesy your way forward. In some ways you hope backward and remember forward if you let the past speak in the present for the sake of the future.

> *Time present and time past*
> *Are both perhaps present in time future.*
> *And time future contained in time past.*
>
> T. S. ELIOT[3]

For Friedrich Nietzsche, what makes humans "human" is the ability at the same time to remember and imagine a future enough to make promises: "To breed an animal with the right to make promises—is that not the paradoxical task that nature has set itself in the case of man? is it not the real problem regarding man?"[4] To be sure, memory and imagination are awkward dance partners, with memory's faulty steps and imagination's wild leaps making every move a challenging choreography. Our minds are wired to forget, not remember, making the foxtrot of memory and imagination an intricate interplay.

Stories act as a kind of memory glue, salvaging what time savages, holding together our recollections and shielding them from the erosive forces of nature. In medieval times, maps played a comparable role, serving not just as directional guides but as narrative frameworks that helped people sequence and spatially orient the stories of Christ's life and the apocalyptic New Jerusalem. By incorporating diagrams, pictures, and itineraries, individuals could better organize and retain these sacred narratives.[5]

Memory isn't just an act of retrieval, but a process of constant reconnection and reconstruction.

WELSH JOURNALIST JUDE ROGERS[6]

Imagine trying to build a skyscraper without a foundation. That's exactly what we're doing when we attempt to construct our future while bulldozing our past. It's like trying to read a novel by starting at the last chapter, or trying to understand a symphony by playing the finale first: you'll hear the grand conclusion, but you'll miss the intricate melodies and harmonies that led to it.

The present isn't a blank slate; it's a palimpsest, layered with the echoes of yesterday. And the future? It's not born from a vacuum of criticism, but from the fertile soil of understanding. Israel's prophets weren't molehunters, looking for things to whack down. Nor were they fortune-tellers. They were master storytellers, their fingers on the pulse of Israel's past and present to move the people forward.

Semioticians are cut from the same cloth. They don't just peer into crystal balls; they dive into the depths of history. Because here's the kicker: memory and imagination aren't rivals—they're (remember?) ... dance partners, moving in perfect synchrony. To dream of what could be, we must first embrace what has been.

Think of Lin-Manuel Miranda's "Hamilton." It's a perfect example of this "dance" between memory and imagination. Miranda didn't just criticize the traditional way American history was told—he reimagined it while deeply respecting its substance. He studied the historical texts meticulously (memory) but then dared to envision what the story could be (imagination): the Founding Fathers rapping, a multiracial cast playing historical figures, hip-hop serving as the soundtrack to eighteenth-century politics.

The musical is literally a palimpsest—it layers modern vernacular and musical styles over historical events. Miranda wasn't trying to "whack down" traditional historical narratives; rather, like those ancient prophets, he was using his deep understanding of both past and present to move people forward. He showed how the immigrant story of Hamilton echoes in today's America, how the political divisions of the 1800s mirror our own.

Through this creative act, he didn't erase history—he made it more vivid and relevant than ever, proving that memory and imagination truly are dance partners, each movement of one inspiring the next step of the other. The result wasn't just criticism of how history had been told; it was a revolutionary new way of understanding our shared story.

Divine Dance of the Seven Veils: May I take a moment of privilege and put aside semiotics and put on homiletics?

Jesus orchestrated Torah like a master conductor, weaving a resounding symphony of sacred narratives. With each bar, he unveiled new depths of holy writ's profound wisdom and transcendent beauty. As the virtuoso artisan (*tekton*), Christ's touch transformed the mundane into the miraculous, revealing eternity.

His insights, like perfectly pitched harmonies, vibrated through the deepest layers of truth, illuminating the heavens and the holy-of-holies of the divine. With every movement, the seven veils of mystery lifted, revealing the celestial duet between memory and imagination.

Thus endeth the sermon.

The Two Universal Plotlines: All literature distills down to two timeless tales of memory and imagination:[7]

> The Journey: A person ventures into the unknown, sparking imagination and growth.
>
> The Stranger: An outsider arrives, prompting reflection, comparison, and a reckoning with memory and the past.

And then there's The Greatest Story Ever Told—The Bible—masterfully weaving both plotlines of imagination and memory into a singular, mesmerizing narrative that expands horizons and resonates universally.

Presentism: We are properly hectored to respect every "otherness" out there, except the "otherness" of the past. We love to judge the past as if they were just like us. That's called "presentism."

Reading history backwards is the cardinal sin for historians, yet it's become a widespread epidemic, infecting even the guardians of the past. To inoculate against this anachronistic plague of presentism, semioticians must rigorously contextualize every fact and statistic, including the tempering fact that we too operate in a world that our descendants will find objectionable and unjust in ways we cannot anticipate.

Let's dissect three examples that expose how numbers, stripped of their historical skin, can lead us astray.

First, let's time-travel to eighteenth-century Britain to see why historical context is crucial. Imagine a world where you could be executed for over 200 different crimes, yet domestic violence was barely on the legal radar. Court records from this era show almost no cases we'd classify as domestic violence today. Why? Because the law was obsessed with protecting pounds and property, not people—especially not women.

Fast forward to the mid-nineteenth century, and we see the first glimmer of change: laws specifically designed to shield women from assault. What we today recognize as domestic abuse or domestic violence was, for centuries, simply dismissed as "domestic affairs"—a private matter beyond public concern or legal intervention. This profound shift in terminology reflects more than just changing vocabulary; it represents a fundamental transformation in how society views these acts. This legal evolution isn't just a footnote in history books; it's a stark reminder of how drastically society's values can shift. So, when we look at domestic violence statistics from different eras, we're not just comparing numbers—we're comparing entirely different worlds. Without this context, we risk misreading the past and misunderstanding our progress.[8]

Now, let's hop over to modern-day China, where headlines scream about the world's largest military. It's easy to picture an unstoppable force of millions, but let's zoom in for a moment.

Imagine an army where many soldiers are "only

SEMIOTIC TELL #21

children"—a quirky consequence of China's four-decade one-child policy. Suddenly, this massive military takes on a new dimension. Each soldier represents not just a fighter, but an entire family's hopes and dreams.

So, what happens when you send these "only sons" into battle? How many casualties could Chinese society stomach before public opinion turns sour? Picture the potential outcry if conflict erupts with Taiwan. This isn't just trivia—it's a game-changer for understanding China's military strategy. By digging into these contextual nuggets, we transform dry statistics into a rich, complex story. It's like putting on 3D glasses; suddenly, we see depth where before we only saw numbers.

Third, let's look at The Great Kindle Vanishing Act of 2009—when "Big Brother" became real. Imagine waking up one day to find your favorite books gone from your Kindle—poof, vanished into thin air. That's exactly what happened in 2009 when Amazon remotely deleted copies of George Orwell's *1984* and *Animal Farm* from customers' devices without warning.

The irony? These were the very books that warned us about totalitarian control and the manipulation of information. Was this incident a sign of another nail in that coffin?

Before we pull that trigger, and rush to judgment, we need to do our homework and understand the full context. The reason for this action was that the digital editions were being sold by a company that did not have the proper rights to the books. In other words, Amazon's intentions weren't sinister—they were addressing a copyright issue. Amazon's CEO apologized and promised better communication in the future.

Yet this incident sparked important conversations about digital ownership and rights that continue to this day. It raised alarming questions: In the digital age, do we truly own what we buy? How much power should companies have over our personal libraries? What are the implications for privacy and freedom of information?

The Harmony of Context, and Learning: "Context is key to creativity" is the dictum of David Byrne, singer-songwriter-filmmaker. He notes how different venues—from the gritty CBGB to the prestigious Carnegie Hall to massive pop concert arenas—each demanded a unique approach to musical composition and performance. This insight, while born in the realm of music, resonates powerfully when applied to semiotics.[9]

Just as musicians adapt their art to different spaces, semioticians must attune themselves to the varying contexts of the past and present and future. But the importance of historical context as a preset for the present and future cannot be minimized. Context keeps interpretation grounded in the story itself. This approach discourages wandering from the narrative or using imagination to "connect imaginary dots" or "vain imaginings."

The modern "pedagogical" model is to learn the labels and categories, and then to find things to match the categories (e.g., "Feature spotting"). The semiotic model of learning is to observe things in in their natural context (in situ), engage the subject directly (intimate distance), and then find fresh ways to understand and describe them. By grounding our understanding in immersion in the actual events and their setting, not from the posture of some imperial, impartial

SEMIOTIC TELL #21

"spectator evidence,"[10] we resist the temptation to impose anachronistic views or fanciful wishing. Instead, we promote a more authentic engagement with trends and trajectories.

The semiotic model aligns beautifully with Byrne's emphasis on context and creativity. It invites learners to immerse themselves in the "venue"—be it Ancient Rome, Renaissance Florence, or Colonial America, or the twenty-first century—and develop interpretations organically, much as a musician might adapt their performance to a new space. This approach equips us with the tools to approach current events and future challenges with greater nuance and creativity.

We all make meaning using our imagination around what we love, not what we think. None of us thinks our way through life; we imagine our way around our deepest desires, passions and loves. It is one of the reasons some Evangelicals can believe "correct" things but are living out their imagination for life that seem to betray their "correct" beliefs with what their hearts are set on.

JASON SWAN CLARK[11]

The Imagination Imperative: "God and the imagination are one." This profound line from poet Wallace Stevens[12] encapsulates a truth that we, in our technological era, have tragically blanked out. The imaginal realm, once the second home of the semiotician, has become a distant shore. We have lost our sensory and imaginative connection to the Living Story, a loss that some may find uncomfortable to confront.[13]

Dom Jean Leclerq's powerful commentary on the decline

of biblical imagination serves as a mirror to our current state and a call to flex the imagination.

> We are fond of abstract ideas. Our imagination, having become lazy, seldom allows us to do anything but dream. But in the men of the Middle Ages it was vigorous and active. It permitted them to picture, to "make present," to see beings with all the details provided by the text: the colors and dimensions of things, the clothing, bearing, and actions of the people, the complex environment in which they move. They liked to describe them and, so to speak, re-create them, giving very sharp relief to images and feelings. The words of the sacred text never failed to produce a strong impression on the mind. The biblical words did not become trite; people never got used to them. Scripture, which they like to compare to a river or a well, remained a fountain that was always fresh.[14]

The faith practices of our medieval ancestors didn't seek to eliminate imagination, but rather to sanctify it, substituting carnal images with holy ones. In doing so, they embodied Stevens' philosophy, uniting God and imagination in a sacred dance of understanding and revelation.

> *Imagination is a good servant, and a bad master. The simplest explanation is always the most likely.*
>
> BRITISH MYSTERY NOVELIST AGATHA CHRISTIE[15]

SEMIOTIC TELL #21

While imprisoned in Reading Gaol in 1897, Oscar Wilde wrote a long letter now known as "De Profundis." In this letter to Lord Alfred Douglas, he shared his conviction that "Christ realized ... that imaginative sympathy which in the sphere of Art is the whole secret of creation."[16] For Wilde, Christ exemplified a profound ability to imaginatively place himself in the position of others, to understand and feel their experiences deeply even when their experience, emotions, and perspectives were different. This capacity to create something that resonates with a broader human experience, according to Wilde, is also the core of artistic creation. Both the life of the spirit and the artistic process require a similar kind of empathetic imagination.

Imagination is encouraged by the Spirit, disciplined by Scripture, informed by the wisdom of the [hermeneutical and] homiletical city and energised by the need of the world.[17]

HOMILETICS PROFESSOR AND HYMN-WRITER THOMAS TROEGER

The Semiotician's Dual Imagination: Sensing and Shaping the Sacred: Imagine a semiotician as a celestial DJ, mixing the music of the spheres with the rhythms of human experience. This cosmic turntablist needs two turntables: the Primary and Secondary Imagination. I steal this from W. H. Auden, who in his Inaugural lecture in Oxford in 1956 as the new Professor of Poetry, distinguished between a Primary and Secondary Imagination.[18]

1. The Primary Imagination: Cosmic Antenna

Picture the Primary Imagination as a mystical antenna, quivering with sensitivity to the sacred frequencies that permeate our universe. It's the part of us that stands in awe before a sunset, shivers at the sound of whale song, or feels the weight of history in an ancient ruin. This is our soul's radar, detecting whispers of the sublime in the everyday.

2. The Secondary Imagination: Divine Translator

Now, envision the Secondary Imagination as a divine translator, taking those raw, cosmic signals and rendering them into forms we can grasp and share. It's the artist's brush, the poet's pen, the priest's ritual. This imagination doesn't just perceive the sacred—it gives it shape, color, and voice.

The Semiotician's Alchemy: To be a semiotician, then, is to engage in a form of metaphysical alchemy. Like the alchemists of old who sought to transmute base metals into gold, the theo-semiotician works to turn the raw ore of divine insight into the precious metals of human understanding.

In this alchemical process, we become cosmic prospectors and master craftsmen. We sift through the sands of experience, panning for glimmers of the sacred. Then, in the crucible of our Secondary Imagination, we heat, shape, and refine these raw nuggets of meaning into jewelry for the soul—symbols, metaphors, and narratives that adorn our shared human experience with glimpses of the divine.

Our laboratory is the world itself, our instruments the

keen eye, open mind, and tender, tending heart. We're not just analyzing symbols—we're synthesizing new ones, combining elements of the seen and unseen to catalyze fresh insights and deeper connections.

So, dear semiotician-alchemist, keep your cosmic senses sharp and your earthly crucible ready. The universe offers endless raw material, and humanity thirsts for the gold you can create.

"Slightest Particulars:" We have already learned so much from French Benedictine monk Jean Leclercq (d. 1993). Here's one more: in his seminal work on monastic culture, *The Love of Learning and the Desire for God*, he observes that, for the medieval monks, "The sanctification of the imagination results in their attachment to the slightest particulars of the text, and not merely to the ideas it contains."[19] The semiotics of scripture is such that the "slightest particulars," the smallest specifics, the innermost details often carry so much weight that to ignore them is to ignore a revelation.

Enfold everything you notice in Scripture like a friend. Hold every detail of your life gently, like a delicate flower. The world of truth reveals its wisdom when you trust in God's quiet guidance. There is wisdom to be exhaled from every experience breathed in.

The biblical holy grail for a semiotician is the detail that is *hapax legomenon* (used only once), or *unerfindbar*, a phrase used by biblical scholars like Adolf von Harnack, a German theologian and church historian. Harnack's usage has a range of connotations: the elusive and exclusive nature of Jesus' personality; the inexplicable essence of Christianity; and certain biblical words that are implausibly inventible, incomprehensible and unfathomable without being true. The word can also mean a level of detail that suggests an origin in historical memory.

Let me help explain this with an example that has haunted me ever since I first heard it. When John's gospel (19:23) mentions that Jesus' tunic was "seamless, woven in one piece from top to bottom," this is exactly the kind of granular, seemingly arbitrary detail that scholars might identify as *unerfindbar*. It's the kind of detail that might seem too specific to have been invented—why would someone fabricating a story include such a minor sartorial observation? The detail serves no obvious theological purpose, doesn't advance any clear agenda, and yet is precise enough that it suggests someone actually saw the garment and wants the mention to convey some meaning. This kind of detail functions like an unintentional fingerprint of authenticity—similar to how a true eyewitness account of a car accident might include a seemingly irrelevant detail like "the driver was wearing a blue plaid shirt with a torn pocket" that wouldn't likely be invented but might stick in the memory of someone who was actually there.

Die Persönlichkeit Jesu ist unerfindbar
(The personality of Jesus is inexplicable)

GERMAN HISTORIAN AND THEOLOGIAN ADOLPH VON HARNACK[20]

"Vain Imaginings:" It is helpful to distinguish between sacred imagination and vain imaginings. Imagination can go awry quickly, with too much lateral thinking, too many

SEMIOTIC TELL #21

free associations, etc. Paul warned about "vain imaginings"[21] which are based on personal vanity, not Christ. A sacred imagination is one that is hallowed by the divine, captured by the biblical story, illuminated by the Holy Spirit, and awakened by the world's yearnings. People's lives are reeled on storylines, making the question of who crafts these narratives critically important.

It's not a "vain imagining" if your imagination is always winging away and wending its way to The Story, to Jesus. Call it

> holy imagination[22]
>
> sacred imagination[23]
>
> sanctified imagination
>
> biblical imagination
>
> apostolic imagination[24]
>
> responsible speculation
>
> sacred learning

Womanist biblical scholar Wilda Gafney at Brite Divinity School defines the sanctified imagination as "the fertile creative space where the preacher-interpreter enters the text, particularly the spaces in the text, and fills them out with missing details: names, back stories, detailed descriptions of the scene and characters, and so on."[25]

A sacred imagination is especially needed when engaging in hermeneutical retrieval, a concept closely associated with theologian David Tracy (d. 2019), who coined and championed this approach as a method for engaging with the past of religious traditions. The core idea of hermeneutical retrieval involves critically re-examining and imaginatively reinterpreting the symbols, narratives, and practices of a tradition in light of current contexts and concerns. It's not simply about passively preserving the past, but rather about imaginatively seeking its ongoing relevance and potential for new insights.

The Allegorical Abyss: Taming the Wild Beast of Interpretation Our atrophied imaginations are precisely why I urge you, my semiotics students, to approach allegory with extreme caution. This seemingly innocuous literary device is a double-edged sword when wielded in biblical or cultural semiotics.

Allegory is the literary equivalent of LSD—a potent, mind-bending substance that distorts reality and blurs boundaries. It opens Pandora's box of limitless interpretation, unleashing a torrent of conjecture that can sweep away reason ("the quality control department," in Iain McGilchrist's phrase)[26] and context. Once you tumble down this rabbit hole, there's no guarantee you'll find your way back to solid ground.

Protestant Reformers didn't just dislike allegory; they saw it as a threat. To them, it was a breeding ground for triviality and fantasy, a "one-to-one correspondence of dissimilars" that perverted the very essence of creative symbolism. "[Allegory] is a mere fable, which has no foundation in the Word of God …. It is a game of wit, not a solid interpretation" declared John Calvin in his *Commentary on Galatians*.[27] Or here is Martin Luther in his *Lectures on Genesis*: "Allegories are empty speculations, and the more subtle they are, the more they lead us away from the truth."[28]

Symbolism vs. Allegory: A Crucial Distinction: Don't

confuse allegory with symbolism. A symbol is a concrete thing that represents a larger abstract idea (like a dove representing peace). An allegory is an extended narrative where the entire story and its elements systematically represent another meaning (like Jesus' Parable of the Sower, where the seeds, soils, and outcomes can be made to represent different types of people and their responses to spiritual teachings). Symbols are bridges and breaches, uniting disparate entities and grounding us in reality. Allegory, in contrast, is a wrecking ball, shattering concrete connections and severing ties to the tangible world. It's the difference between a multifaceted gem (symbolism) and a rigid, one-dimensional construct (allegory).

Some early church fathers, as well as monastic traditions, fell into the allegorical trap, producing interpretations so detached from reality they might as well have been plucked from thin air. For Origen the "breasts" in Song 1:13 were the "Old and New Testaments" at which we should "suckle" every day.[29] For St. Gregory the Great (d. 604), Noah's ark was an allegory of the church. He saw the ark's:

> Length as representing the Church's temporal journey
>
> Width as symbolizing the Church's breadth of charity
>
> Height as representing the Church's aspiration to heavenly things
>
> Gopher wood as signifying the Cross
>
> Pitch as representing the unity of the faithful

Noah's wife as symbolizing the Synagogue (Judaism)

Such flights of fancy serve as a cautionary tale of allegory's seductive power to lead us astray.

Allegory, like a powerful hallucinogen, dissolves the boundaries between meaning and fantasy, tempting interpreters to impose rigid one-to-one correspondences that shatter authentic connections to reality. While symbolism builds bridges between the concrete and abstract, allegory's unrestrained application typically leads to interpretive chaos, transforming sacred texts into playgrounds for untethered speculation. Allegory breeds misunderstandings and fantastical readings that bear little resemblance to original contexts and meanings.

While allegory can be a powerful tool in disciplined hands (and some preachers excel at it), its untutored, unbridled use in semiotics is a recipe for disaster. Instead, we must anchor ourselves in historical context and the raw power of the story itself.

Only when our imaginations are tempered by the Holy Spirit can we safely navigate the treacherous waters of allegorical interpretation.

Until then, tread carefully, for there be dragons.

Grand Narrative: For the theo-semiotician, life is a grand story, with each of us as living, breathing pages. The ink that writes our tale? Scripture itself, flowing from the divine Author's pen.

Every thought becomes a verse, every action a chapter, all pointing to the ultimate Protagonist—the Logos of God.

Picture your mind as a mirror, constantly reflecting Christ

SEMIOTIC TELL #21

in every facet of your being. Your very essence becomes a living anamnesis—a vibrant retelling of the Greatest Story Ever Told, not just on Sundays, but in every breath and heartbeat.

Envision your daily routines transforming into sacred rituals. That morning coffee? A communion cup. Your commute? A pilgrimage. Every task, no matter how routine, becomes infused with holy purpose when viewed through the lens of divine imagination.

When we allow ourselves to be captivated by Christ's vision, the world shifts from a fading photograph to a canvas bursting with potential. Suddenly, we see creation not as a lost cause, but as the first brushstroke of a masterpiece still in progress—a New Creation waiting to be fully revealed.

In this reimagining, we move from mere observers to conceivers, our lives a testament to the power of story, memory, and holy imagination.

Anyone who has been trained by history and knows
the immense complexity of forces in human society
will be suspicious of a scheme which reduces everything
to a single cause and a single remedy.

WALTER RAUSCHENBUSCH IN 1913[30]

Dance the Memory-Imagination Tango.

Source Code Interactives

1. Half of the *Mayflower* passengers died during that first winter (this includes both adults and children). This prompted the original Plymouth settlers to call their children and grandchildren "Increasings."[31] It was a word of prophesy as much as affection: The Increasings.

    How does the legacy of the "Increasings" shape our understanding of perseverance, community, and faith?

    Who would you consider to be the modern-day "Increasings"?

    What are some of the biggest challenges facing young people today? How can we better support and protect them?

    How can we ensure that all "Increasings" have access to quality education and opportunities for success?

    What role does mental health play in the development of our "Increasings"? How can we promote mental health awareness and support?

    How can we teach our "Increasings" the importance of environmental stewardship and sustainable practices?

2. Some religious leaders, like T. D. Jakes, have used allegory effectively in sermons. Check out a couple of his sermons and discuss how he allegorizes responsibly.

3. Early church fathers sometimes employed allegory (e.g., interpreting the seven demons cast out of Mary Magdalene as representing the seven deadly

SEMIOTIC TELL #21

sins). A sample of some other early church allegorical interpretations?

1) Origen (c. 185–254):
   - Interpreted the "breasts" in Song of Solomon 1:13 as the Old and New Testaments
   - Saw the Israelites crossing the Red Sea as representing baptism
   - Read the battle of Jericho as the triumph of Jesus over the world

2) Augustine (354–430):
   - Interpreted the Good Samaritan parable where the man represents Adam, Jerusalem is paradise, Jericho is mortality, robbers are the devil, the Samaritan is Christ, and the inn is the Church
   - Saw Noah's Ark as a prefiguration of Christ's body/Church, with its measurements representing spiritual truths

3) Gregory the Great (540–604):
   - Interpreted Noah's Ark extensively:
     - Length = Church's temporal journey
     - Width = Church's charity
     - Height = Heavenly aspirations
     - Pitch = Unity of faithful
     - Noah's wife = The Synagogue

Early church fathers often used such allegory to uncover "deeper spiritual meanings" in scripture. However, as we've seen, this approach risks severing texts from their historical context and original meaning. Consider the following question: At what point does allegorical interpretation become an exercise in "vain imagining" rather than faithful semiotic exegesis? Support your view by analyzing one of the examples above, discussing both its potential insights and its interpretive risks.

4. Jesus himself used allegory in some parables (e.g., Matthew 13:1–9, 18–23). Study these cases and discuss the difference in how Jesus uses it vis a vis others' mentioned above.

5. Charles A. Foster is an English writer, veterinarian, taxidermist, barrister, philosopher, and a Fellow of Exeter College, Oxford. He is known for his books and articles on Natural History, theology, law and medical ethics. Discuss this quote from him:

> How many other humans are in the same room with you now? Two? Then next to you are two other universes, almost unimaginably different from yours. The exploration of those universes is more difficult and more important than the exploration of distant galaxies. Though the exploration of other human worlds is hard—and often confounded by the human tendency to lie—it is a good deal easier than the attempt to enter the Umwelten of non-humans, like a catfish, which has taste buds all over its body

(It's one big tongue). Or an octopus, which has a brain, but delegates much of is sensation and action to its tentacles. Perhaps its arms live in a world of touch and taste, and the head alone 'sees'? Where, then, is the octopus itself? Is that a meaningless question?³²

6. Is imagination the opposite of imitation?

7. *Pilpul* (לופלפ) [Pill Pool] is a method of studying the Talmud and Jewish texts developed by Jewish scholars in the 14th–16th centuries. It involves extensive back-and-forth debate and argumentation about fine parsing of texts. Discuss each of these key features, and how they might be better integrated into your exegesis of the Scripture:

    a. Focus on intense textual analysis—Every word and nuance is examined in great detail.

    b. Use of logic and critical questioning—Students vigorously debate meanings and reason through implications using logic.

    c. Mental gymnastics—Those trained in pilpul develop great agility in analyzing texts from all angles.

    d. Seeing multiple interpretations—Students are encouraged to come up with creative readings and new perspectives.

    e. Exhaustive discussion—Debates can go on at length until all aspects of a text are thoroughly debated.

    f. Protection of tradition—At its core, pilpul aims to

deeply understand and defend traditional Jewish teachings.

8. The "discipline of historical context" (as Sweet defines it) is not easy. Here is an example of how difficult it can be:

There is a big debate as to whether Mary Mother of Jesus was at the cross. Only one of the gospels mentions her by name. One biblical scholar said of course she was, and added: "Have we ever heard of a mother not going to her own son's funeral?"

Well, yes. I was one of the preachers at the funeral of a young black man and as the service began with a song, she was so wrought with grief that she passed out and had to be taken out of the crowded church by passing her over the heads of those present like in a rock concert.

Furthermore, there is a saying that is relevant in lots of cultures around the world, "White hair does not see of black hair" or literally "White does not see of black." In other words, parents don't go to funerals of their children. This applies to about 1 billion people worldwide. So what can seem obvious in our context is not so much if put in a wider cultural context.

What are some current examples of this?

9. Why does Matthew's gospel in chapter 28 call the eleven men "disciples" (28:7, 8, 13, 16) but Jesus calls them instead "brothers" (vs. 10). Is this just a copy-editor's issue, or is this a "sign" that he forgave them and gives them official status in the new family of God?

10. If the key to successful communication is making the familiar strange so it can be fresh again, discuss the Russian concept of *ostranenie*, developed by Victor Shyklovsky. How important do you think defamiliarization is, and how important is the imagination in the practice of ostranenie?[33]

11. Is the imagination more important when you take a bird's eye view or a frog's eye view?

12. Discuss the Amazon Kindle fiasco discussed in this chapter. How might this event serve as a powerful "sign" for our times? Here are some things to talk about:

> Value physical books and diverse sources of information
>
> Be vigilant about our digital rights
>
> Consider the broader implications of our increasingly digital world
>
> As Christians, can we use this incident to . . .
>
> Highlight the importance of truth and its preservation?
>
> Discuss the value of wisdom literature, both ancient and modern?
>
> Emphasize the need for discernment in our digital age?

In our fast-paced digital world, let's not forget the timeless wisdom found in both our Bibles and great literature—wisdom that can't be deleted with the click of a button.

13. Western populations are also aging to the point where by 2050 half of the world's population growth is likely to come from just eight countries: the Democratic Republic of Congo, Egypt, Ethiopia, India, Nigeria, Pakistan, the Philippines and Tanzania.[34]

    What does an aging population portend about the future, most especially in terms of healthcare and social services? What does this shift in population growth say about the products and processes of the future—how we eat, what we buy, where we hang out, etc.?

14. Do you think the ability of Hubble to generate images that captured the public's imagination accounted for its eventual success as much as did the data it produced?

15. If we combine elements of Hebrew linguistics, numerology, and typology in an allegorical interpretative framework, this is what we get.

    Yahweh (הוהי) is spelled with four Hebrew letters: Yod (י), Hei (ה), Vav (ו), and Hei (ה).

    Hebrew letters also serve as numbers: Each letter in the Hebrew alphabet does have a numerical value (gematria). Yod is 10, Hei is 5, Vav is 6, and the final Hei is again 5.

    Hebrew Pictograms and their Meanings:

    > Yod (י): In Hebrew pictographic interpretations, Yod is sometimes represented as a hand or an arm.

    > Hei (ה): Hei is often associated with a window or an opening. In theological contexts, it's

SEMIOTIC TELL #21

sometimes interpreted as representing revelation or grace.

Vav (ו): Vav can be represented pictographically as a nail or a hook, symbolizing connection or joining.

Final Hei (ה): As before, the second Hei can also represent grace or revelation, depending on interpretation.

Allegorical Interpretation: The phrase "Hand of Grace, Nailed in Grace" is an allegorical interpretation where Yahweh (יהוה) is connected to the crucifixion of Jesus (hand, nail, grace).

How does this allegorical interpretation of the name of YHWH effect you? Does this kind of allegorizing make you nervous? Are you comfortable saying, after this devotional allegorizing, "Even the spelling of His name reveals His Glory?"

16. Nothing tears apart the social fabric more than the guilt/honor-by-association meme. Everyone likes what they like. Even despots and dictators like what they like. Just because Adolph Hitler loved Mickey Mouse, and underlings like Joseph Goebbels presented him with Disney movies and cartoon strips for Christmas, doesn't mean that I can't like Disney and Mickey Mouse without feeling like or being accused of being a Nazi. This kind of reasoning, which dominates social media and political discourse, is a source of hate and is sourced in hell.

   a. Why do you think the "guilt/honor-by-association"

meme is so powerful in today's social and political discourse? Can you think of examples where this type of reasoning has been applied?

b. How do we differentiate between liking something (e.g., a brand or artwork) and endorsing the values or actions of those who are associated with it? How do we maintain this distinction in public conversations?

c. How does social media contribute to the spread of guilt-by-association thinking? Do you think it is possible to reverse or minimize this tendency on social media platforms?

d. Does knowing the personal likes or dislikes of a historical figure, especially a negative one, affect your opinion about those things today? Should it?

e. The paragraph mentions that this reasoning is "the source of hate." Do you agree or disagree? How does guilt by association contribute to division in society, and how can we challenge this mindset?

f. If you could reshape social media and political discourse to minimize guilt-by-association thinking, what practical steps would you suggest for individuals and society?

Semiotic Tell #22

The Levitation of Signs

A Semiotic Approach to Faith: Semioticians are masters of mental acrobatics, expertly juggling ideas in mid-air. To live in suspense is to embrace two core tenets:

Acknowledge the abyss of your ignorance

Resist the siren call of premature understanding

Allow epiphanies to bloom organically, in their own season. This process may span moments or millennia, but you learn to dance within the ellipsis of thought. Every story, after all, trails off into a tantalizing whisper of dot-dot-dots ....

At any given moment, I'm a circus performer, keeping dozens of these suspended dots aloft. Behold, a menagerie of levitating enigmas:

> ***The Fishermen's Quartet:*** Why did Jesus cast his net for four fishermen among his twelve disciples? Was it merely for their boats, or did their profession harbor deeper currents?

> ***The Seamless Robe:*** What's the thread connecting Jesus to his seamless garment? A mother's loving handiwork, or a symbol woven with divine intention?

Judas' Paradoxical Demise: How do we untangle the knot of Judas Iscariot's fate, strung between Matthew 27:5 and Acts 1:18?

The Last Supper's Phantom Chef: Who seasoned the flavors of fate at this pivotal moment in Christian history?

Mary Magdalene's Fractured Reflection: Is she a kaleidoscope of biblical Marys, or a singular, misunderstood disciple?

The Vanishing Family: Why do Jesus' relatives evaporate from the Gospel narratives, leaving only Mary's silhouette?

David's Prophetic Orchestra: Who were these mystical musicians, ordained to "prophesy with lyres, harps, and cymbals"[1]

The Melchizedek Conundrum: Who was this priest-king of Salem, bridging Old and New Testaments like a spectral pontifex?

The Urim and Thummim: What power crackled within these cryptic divinatory stones of the Israelite priests?

The Nephilim Enigma: Were these "giants" of Genesis 6:4 fallen angels, alien interlopers, or metaphors for a lost age of heroes?

Samson's Bestiary: Why does his tale bristle with lions, goats, bees, and foxes? A divine menagerie or coded allegory?

The Temple Tantrum's Twisted Cords: What

exactly did Jesus wield? Mere rope, or palm fronds charged with symbolism?

The Staircase Paradox: Why do memories of descending cellar steps and ascending attic stairs etch themselves so vividly in our minds? #UpTheDownStaircase

This list could spiral endlessly, each question a new tendril in faith's ever-growing vine.

Living in suspense transcends Samuel Taylor Coleridge's (1772–1834) "willing suspension of disbelief"[2] for "poetic faith," or even the traditional "leap of faith." Instead, it's about:

> Embracing the intellectual and spiritual squirm like a contortionist of the soul
>
> Recognizing the vast unknown while nurturing hope in the knowable
>
> Affirming that life is a perpetual apprenticeship in wisdom
>
> Cultivating a mind as open and receptive as a parachute in free fall

A shallow faith is a rusty spring, unable to absorb the shocks of doubt and questioning. Semiotics, however, provides the ultimate shock absorbers for any spiritual monster truck rally. It equips us to navigate the labyrinth of belief, holding contradictions like a juggler's flaming torches, exploring ambiguities like a spelunker in unmapped caves, and finding meaning in the quantum foam between certainties.

In this way, semiotics doesn't just inform our faith—it performs alchemy upon it, transmuting leaden dogma into golden wonder. It creates a faith as dynamic and resilient as a cat with nine lives, thriving on questions as much as answers. It teaches us to live within life's greatest mystery: existence itself.

Silas Weir Mitchell (d. 1914), a neurologist and poet, urged us to see "hysteria" as "mysteria"—a call to resist the urge to categorize the incomprehensible too hastily.[3]

A Semiotic Finale: The Suspension Bridge to Wonder As we reach the end of these lecture notes, we find ourselves not at a conclusion, but at a launching point. The art of suspended levitation is not about finding all the answers, but about learning to thrive in the questions.

Imagine faith as a suspension bridge, its cables the strands of inquiry we've explored. Each question, each doubt, each moment of wonder adds tensile strength to the structure. The bridge sways and flexes under the winds of uncertainty, but it does not break. Instead, it carries us across the chasm between the known and the unknown, between the earthly and the divine.

As you step onto this bridge, feel the gentle sway beneath your feet. Look out over the misty abyss of the unexplained. Breathe in the crisp air of possibility. This is where faith truly lives—yes, anchored in the solid ground of certainty, but suspended in the exhilarating expanse of the unknown.

Remember, dear students, that you too are a theo-semiotician like Jesus, a meaning-maker in a universe bursting with signs and symbols. Your questions are not weaknesses, but the very sinews that give your faith its strength and flexibility.

So go forth, my esteemed students. Ask. Wonder. Doubt. Believe. Let your faith dance on the high wire of inquiry,

SEMIOTIC TELL #22

balanced between heaven and earth. For it is in this suspended state, this holy vertigo, that we truly touch the face of the divine.

And as for all those questions we've raised? They remain suspended, glittering like stars in the night sky of our collective imagination. They are not problems to be solved, but koans to be lived.

So we end this lecture as we began, in the midst of a thought, in the heart of a mystery, trailing off into that most potent of semiotic punctuations ...

Live in suspended levitation.

Source Code Interactives

1. Ludwig Wittgenstein concluded that "Life can educate one to a belief in God."[4] Do you agree that personal experiences and life's journey, especially "sufferings of various sorts," can lead one to develop a belief in God, rather than through philosophical or intellectual arguments alone?

2. "Living in suspense transcends Coleridge's willing suspension of disbelief." How does the concept of semiotic levitation differ from traditional approaches to faith and belief? What makes it unique?

3. The text presents faith as a "suspension bridge." Analyze this metaphor—how does it capture both the stability and flexibility required in religious understanding?

4. Examine the paradox of "holy vertigo" mentioned in the text. How can spiritual uncertainty lead to deeper religious experience?

5. Sweet lists several biblical enigmas, including "The Fishermen's Quartet" and "The Seamless Robe." Choose one of these mysteries and explore its potential symbolic meanings and theological implications.

6. "A shallow faith is a rusty spring, unable to absorb the shocks of doubt and questioning." Discuss how doubt might strengthen rather than weaken religious faith.

7. Compare Mitchell's reframing of "hysteria" as "mysteria" to the broader theme of embracing uncertainty in

SEMIOTIC TELL #22

religious thought. How does this perspective challenge traditional approaches to religious mystery?

8. The text describes semiotics as providing "ultimate shock absorbers for any spiritual monster truck rally." Analyze this vivid metaphor—what does it reveal about the relationship between academic study and lived faith?

9. Consider the "menagerie of levitating enigmas" presented in the text. How do these unresolved questions serve as tools for spiritual growth rather than obstacles to faith?

10. "To live in suspense is to embrace two core tenets: Acknowledge the abyss of your ignorance; Resist the siren call of premature understanding." How might these principles be applied to interfaith dialogue?

11. The text suggests we should be "holding contradictions like a juggler's flaming torches." Explore how this approach to religious paradox differs from traditional theological methods of resolving contradictions.

12. Analyze the role of questions in this approach to faith. How does the text's emphasis on "questions as much as answers" challenge conventional religious education?

13. Sweet describes you, the reader, as a "theo-semiotician like Jesus." What implications does this have for personal religious authority and interpretation?

14. Examine the text's use of performance metaphors (circus performer, contortionist, juggler). How do these images reshape our understanding of religious practice?

15. "Every story trails off into a tantalizing whisper of dot dot dots ..." Discuss how this perspective might change our approach to reading and interpreting sacred texts. You might listen to the "Unfinished Symphony" when answering this.

16. The text presents faith as "a perpetual apprenticeship in wisdom." How does this framing challenge both religious fundamentalism and secular skepticism?

semiotic Tell #23

The Sentinel's Threshold

Blessed is the man that heareth me,
Watching daily at my gates,
waiting at the posts of my doors.

PROVERBS 8:34 KJV

THE PHENOMENON OF THRESHOLDS FORMS a timeless bridge, a sacred pathway connecting ancient traditions to daily relevance. From the gates of Solomon's temple to the portals of our current understanding, thresholds stand as powerful symbols of transition, revelation, and awakening. Thresholds traverse the landscape of human experience, linking past to present.

The Book of Revelation, that enigmatic finale to the biblical narrative, presents us with a threshold of cosmic proportions. The semiotician advocates a cosmic view of life. The apostle John, exiled on Patmos (the first century equivalent of Devil's Island), stands before a mystical doorway:

> After this I looked, and, behold, a door was opened in heaven: and the first voice which I heard was as it were of a trumpet talking with me; which said, Come up hither, and I will

shew thee things which must be hereafter. And immediately I was in the spirit: and, behold, a throne was set in heaven, and one sat on the throne.[1]

This celestial threshold serves as a portal through which divine mysteries flow. It marks a transition from the earthly to the heavenly, from the known to the unknown to the unknowable. John, invited to "come up hither" and witness the events that will unfold in the future, becomes our eyes and ears at the precipice of eternity.

Guardians of Sacred Space: Throughout history, thresholds have been more than mere architectural features. They have been liminal spaces, charged with semiotic significance, interpreting the signs and symbols that transition between different realms of being.

In the Jerusalem Temple and beyond, there were ten levels of holiness.[2] A complex hierarchy of thresholds separated the profane from the sacred and escalated the levels of the sacred, some of which included:

> The Outer Court: A space of initial separation
>
> The Court of Women: A threshold of gender and ritual purity
>
> The Court of Israel: Reserved for ritually pure Jewish men
>
> The Court of Priests: An elevated space for those who serve
>
> The Temple Entrance: The gateway to the Holy Place

SEMIOTIC TELL #23

The Veil: The final threshold before the Holy of Holies

Each threshold represented not just a physical boundary, but a spiritual one. To cross a threshold was to undergo a shift of being, to ascend in holiness, to draw nearer to the divine presence.

In the Jerusalem Temple, sentinels were honored positions. Although the Hebrew word "Shomrei" is usually translated as "Guardian" or "Keeper" or "Watchmen," the word Sentinel is actually the best translation.

> Sentinel of the Threshold (*Shomrei HaSaf*): Also known as the "Gatekeepers" or "Doorkeepers" or "Guardians," they guarded the Temple entrances, ensuring only authorized personnel and ritually pure individuals entered.

> Sentinels of the Gate (*Shomrei HaAbarah*): "Gatekeepers" or "Watchmen" were specifically responsible for guarding the Temple gates, controlling access, and maintaining order.[3]

Both roles were essential for maintaining the Temple's sanctity and security. These officials were either descendants of Levi (Sentinels of the Gate) or specifically the Kohathites (Sentinels of the Threshold). The Sentinels of the Gate and Threshold played vital roles in preserving the Temple's sanctity and safety. Crossing each threshold in the Temple was a liminal experience—a moment of being "betwixt and between."

Thresholds also served practical purposes in the past, such as:

> Water and sand barriers: Thresholds in the form

of doorway sills helped prevent water and sand from entering homes, especially in areas with heavy rainfall or flooding. The raised barrier kept the interior dry and protected from the elements.

As draft stoppers, thresholds also helped reduce drafts and airflow between inside and outside spaces, conserving heat and energy.

These practical functions of thresholds highlight their role as a transitional space, separating the controlled environment within from the unpredictable outside world. Similarly, semioticians as threshold sentinels can be seen as protecting and guiding others through the turbulent waters of complex information and meanings, preventing the influx of misinformation and helping to conserve valuable intellectual energy.

Semioticians, as threshold sentinels, stand at the forefront of understanding, interpreting, and navigating the complexities of meaning and communication as we face the future.

Sentinels of the Threshold: In our twenty-first century world, the role of threshold guardian takes on new meaning. Semioticians are called to be sentinels, not of stone edifices, but of stories, understanding and insight. Semioticians who decipher the signs and symbols of our culture must stand at the boundary between the familiar terrain and the terra incognita.

As sentinels of the threshold, semioticians are called to:
Face Forward: Embrace the future with courage and discernment.

Stand on the Brink: Position ourselves at the

edge of new discoveries, anticipating and analyzing emerging trends and trajectories.

Usher Others: Guide those seeking wisdom across the thresholds of understanding.

The Synergy of Sentinels and Bridgers: While sentinels guard the thresholds, bridgers span the gaps between worlds. Together, they form a powerful alliance:

Sentinels provide vigilance and discernment and direction

Bridgers facilitate connection and comprehension. But even bridgers need to be semioticians: The only way you can stay on a bridge is to look beyond the bridge; and the faster you go, the farther down the bridge you need to look.

This synergy of sentinels and bridgers propels us forward, navigating the complex landscape of human knowledge and divine revelation.

Crossing the Final Threshold: As we conclude our journey through the "23 Tells" of "Decoding the Divine," we stand at a threshold ourselves. We have explored ancient wisdom and modern insights, seeking to decipher the language of the sacred in our lives.

The call to "sentinel the thresholds" is more than a tell or a commandment—it is an invitation. An invitation to stand at the frontier of understanding, to peer into the mysteries that lie beyond our current comprehension. It challenges us to be both guardians and guides, protecting sacred knowledge while ushering others into new realms of insight.

In a world often fragmented by misunderstanding, we are called to be interpreters of the divine semiotics—the signs and symbols through which eternal truths are communicated. As we cross this final threshold, may we carry with us the wisdom gained from each tell, using it to illuminate the path for others.

Let us go forth as sentinels and bridgers, decoding the divine in every aspect of our lives. For in doing so, we not only gain understanding for ourselves but become beacons of light, guiding others across the thresholds of wisdom, compassion, and spiritual awakening.

The journey of decoding the divine is never-ending. Each threshold crossed reveals new mysteries, new challenges, and new opportunities for growth. As we close this book, may it be not an end, but a beginning—a stepping stone to deeper understanding and a more profound connection with the divine.

Stand tall, sentinels of the threshold. Your watch has just begun.

SEMIOTIC TELL #23

Source Code Interactives

For ancient worshipers, moving forward through the thresholds could evoke experiences of: anticipation and awe; a sense of personal transformation and increasing holiness; a heightened sense of caution and mindfulness; leaving the everyday world and entering sacred space; a growing sense of reverence and spiritual intensity; increased awareness of one's own state of purity or impurity; a closer connection to the divine presence. Often, crossing a threshold involved some form of ritual or purification. This could lead to a feeling of cleansing or renewal; mental preparation for encountering the divine; a sense of communal identity for those allowed to cross. Since not everyone could cross every threshold. This could create a sense of belonging for those included; feelings of exclusion or longing for those kept out; reinforcement of social and religious hierarchies. In many ancient Near Eastern cultures, including Judaism, temples were seen as microcosms of the universe. Thresholds could represent transition between earthly and heavenly realms; movement through different levels of creation; a journey towards the center of the cosmos.

Here are some discussion questions to explore the concept of "crossing the threshold" in daily life, drawing parallels from ancient Temple practices:

Personal Reflections:

1. What thresholds do you cross daily (e.g., entering a sacred space, starting a new project)? How do you prepare mentally or spiritually?

2. Describe a moment when crossing a threshold brought

transformation, awe, or reverence. What triggered this response?

3. How do you maintain a sense of mindfulness and caution when transitioning between different aspects of life?

Spiritual Growth:

1. What rituals or practices help you feel cleansed, renewed, or prepared for meaningful experiences?

2. How do you cultivate a sense of reverence and spiritual intensity in daily life?

3. Reflect on times when you felt a deeper connection to the divine. What thresholds did you cross to reach that state?

Community and Belonging:

1. What communities or groups do you belong to, and what "thresholds" define membership?

2. How do you navigate feelings of exclusion or longing when facing inaccessible thresholds?

3. Discuss how social hierarchies or religious structures impact your sense of belonging.

Transitions and Transformation:

1. What life transitions (e.g., career change, moving) have required you to cross significant thresholds? What did you learn?

2. How do you mark important life transitions to signify crossing into a new phase?

SEMIOTIC TELL #23

3. Reflect on times when crossing a threshold brought increased self-awareness or personal growth.

<u>Symbolic Thresholds:</u>

1. What symbolic thresholds (e.g., entering a new decade, recovering from adversity) have you crossed? How did you navigate them?

2. Discuss how everyday spaces (e.g., home, workspace) can become sacred or threshold-like.

3. How do cultural or personal traditions influence your perception of thresholds?

<u>Inward Journey:</u>

1. What inner thresholds (e.g., overcoming fears, embracing change) must you cross for personal growth?

2. Describe your inner journey toward greater self-awareness and spiritual depth.

3. How do you integrate lessons from crossing inner thresholds into daily life?

4. Before he died in 2001, semiotician and linguist Thomas Sebeok searched desperately for a lasting, universal deterrent "that would prevent people from breaking into radioactive waste repositories" 10,000 years from now.[4] Can anyone read cave paintings? Can anyone read all the hieroglyphics? Language changes so fast, how will we tell future generations not to dig up or get near certain radioactive waste dumps? Since he could come up with no warning sign that would still be understood after 10,000

years, he concluded we needed to inaugurate an "atomic priesthood" who could relay the dangers by using folklore, legend, and ritual.

    a. How can we effectively communicate important messages to future generations, considering the rapid evolution of language and the potential for cultural and technological changes?

    b. Do you agree with Thomas Sebeok's idea of establishing an "atomic priesthood" to convey the dangers of radioactive waste through folklore, legend, and ritual? Why or why not?

    c. Can written signs or messages be relied upon to convey critical information over extremely long periods, such as 10,000 years? What are the limitations of this approach?

    d. What alternative strategies could be employed to prevent people from accessing radioactive waste repositories in the distant future, and what are the potential advantages and disadvantages of each approach?

5. The British social philosopher Gillian Rose (d. 1995) once claimed Miss Marple was the nearest literary representation of the Holy Spirit.[5] What are some possible reasons why Rose might have made this claim?

6. Here are several theological parallels to prime the conversational pump:

She discerns truth through seemingly minor details and patterns, similar to how the Spirit reveals divine truth through everyday signs

SEMIOTIC TELL #23

She operates quietly in the background while bringing justice and resolution

She's often underestimated/invisible yet powerfully effective

She serves as a "counselor" and guide (paraclete) to others

She brings hidden sins to light

7. What are some other literary Holy Spirit candidates?

Connect with Leonard

For more from Leonard Sweet:

Websites:
  www.leonardsweet.com
  www.preachthestory.com
  www.sanctuaryseaside.com

Instagram: @leonard.sweet

Facebook:
  facebook.com/lensweet
  facebook.com/preachthestory
  facebook.com/sanctuaryseaside

Twitter: @lensweet

YouTube: www.youtube.com/@leonardsweet1

Podcast: www.leonardsweet.com/podcasts

Napkin Scribbles Podcast:

  Spotify:
  https://open.spotify.com/show/2vt6wEi70dQEpW37CypfvY

  iTunes:
  https://podcasts.apple.com/gb/podcast/
  napkin-scribbles-a-podcast-by-leonard-sweet/id1436743015

Scripture Versions

Scripture quotations marked NIV are taken from the Holy Bible, New International Version®, NIV®. Copyright © 1973, 1978, 1984, 2011 by Biblica, Inc.™ Used by permission of Zondervan. All rights reserved worldwide. www.zondervan.com. The "NIV" and "New International Version" are trademarks registered in the United States Patent and Trademark Office by Biblica, Inc.™

Scripture quotations marked KJV are taken from the Holy Bible, King James Version.

Scripture quotations marked NASB are taken from the NASB® New American Standard Bible®, Copyright © 1960, 1971, 1977, 1995, 2020 by The Lockman Foundation. Used by permission. All rights reserved. lockman.org

Scripture quotations marked NKJV are from the New King James Version.® Copyright © 1982 by Thomas Nelson, Inc. Used by permission. All rights reserved.

Scripture quotations marked ESV are from The Holy Bible, English Standard Version® ESV®, copyright © 2001 by Crossway, a publishing ministry of Good News Publishers. Used by permission. All rights reserved.

Scripture quotations marked NLT are taken from the Holy Bible, New Living Translation, copyright ©1996, 2004, 2015 by Tyndale House Foundation. Used by permission of Tyndale House Publishers, Carol Stream, Illinois 60188. All rights reserved.

Scripture quotations marked MSG are taken from The Message, copyright © 1993, 2002, 2018 by Eugene H. Peterson. Used by permission of NavPress. All rights reserved. Represented by Tyndale House Publishers.

Scripture quotations marked NRSV are from the New Revised Standard Version Bible, copyright © 1989, Division of Christian Education of the National Council of the Churches of Christ in the United States of America. Used by permission. All rights reserved.

Scripture quotations marked TLV are taken from the Holy Scriptures, Tree of Life Version. Copyright © 2014,2016 by the Tree of Life Bible Society. Used by permission of the Tree of Life Bible Society.

Scripture quotations marked (MOF) are from the James Moffatt, A New Translation of the Bible, Containing the Old and New Testaments. New York: Doran, 1926. Revised edition, New York and London: Harper and Brothers, 1935. Reprinted, Grand Rapids: Kregel, 1995.

Notes

FRONT MATTER

1. Kenneth Laine Ketner, "A Thief of Peirce: The Letters of Kenneth Laine Ketner and Walker Percy," *The Modern Schoolman*, 69 (May 1992), 315–335.

2. See Saint Augustine, *Teaching Christianity* (translated by Edmund Hill, edited by John E. Rotelle, 1996), 107.

3. Hugh MacDiarmid said this in his long poem "A Drunk Man Looks at the Thistle" written in Scottish and first published as a standalone volume, *A Drunk Man Looks at the Thistle* (1926).

   See also *Collected Poems of Hugh MacDiarmid*, revised edition with enlarged glossary prepared by John C. Weston (1967), 151–255.

4. From 1984 to 1995 I wrote the entire content for the lectionary-based preaching journal *Homiletics*, published by Communications Resources. That alone is 600+ published sermons. In 1995 I started the first free open-source preaching website called wikiletics.com, and contributed a sermon a week to that resource from 1996 to 1998. That's 100+ sermons. From 1998 to 2005 I wrote a sermon a week for preachingplus.com published by Group Publishing. That's 300 published sermons. From 2005 to 2013 I contributed a sermon a week to sermons.com. That is another 400+ sermons. Then in 2013 I started a new preaching resource online and on YouTube called PreachTheStory.com, to which I've contributed another 500+ sermons. This does not include my contributions to other journals like *Pulpit Resource* and varied collections of sermons. After publishing over 2000 sermons, you'd think I'd have run out of things to say … but it turns out the Greatest Story Ever Told is also a Never-Ending Story.

5. See Charles M. Nielsen's "Communion for Dogs," *Perspectives in Religious Studies*, 10 (Spring 1983), 51–61, 51–52.

6. Plants are masters of semiotics. When they are under attack, they immediately start sending signals of help and warning to neighboring foliage and fauna. They secrete hormones that trigger the release of

compounds that gird up its immune system, and these hormones are invasion specific, depending on the insect. Not just on "Avatar" do plants communicate with each other.... They send biochemical messages via the root system, or they deploy symbiotic fungal connections in the soil. They also release chemicals in the air. These signs and signals of the "Wood Wide Web" are read by the whole forest family.

7. Jesus says this in Matthew 26:41. Thanks to Nathan Nordine for the "watch and wag" inspiration.

8. In *Emily in Paris*, Emily meets a professor of semiotics named Thomas in Season 1, Episode 6, titled "Ringarde." This is where she encounters Thomas (played by Julien Floreancig), a charming but ultimately self righteous and pretentious semiotics professor. They start a fleeting relationship after meeting at a café, but the relationship quickly sours when Thomas reveals his snobbish attitude, especially when he dismisses *Swan Lake* as beneath him. Emily dumps him by the end of the episode, calling him out for his pretentious behavior.

9. *Collected Papers of Charles Sanders Peirce* (1931–1960), Book 2 Chapter 2, Section 1, Paragraph 228.

10. When I saw, in some of my doctoral professors, a high commitment to theory, and suddenly realized that a lot of scholarship was interpretive choice, not historical fact—I learned when to open and close the doors of the ivory tower. I have steered away from interpretitis ever since.

11. If you want to explore further the godfather of semiotics, Charles Sanders Peirce, I recommend starting with his triadic nature of reality.

    Firstness is founded on unrealized possibilities which color the world with irregularities and imprecisions, whose ontological foundation, chance, maintains all variety and novelty.

    Secondness takes as its principle the brute force that collides with experience and imposes its dual character, of action and reaction, what in metaphysics is called existence.

    Finally, Thirdness is every representative and conformist character that announces facts and possibilities and arranges them under the roof of determination and predictability, whose ontological repertoire describes as law or habit. For more see: Ivo Assad Ibri, *Kósmos Noetós: The Metaphysical Architecture of Charles S. Peirce* (2015). Also see "The Philosophical Melody of Symbols's Evolution in Peirce's Thought" by Renan Henrique Baggio of the Pontifícia Universidade Católica de São Paulo.

12. Common rendering of 1 Chronicles 12:32.

NOTES

13. Roman Jakobson, "Closing Statement: Linguistics and Poetics," in *Style in Language*, Thomas A. Sebeok, ed., (1960), 353.

14. Leonard Sweet, *Soul Tsunami: Sink or Swim in New Millennium Culture* (1999), 23.

15. Leonard Sweet, *Nudge: Awakening Each Other to the God Who's Already There* (2010), 276–277.

16. See Augustine's autobiographical work *Confessions* (397–400), Book X, Chapter 27.

17. Here is a more detailed account of this story:

    Bishop Ambrose of Milan had a major influence on Augustine's life as he journeyed from heresy to orthodoxy and from sexual immorality to celibacy. Ambrose, by living an exemplary life worthy of Augustine's admiration, was able to attract him to his services. There he was able to help Augustine overcome his disdain for the Old Testament Scriptures by the use of allegorical interpretation to reveal the deeper meanings of the Bible passages.

    Fearing an outbreak of hostilities, Ambrose, acting as governor, attended the meeting held for the election of the new bishop. During his address to the assembled crowd, through which he sought to defuse the potentially explosive situation, legend has it that a child cried out, "Ambrose Bishop!" Those in the crowd, both Arians and Catholics, forgot their differences and took up the chant, "Ambrose Bishop! Ambrose Bishop!"

    In spite of the wishes of the congregation, Ambrose had no intention of becoming the bishop. He returned to his court, and had some prisoners tortured in the hopes that those favoring his appointment as bishop would be dissuaded by a show of violence. When that failed, he announced that he intended to retire and spend the rest of his days in meditating in solitude. When that did not work, he had some prostitutes brought to his home, but the crowd saw through that ruse as well. Next, Ambrose tried to flee Milan at midnight, but he became lost in the dark and never got very far. To prevent him from trying to flee again, the people of Milan captured him and kept him under guard at his own house.

    Meanwhile they sent a message to Emperor Valentinian, who was at Trier, asking him to ratify their choice as bishop. Valentinian, pleased that there was an unanimous choice, willingly agreed, but, in the meantime, Ambrose had escaped and fled to the country estate of a friend, Leontius. The Pope then issued a proclamation which threatened anyone harboring

Ambrose with severe punishment. Leontius confessed and Ambrose was taken back to Milan.

Even when the appointment was confirmed, Ambrose tried to have the ordination delayed. Finally, Valentinian promised Ambrose that he would not be harmed by the Arians and Ambrose agreed to serve as Bishop of Milan. He was baptised on November 24, AD 373, went through various levels of the priesthood during the next six days, and was consecrated bishop on the following Sunday, December 1.

Here are Augustine's words:

> I had thought that nothing could be said for the Catholic faith in the face of the objections raised by the Manichees, but it now appeared to me that this faith could be maintained on reasonable grounds—especially when I had heard one or two passages in the Old Testament explained, usually in a figurative way, which when I had taken them literally, had been a cause of death to me (*Confessions*, Book 5, Chapter 14, translated by R. S. Pine-Coffin [1961]).

Ambrose through his sermons showed Augustine how to read the Bible "figuratively." Most scholars read this as "allegorically," but it is more accurately rendered semiotically.

> I was glad ... that the old Scriptures of the Law and the Prophets were set before me in such a way that I could now read in a different spirit from that which I had had before, when I used to criticize your holy ones for holding various views which, plainly, they never held at all. And I was happy when I heard Ambrose ... recommend most emphatically ... this text as a rule to go by: The letter killeth, but the spirit giveth life. So he would draw aside the veil of mystery and explain in a spiritual sense the meanings of things which, if understood literally, appeared to be teaching what was wrong (*Confessions*, Book 6, Chapter 4, translated by R. S. Pine-Coffin [1961]).

From this point onward, Augustine "began to prefer the Catholic faith."

While at Milan, Augustine only had superficial contact with Ambrose. Ambrose had greeted Augustine warmly and welcomed him to Milan and was very kind and generous towards him, but he was also a very busy man. Augustine writes:

> I was not able to ask him the questions I wanted to ask in

the way I wanted to ask them, because I was prevented from having an intimate conversation with him by the crowds of people, all of whom had some business with him and to whose infirmities he was a servant. And for the very short periods of time when he was not with them, he was either refreshing his body with necessary food or his mind with reading. When he was reading, his eyes went over the pages and his heart looked into the sense, but voice and tongue were resting. Often when we came to him (for no one was forbidden to come in, and it was not customary for visitors even to be announced) we found him reading, always to himself and never otherwise; we would sit in silence for a long time, not venturing to interrupt him in his intense concentration on his task, and then we would go away again . . .

Anyhow, I was given no chance of making the inquiries I wished to make from that holy oracle of yours [referring to God], his breast. I could only ask things that would not take long in the hearing.

18. With thanks to David Sunde for inspiring this synesthesia section.
19. People ask me all the time why I like to create new words. I usually respond that new times and new realities require new words. But I'd rather quote Peirce: "He who introduces a new conception into philosophy is under the obligation to invent acceptable terms to so express it." *Collected Papers*, Volume 5, ed. Charles Hartshorne and Paul Weiss (1905), 411.
20. For more on "narraphors" and their role in preaching, see my homiletics text *Giving Blood*.
21. See Pope Francis' *Desiderio Desideravi* (2022). For the commemorative edition, see Cardinal Jospeh Ratzinger and Romano Guardini, *The Spirit of the Liturgy* (2020).
22. John Vervaeke, Timothy P. Lillicrap, and Blake A. Richards, "Relevance Realization and the Emerging Framework in Cognitive Science," *Journal of Logic and Computation*, 22 (February 2012), 79–99, https://doi.org/10.1093/logcom/exp067. Also see the John Vervaeke's popular YouTube series, "Awakening from the Meaning Crisis," in which he explores the roots of the contemporary sense of disconnection and meaninglessness and proposes strategies for cultivating a deeper sense of purpose and significance in life.

SEMIOTIC TELL 1

1. 1 Chronicles 12:32 NIV.
2. I am grateful to Mark Chironna for pointing this out to me.
3. See his 1982 speech "Utopia and Prophecy in Latin America:" "Only a Church that recovers the life of its Founder and lets itself be invaded by the Spirit that urges it to announce the good news to the poor and liberty to the oppressed, only a Church under the perpetual sign of conversion and under the standard of radical change, only such a Church will be capable of helping to establish a new society in Latin America."
4. A "cricket fingerprint" is a key indicator of the health of your landscape and the impact of climate change. Can you still hear the crickets?
5. Matthew 16:2–3 LIS. The earliest known written records of this phrase date back to the first century BCE, in the works of the Roman poet Virgil: "Red sky at night, the sailor's delight; Red sky in the morning, the sailor's warning." Virgil, *Georgics*, Book 1, lines 424–425. This similarity suggests that the phrase might have been a common proverb or saying in the ancient Mediterranean world. It's possible that: 1) Jesus was referencing a familiar saying: He might have used a well-known phrase to illustrate a point about discerning signs and understanding the times. 2) Early Christian writers were influenced by Roman literature: The Gospel of Matthew, written decades after Jesus' time, might have incorporated elements from Roman culture and literature, including Virgil's works. While one can't confirm direct influence, this connection highlights the cultural exchange and shared wisdom of the ancient world.
6. Matthew 16:3; Luke 12:56, NLT.
7. For the identification of "understanding" and "wisdom," see Job 38:4 NIV: "Where were you when I laid the foundation of the earth? Tell me, if you have understanding." Or Esther 1:13 NIV: "Then the king said to the wise men who knew the times for this was the king's procedure toward all who were versed in law and judgment."
8. "Leah said, 'God has given me my wages because I gave my servant to my husband. So she called his name Issachar'" (Genesis 30:18 NIV).
9. With gratitude to Lutheran scholar Ralph W. Klein's work here as found in *1 Chronicles: A Commentary* (2006), 321–326.
10. 1 Chronicles 12:39–40.
11. Other contenders for smartest animal include, Primates (chimpanzees, gorillas, orangutans), Dolphins, Elephants, Ravens, Octopuses.

12. Judges 5:10, 10:4. I am not happy that the story of Balaam's ass is not included in the Revised Common Lectionary or the Narrative Lectionary.
13. Genesis 49:13, Deuteronomy 33:18–19. The blessing of Moses in Deuteronomy 33:18–19 ESV highlights Zebulun's unique role, and its close ties to Issachar: "Rejoice, Zebulun, in your going out, and Issachar in your tents. They shall call peoples to the mountain; there they shall offer sacrifices of righteousness; for they shall draw from the abundance of the seas and the hidden treasures of the sand."
14. Joshua 19:10–16.
15. In terms of tribal distribution of land, Zebulun was on the South of the Sea of Galilee, Issachar on the Southeast of the Sea of Galilee.
16. Genesis 49:14–15.
17. John 3:8.
18. Revelation 16:1.
19. Matthew 4:19.
20. Ephesians 5:16.
21. Here is a brief overview of where these concepts are discussed:

    Danger of Overinterpretation: See the essay "Interpretation and History" (23–43) and "Overinterpreting Texts" (45–66).

    Contextualization: The importance of context is emphasized in the essay "The Pragmatics of Interpretation" (67–91).

    Denotation vs. Connotation: Eco delves into the distinction between in "On the Semiotic Analysis of Culture" (103–119).

    Intention of the Author: see Eco's essay "Intentio Lectoris: The State of the Art" (135–154).

    Role of the Interpreter: their biases are discussed in "Unlimited Semiosis and Drift" (151–160).
22. Judith Levin, *Soda and Fizzy Drinks: A Global History* (2021). The "Perfect Harmony" was devised in 1971 by McCann Erickson advertising agency.
23. Matthew 10:41–42 MSG.
24. Of course, ancient civilizations, including the Romans, had public fountains that served both decorative and practical purposes, including providing drinking water. But in terms of modern public drinking fountains, NYC the first in 1832, then in 1859 in London, the

Metropolitan Free Drinking Fountain Association was established in 1859. This organization began installing public drinking fountains throughout London to provide free, clean drinking water to the public partly for public heath reasons, because access to clean drinking water was limited and waterborne diseases common, but the Temperance movement saw public water fountains as an alternative to alcoholic beverages, encouraging people to drink water instead of alcohol.

25. Matthew 5:41.
26. St. John Climacus, also known as St. John of the Ladder, *The Ladder of Divine Ascent* (600). This seminal work serves as a guide to ascetic life, outlining a spiritual journey through thirty steps, each representing a specific virtue or spiritual practice leading toward divine union. The quote comes from *Metropolitan Anthony Bloom, Living the Christian Creed: Theology as Encounter* (2024), 277.
27. See my book *11: Indispensable Relationships You Can't Be Without* (2012).
28. A. A. Berger, "The Science of Signs," in *The Objects of Affection: Semiotics and Consumer Culture* (2010).
29. Genesis 49:14 NIV.

SEMIOTIC TELL 2

1. *The Living Reminder* (1977), 83.
2. Luke 21:6 NIV.
3. Crystal Downing, *Changing Signs of Truth* (2012), 91.
4. Daniel Chandler, *Semiotics: The Basics, 3rd ed.* (2017), 13–15.
5. David Bentley Hart, *The Beauty of the Infinite: The Aesthetics of Christian Truth* (2003), 327–28.
6. Hawthorne returned from the transcendentalist commune at Brook Farm in West Roxbury, Massachusetts in 1842, and married Sophia Peabody shortly thereafter. See Dale Salwak, *Nathaniel Hawthorne* (2024).
7. Latin: "*Non potest homo intelligere sine phantasmatibus*" in *Summa Theologica*, Part I, Question 84, Article 7.
8. Tertullian in the third century gave us the association of "sacrament" with water.
9. My first treatment of abductive reasoning was in *A is For Abductive: The Language of the Emerging Church* (2003). I then expanded "abductive" to

NOTES

embrace "transductive" in my homiletics textbook called *Giving Blood: A Fresh Paradigm for Preaching* (2014).

10. For Peirce, abductive reasoning was the basis of all cognitive thought and life. Unfortunately, Peirce never developed a unified theory of abduction, but a metaphor for abductive reasoning I have found helpful is Sherlock Holmes, a master of abduction. An inference is drawn from observed clues to reach a hypothesis which explains all the data. German astronomer Johannes Kepler was a master of abduction: he observed irregularities in the movement of Mars and hypothesized an elliptical path for Mars. In a sense, every physician needs to be a master of abduction: medical diagnosis is drawn from symptoms and a hypothesis is made about the cause of those symptoms which is then tested and treated.

11. Italian screenwriter Roberto Benigni's "formula" is a distillation of the core themes of his Holocaust comedy-drama film "Life is Beautiful" (1997).

12. See my *The Well-Played Life* (2014).

13. For Ferdinand de Saussure's dyadic model of sign, see *Course in General Linguistics* (*Cours de linguistique générale*) (1916). The book was published posthumously in 1916 by his students Charles Bally and Albert Sechehaye, based on notes from his lectures. See chapter 1, "Signs and Signification," and more precisely the section "The Sign as a Dyadic Unit."

14. *Troubled: A Memoir of Foster Care, Family, and Social Class* (2024) operates on multiple semiotic registers: at once a memoir of Henderson's "troubled" childhood in foster care, an analysis of our "troubled" social order, and an exploration of how elite "luxury beliefs" trouble the waters of class mobility. The title's polysemy mirrors the complex interplay between personal and societal dysfunction, as Henderson's lived experience of social disruption becomes a lens for examining how privileged ideological positions can ripple outward to create broader societal turbulence. His journey from "troubled child" to social analyst reveals how the very notion of being "troubled" shifts meaning across class lines—from the personal troubles of poverty to the troubling beliefs that perpetuate social inequality.

15. Painter and aspiring architect Adolph Hitler was a design genius, and no movement understood the importance of design more than the Nazis. Most of the symbols they used they stole from others, but they then restylized them, restructured them, and re-harmonized them into coherent theater of madness.

16. Here is the full quote: "All instruction is either about things or about

401

signs; but things are learned by means of signs ... and hence may be understood what I call signs: those things, to wit, which are used to indicate something else." Augustine of Hippo, *On Christian Doctrine*, Book I, Chapter 2.1.

17. Here is the full quote: "Signs are given to men, to whom it is proper to discover the unknown by means of the known. Consequently a sacrament properly so-called is that which is the sign of some sacred thing, pertaining to man; so that properly speaking a sacrament, as considered by us now, is defined as being the 'sign of a holy thing so far as it makes men holy.'" Thomas Aquinas, *Summa Theologiae*, III.60.2.*responsio.*

18. As far as his writing life is concerned, Arthur has taken the essay and filled it, over and over, with his singular insights and perceptions. The form is especially suited to his temperament. Beginning in 1999 with Irish Nocturnes, he has shown, through many collections, how wide-ranging, compelling and illuminating this particular, and often undervalued, brand of literature can be. It is partly a matter of connections. "My writing," he says, "stems from specific objects and events": and from these starting points, his essays branch out into a web of allusions, without sacrificing their hold on the particular. What he is aiming for, and achieves, is "a closer, deeper reading of a few fragments of experience." As with Joyce Cary in A House of Children, for example, a branch of fuchsia and its fallen petals transports Chris Arthur, in imagination, back to long-ago Donegal and—in his case—a cottage on Horn Head. At the same time, Arthur's fuchsia sparks off a botanical exploration, some literary sidelights, a couple of paragraphs on Robert the Bruce's daughter Marjorie, and serious thoughts about suspension bridges. It's all exhilarating.

An autobiographical element, muted and evocative, runs through Arthur's essays. It's inevitable, he says, that an Irish perspective should colour his thinking, even though it's overlaid by the effect of years spent living elsewhere. He was born in Lisburn, Co Antrim, into a middle-class family, and grew up during the worst phase of the Troubles. (He remembers helping to crisscross his classroom windows with clear tape, in order "to minimise glass shrapnel in the event of explosions".) It was a Protestant upbringing—and for all his equable disposition, Arthur put himself at odds with some of his family members by washing his hands of sectarian rules and responses. An uncle looked askance at his reading of Flann O'Brien—the same uncle, perhaps, who held that "You can always tell them, i.e., Taigs or Fenians, by their faces." If "O'Brien" was bad enough, however, as a pointer to tribal affiliation, "Seamus" was infinitely worse. "'Seamus' would have acted as a red rag ... to the bull of my uncle's

NOTES

prejudices." Not to upset his relative, then, the young Chris Arthur didn't disclose his great enthusiasm for the recently published Heaney.

19. Link to Luther Rose: https://en.wikipedia.org/wiki/Luther_rose#/media/File:Lutherrose.svg.

20. *Luther's Works*, American Edition, volume 49, 358–359.

21. Podcast with Paul Patton via Robert Woods: Series No. 1: "Stewarding the Stirrings of the Soul":

    Episode 1: (Series 1, Episode 1). Patton explores what it means to "steward the stirrings of one's soul," and how it contributes to spiritual growth.

    Episode 2: "steward the stirrings of one's soul," and how it contributes to a growing sense of "sacred interiority."

    Episode 3: Paul reflects on what is meant to be an ultimate "soul stirring," a dominant truth that serves as the hub of our cognitive wheel, what the ancient Jews called a "Shema." He offers that our Shema prioritizes our truth assertions and is meant to be memorized, even recited aloud twice each day, consistent with the practice of the recited Shema in ancient Israel. What is your "Shema?" What truth assertion is so central that it is the hub of your cognitive wheel?

    Episode 4: identifying a central confession, a "shema." In so doing, Paul suggests, we begin the intentional process of strengthening our sacred interiority. British philosopher and pastor, John Peck's "I Have a Vision."

    Episode 5: Patton offers more biblical examples and stories from church history surrounding the mind-building exercise of memorizing central confessions and soul-stirring inspirations.

SEMIOTIC TELL3

1. Caryll Houselander, *The Reed of God* (1955), 73.

2. Gareth Herincx, "Loosen Up and Speak More Freely in a Car," AutomotiveBlog.co.uk, 19 August 2020. More than three quarters of Brits have their deepest and most meaningful conversations in cars. https://automotiveblog.co.uk/2020/08/loosen-up-and-speak-more-freely-in-a-car/. See also https://symptomsofliving.com/blog/why-are-cars-the-best-place-for-deep-conversations/?form=MG0AV3&form=MG0AV3.

3. Michael Lobel, *Van Gogh and the End of Nature* (2024).

4. Rebecca Solnit, *Recollections of My Non-Existence* (2021).

5. A. C. Grayling, *The Frontiers of Knowledge: What We Know About Science, History, and the Mind* (2021).

6. Leonard Sweet, *Carpe Manana* (2001).

SEMIOTIC TELL 4

1. I enjoyed Shauna Pilgreen's *Translating Jesus: How to Share Your Faith in Language Today's Culture Can Understand* (2023), especially her statement: "Sundays are for swapping stories."

2. Mark 4:33–34 NRSV.

3. Leonard Sweet and Michael Adam Beck, *Contextual Intelligence* (2020).

4. George Lakoff and Mark Johnson, *Metaphors We Live By* (2003), 239.

5. There is a wonderful TED Talk by Christoph Niemann that talks about this: https://www.ted.com/talks/christoph_niemann_you_are_fluent_in_this_language_and_don_t_even_know_it?language=en.

6. Latin: "*Non potest homo intelligere sine phantasmatibus*" in *Summa Theologica*, Part I, Question 84, Article 7.

7. Richard Rorty, *Philosophy and the Mirror of Nature* (1979), 12.

8. Entitled *Paradigmen zu einer Metaphorologie* (1960). The book was translated into English in 2010 as *Paradigms for a Metaphorology*.

9. Goethe, *Faust*, Part II, Act V, Scene 7 (Faust, Der Tragödie zweiter Teil). The exact quote is the final line of the entire work, part of the "Chorus Mysticus" that concludes the work.

    The Nietzsche quote comes from *Also Sprach Zarathustra* (Thus Spoke Zarathustra), specifically in the section titled "Auf den Glückseligen Inseln" ("On the Blessed Isles"). This work is one of Nietzsche's most famous philosophical texts.

10. Eugene Peterson, *Answering God: The Psalms as Tools for Prayer* (1991), 73.

11. Here are some examples of how CMA has been used to analyze the use of metaphor in discourse: Charteris-Black's, *Corpus Approaches to Critical Metaphor Analysis* (2004) analyzed the use of metaphor in political speeches by Margaret Thatcher and Tony Blair. He found that Thatcher used more metaphors that dehumanized her opponents, while Blair used more metaphors that naturalized inequality. Norman Fairclough's *Analyzing Discourse: Textual Analysis for Social Research* (2003) analyzed the use of metaphor in advertising. He found that advertisers often

use metaphors to create a sense of desire and longing in consumers. Raymond Gibbs and Lynne Cameron's analysis of metaphors in everyday conversation is titled "The Social Cognitive Dynamics of Metaphor Performance," *Cognitive Systems Research*, (9 March 2008):64–75. They found that people often use metaphors to make sense of their experiences and to communicate their ideas to others. CMA is a growing field of research, and it is being used to explore a wide range of issues, from the construction of identity to the representation of gender and race.

12. For the participatory nature of signs, see Charles Sanders Peirce, who sees a relational base to everything in existence. Charles S. Peirce, *Collected Papers of Charles Sanders Peirce*, eds. Charles Hartshorne, Paul Weiss, and Arthur W. Burks (1931–1935/1958), Volume 2, "Elements of Logic," 227–272. Peirce explicitly talks about the nature of signs as inherently relational on pp. 230–233.

13. With thanks to Bob Reardon.

14. Psalm 121:8.

15. Matthew 11:2–6.

16. Matthew 11:4–5 MSG.

17. With thanks to Robert Castro. Here is not the full episode, but a few bites that give the picture: https://youtu.be/MyQ8WDUYX-Y?si=HWbcoT7DA9iiimQL.

https://youtu.be/WQ8_F6jYWv4?si=zP1Ylo_iaQmMV4AM.

SEMIOTIC TELL5

1. See W. W. Wiersbe, *The Bible Exposition Commentary*, Vol. 1 (1996), 639.

2. A piece of the puzzle means nothing until you link the piece to other pieces and make it into a whole. "The pieces are readable, take on a sense, only when assembled; in isolation, a puzzle piece means nothing—just an impossible question, an opaque challenge." (p. xv of the Preamble to Georges Perec, *Life: A User's Manual* Translated from the French by David Bellos [2009]; originally published in 1978).

3. John 1:18.

4. John Wesley, *Explanatory Notes upon the New Testament* (1755), Preface.

5. For example, the FBI is our Secret Police. But the FBI failed to connect obvious dots from the trackings of Zacarias Moussaoui to the 9/11 plot.

The FBI even neglected to search his computer even after they had him in custody.

6. Mark 2:1–12.
7. Peter walking on water is only in the story in Matthew 14:22–33, although the event is told in every gospel but Luke. See Mark 6:45–53, John 6:15–21.
8. As told by Carl Zimmer, *Life's Edge: The Search For What It Means To Be Alive* (2022).
9. I first introduced this semiotic matrix in the foreword to *The Story Lectionary*, ed. David McDonald (2017).
10. This is my argument in *From Tablet to Table* (2015).
11. First formulated in Edwards' *The Distinguishing Marks of a Work of the Spirit of God* (1741), Edwards outlined five principal signs or "tests" to evaluate whether a religious experience or revival was genuinely from the Holy Spirit:

    The experience exalts Jesus Christ: True spiritual experiences will elevate the person and work of Jesus Christ, not diminish or replace Him.

    The experience opposes Satan's kingdom: Genuine revivals will work against the interests of sin, worldliness, and the devil.

    The experience increases regard for Scripture: True spiritual movements will lead people to a greater love and respect for the Bible as God's Word.

    The experience leads people to truth: Authentic experiences will guide individuals towards sound doctrine and a proper understanding of God's nature.

    The experience produces love for God and others: True revivals will result in greater love for God and increased charity towards fellow humans.

    Edwards further expanded on these ideas in his later and more comprehensive work, *A Treatise Concerning Religious Affections* (1746).

12. The Blood Test reminds us of Christ's sacrifice and the tangible, historical reality of the Gospel. It grounds our faith in the concrete events of Jesus' life, death, and resurrection. The Water Test speaks to the cleansing and life-giving nature of the Spirit's work, often associated with baptism and spiritual rebirth. It verifies the life-changing power of the narrative in our lives. The Wind (or Fire) Test alludes to the dynamic, often unpredictable movement of the Holy Spirit, as seen at Pentecost. It confirms the

NOTES

ongoing, living nature of our faith story, constantly renewing and empowering Jesus humans.

13. William Williams, hymn published in 1745.
14. From the collection *Labyrinths: Selected Stories and Other Writings* (1964 edition), translated by James E. Irby, 193–196. Borges is also known for a similar quote: "The Library is unlimited and cyclical. If an eternal traveler were to cross it in any direction, after centuries he would see that the same volumes were repeated in the same disorder (which, thus repeated, would be an order: the Order)."
15. Daniel Kahneman, *Thinking, Fast and Slow* (2011). See chapter 35 "The Focusing Illusion" and chapter 36 "The Remembering Self."
16. Adapted from Richard Leonard, SJ, *Where the Hell is God?* (2010), 54–56.

SEMIOTIC TELL 6

1. From Antoine de Saint-Exupéry's novella *The Little Prince* (*Le Petit Prince*) (1943), Chapter 21.
2. Owen Barfield, *Romanticism Comes of Age* (1944).
3. As found in his discussion of "embodied cognition" in *Being There: Putting Brain, Body, and World Together Again* (1997).
4. Guy Consolmagno, "Life on Mars?" *The Tablet*, 278 (03 August 2024), 32. I love his last line of the article: "Anyone who thinks that faith and science are opposed, knows nothing of either."
5. George Orwell, "In Front Of Your Nose," article in *Tribute*, 22 March 1946.
6. Meister Eckhart, Sermon 57 of *The Complete Mystical Works of Meister Eckhart* (2009), 298.
7. Jules Verne, *Michael Strogoff: The Courier of the Czar* (1876).
8. Jeremy Mynott, "Spreading Their Wings," *Times Literary Supplement*, 23 June 2017, 32.

SEMIOTIC TELL 7

1. See especially Orwell's novels *1984* and *Animal Farm*, which explore themes of truth, propaganda, and the manipulation of information by those in power.

2. This was, most famously, the position of Pseudo-Dionysius the Areopagite (sixth century).

3. "Nobody knows anything" is attributed to screenwriter William Goldman (1931–2018). It's the opening lines of his *Adventures in the Screen Trade* (first published 1983) and is often used to express the unpredictability and uncertainty of the film industry. It suggests that even those with extensive experience in the field cannot consistently predict which films will be successful and which will fail. The quote highlights the inherent risk and gamble involved in filmmaking, as even the most well-crafted and promising films can sometimes fall short of expectations.

   Goldman himself used the quote to reflect on his own experiences in Hollywood, having witnessed the successes and failures of countless films throughout his career. He recognized that even with his insider knowledge and expertise, he could not always accurately predict how a film would be received by audiences. The quote serves as a reminder that even in an industry driven by data and analytics, there is still a significant element of chance and unpredictability.

   In a broader sense, the quote can also be interpreted as a commentary on the nature of knowledge and human understanding. It suggests that despite our vast accumulation of information and insights, there will always be gaps in our knowledge and areas that remain beyond our comprehension. The quote encourages humility and a willingness to embrace uncertainty, acknowledging that there are limits to what we can know.

   The quote "Nobody knows anything" has resonated with many in the film industry and beyond, capturing the essence of the creative process and the inherent risks involved in pursuing artistic endeavors. It serves as a reminder that even with expertise and experience, there is no guarantee of success, and that embracing uncertainty is an essential part of the creative journey.

4. In a conversation recorded in the journal *Contemporary Literature* (1999). The conversation was with the poet and critic Charles Bernstein, and it was published in the journal's fortieth anniversary issue.

   In the conversation, Waldrop was talking about her approach to poetry and her belief that the gaps and spaces between words are just as important as the words themselves. She said:

   > What matters is not things but what happens between them. Or if you take the linguistic model, it is not the phoneme but the connection of phonemes that makes language, the

differences in the sequence ... The gaps keep the questions in relation.

Waldrop's belief that the spaces between things are important is reflected in her poetry, which often uses juxtaposition and collage to create new meanings. Her poems are full of gaps and silences, which force the reader to fill in the blanks and create their own interpretations.

5. See Louise Gluck's poem "Nostos" in *Meadowlands* (1996).
6. See Ernest Hemmingway's *The Sun Also Rises* (1926), Book III, chapter 13. The theme of things deteriorating slowly before a sudden collapse is a recurring theme in Hemmingway. See also *The Old Man and the Sea* (1952), especially towards the end of the book.
7. See my book *The Well-Played Life*.
8. 1 Thessalonians 5:19 KJV.
9. Matthew 18:3.
10. John 1:12 KJV.
11. Immanuel Kant defined genius as "a talent ... entirely opposed to the spirit of imitation" in his *Critique of Judgment*, specifically the Third Critique, where he discusses the concept of aesthetic judgment. Kant argues that genius is a unique creative ability that transcends mere imitation or rule-following. See Immanuel Kant, *Critique of Judgment* Translated by James Creed Meredith (1952).
12. Petit committed "the artistic crime of the century" in August 1974 when he walked back and forth on a cable strung between the Twin Towers 1,350 feet (411 meters) above the ground.

SEMIOTIC TELL 8

1. Stanislaw Lew, *The Futurological Congress* (1985) (Polish: "Kongres futurologiczny"), (1971).
2. The quote "Science fiction is not prophecy" is from the second paragraph of his "Pandora's Box," the introduction to *The Worlds of Robert A Heinlein* (1966).
3. Isaiah 55:8 KJV.

SEMIOTIC TELL 9

1. I have written before, from a different perspective, on this trinitarian aspect to human existence. See my *The Three Hardest Words in the World to Get Right* (2006).

2. Adam Gopnik, *The Table Comes First* (2012), 188.

3. The main difference between dogma and doxa is that dogma is considered an absolute, unquestionable truth, often associated with religious or ideological doctrines, while doxa refers to the commonly held beliefs and opinions within a society, which may not necessarily be considered absolute truths. Dogmas are typically enforced by an authority, whereas doxa arises from societal norms and conventional wisdom.

   In ancient Greek philosophy, particularly in the works of Plato and Aristotle, doxa was not only associated with common belief or popular opinion but also with the concept of glory, fame, or reputation. In this context, doxa referred to the esteem, honor, or glory that one could attain in society through public recognition of their achievements, status, or character. It was often linked to the idea of being held in high regard by others and having a good reputation.

   This concept of doxa as related to glory or reputation is distinct from the more modern sociological understanding of doxa as the taken-for-granted, unquestioned beliefs and assumptions that shape social reality, as proposed by French sociologist Pierre Bourdieu in the twentieth century.

4. Scholars and theologians who have explored the resonance between Charles Sanders Peirce's triadic thinking and trinitarian theology include my esteemed colleague at Drew University, philosopher Robert Corrington, who knows more about Peirce than anyone alive, and has written extensively on the connections between Peirce's philosophy and Trinitarian theology. So too has Peirce scholars Nathan Houser and Michael Raposa.

5. Joshua Mobley, *A Brief Systematic Theology of the Symbol*, 1st edition (2022), 990, Kindle.

6. This is called synechism. Peirce's concept of synechism refers to the idea that continuity and discontinuity are interconnected and necessary for understanding reality. This synechistic approach can be seen as a way of embracing paradox, as it acknowledges the coexistence of opposing aspects.

7. See chapter 6 on "The Paradoxes of Christianity" in Chesterton's *Orthodoxy* (1908).

8. See his book *The Celestial Hierarchy* (circa 500 AD), where Dionysius describes the hierarchical structure of angels and heavenly beings, which he divides into triads: The highest triad, consisting of Seraphim, Cherubim, and Thrones; The middle triad, consisting of Dominions, Virtues, and Powers; The lowest triad, consisting of Principalities, Archangels, and Angels. Throughout his writings Dionysius uses triadic structures and emphasizes the significance of the number three.

9. See William Blake's book *The Marriage of Heaven and Hell* (1790–1793), Plate 14.

10. Luke preserves both sayings: 9:50, 11:23.

11. Jean Grondin. *Introduction to Philosophical Hermeneutics* (1994), 30.

12. See Saint Augustine, *Teaching Christianity* (translated by Edmund Hill, ed. John E. Rotelle) (1996), 107.

13. See Jen Pollock Michel, *Surprised by Paradox* (2019).

SEMIOTIC TELL 10

1. 1 Corinthians 3:11 NIV.

2. Colossians 1:27 NIV.

3. Rowan Williams, "The Nature of a Sacrament," in *Signs of Faith, Hope and Love: The Christian Sacraments Today* (1987), 44. See also p. 32: "St. Thomas Aquinas's admirably and typically simple observation that what makes sacraments distinct is what they are for, the activity in which they are caught up, which is making humans holy!"

4. As portrayed in Cornelius Plantinga's *Gratitude* (2024), a book which inspires and challenges Jesus' followers to look for the fresh footprints of Jesus in our world.

5. Thanks to Loren Kerns for pointing out this connection between Arianism and what I call examplism. See also Roger E. Olson, *Arminian Theology: Myths and Realities (2006)*.

6. As quoted by Rupert Shortt, *Outgrowing Dawkins: God for Grown-ups* (2019).

7. Hans Urs van Balthasaar, *A Theology of History* (1950), 95.

8. Genesis 49:14–15 ESV.

9. Philippians 1:21 NIV.

10. As quoted in Kevin M. Cahill's scholarly essay on Wittgenstein's *Tractatus*

Logico-Philosophicus in D. Z. Phillips and Mario von der Ruhr, eds., *Religion and Wittgenstein's Legacy* (2005), 276.

11. David Martin's review "Core Process" in *Times Literary Supplement*, 11 May 2012, 24.

SEMIOTIC TELL 11

1. John 21:18 NIV.
2. Mary Oliver, in her poem "The Summer Day," asks a question that sounds like a Jesus question. See *House of Light* (1992), 60.
3. See my article "Red Skies, White Elephants, Gray Rhinos, and Black Swans: A Minyan of Trends, Terrains, and Trajectories," in Rowland Smith, ed., *Red Skies: 10 Essential Conversations Exploring our Future as the Church* (2022).
4. For more see Leonard Sweet, *Rings of Fire* (2019), Joseph Tainter, *The Collapse of Complex Societies* (1990), and Nassim Nicholas Taleb, *The Black Swan: The Impact of the Highly Improbable* (2007).
5. See Leonard Sweet's festschrift article for South African biblical scholar Stephan Joubert, "From semiotic exegesis to contextual ecclesiology: The hermeneutics of missional faith in the COVIDian Era," *HTS Theological Studies* 77 (4):1–14 (2021).
6. Robert D. Dale, *Seeds for the Future: Growing Organic Leaders for Living Churches* (2005), 34.
7. John 3:8 NIV.
8. Charles Sanders Peirce once said "A symbol is something that has the power of reproducing itself." See his "*Notes on the Categories*" (1902) in *The Essential Peirce, Volume 2: Selected Philosophical Writings* (1998), edited by the Peirce Edition Project, 258–266, 260.
9. Proverbs 16:9, paraphrased.
10. Proverbs 3:5–6 NKJV.
11. This quote is often cited as being from a 1955 interview with William Miller, but some sources suggest that it may have been from a letter to William Miller, or even from an unpublished manuscript.
12. "Buffett's Cash Hoard," *The Economist*, 10 April 2024, 60.
13. For more information on preparing for the workplace of the future and how to successfully work alongside AI, check out Bernard Marr, *Future*

NOTES

Skills: The 20 Skills and Competencies Everyone Needs to Succeed in a Digital World (2022).

SEMIOTIC TELL 12

1. Genesis 2:15.
2. For how this works in the political and economic arenas, see "The Fraught Balance: Political Instability is an Economic Problem, But So Is Political Stability," *The Economist*, 20 July 2024, 63.
3. Mary Douglas, *Thinking in Circles* (2007).
4. Iain McGilchrist, *The Matter with Things*, Volume 2, beginning of chapter 20.
5. Alan E. Lewis, *Between Cross & Resurrection: A Theology of Holy Saturday* (2001), 13.
6. In "The Dialectical Theology of St. John," *New Testament Essays* (1972), 49–69.
7. Rudolph Bultmann, "The Significance of 'Dialectical Theology' for the Scientific Study of the New Testament," *Faith and Understanding* (Volume 1), Robert Funk, ed. (1969), 145–164, 146.
8. Thomas Jefferson made this remark in a letter to his friend, David Humphreys, dated 18 March 1789. See *The Papers of Thomas Jefferson, Volume 14: 8 October 1788 to 26 March 1789* (1958), edited by Julian P. Boyd, 676–677.

SEMIOTIC TELL 13

1. Hear Clarke say these words in his 1964 interview at the New York World's Fair, broadcasted on BBC, in ARTHUR C CLARKE predicts the FUTURE | Horizon | Past Predictions | BBC Archive. https://www.youtube.com/watch?v=YwELr8ir9qM.
2. This quote is widely attributed to Wells, but no exact citation has been found by me or others. It is, however, a classic *Star Trek* memorable quote: "I told you so, you damned fool" from the episode "I, Mudd" (Season 2, Episode 8). Harry Mudd, played by Roger C. Carmel, was a charismatic con artist and smuggler who appeared in two original *Star Trek* episodes.
3. Deliberate mutilation—like ear-cropping (William Prynne had both ears cut off in 1634 for writing *Histriomastix*, and Alexander Leighton had his ears cut off, his nose slit, and was branded on the face in 1630

for publishing *Zion's Plea*) and hand-chopping (John Stubbs had his right hand chopped off in 1579 for writing "The Discovery of a Gaping Gulf," finger-cutting, etc.—these practices largely ended in Europe and America by the late eighteenth century. But Salman Rushdie was stabbed multiple times in 2022 at one of my favorite places to lecture, Chautauqua Institution, losing sight in one eye and the use of one hand; and in Myanmar, numerous journalists have been tortured in prison since the 2021 military coup for their writing and reporting. Russian poisoning of journalists (like Vladimir Kara-Murza, imprisoned in 2022), are taken as facts of life. The physical punishment of writers through imprisonment, torture, and assassination continues in various parts of the world today.

4. The original introduction to *Animal Farm* (1945), never published in George Orwell's lifetime, first appeared in the *Times Literary Supplement* on 15 September 1972, and was penned early in 1945 (we think). The quote goes on: "If the intellectual liberty which without a doubt has been one of the distinguishing marks of western civilization means anything at all, it means that everyone shall have the right to say and to print what he believes to be the truth, provided only that it does not harm the rest of the community in some quite unmistakable way."

5. N. T. Wright, *What Saint Paul Really Said: Was Paul the Real Founder of Christianity* (1997), 94.

6. Timothy Garton Ash has discussed these three vetoes to free speech in various writings and interviews. Specifically, he has mentioned them in: *Free Speech: Ten Principles for a Connected World* (2016); his article in *The Guardian* titled "The Three Vetoes That Threaten Free Speech" (2016); and a lecture at the Oxford University's St. Anne's College, "Free Speech in the Age of Social Media" (2019).

7. Matthew 11:6 NASB.

8. Matthew 13:57; Mark 6:3 NIV.

9. The very nature of Christian theology is offensive because of "the offense of the cross" (Galatians 5). The gospel is an "offense" to both Jews and Greeks," Paul said (1 Corinthians 1:23; Romans 9:33). Even Jesus' home town "took offense at him" (Matthew 13:57; Mark 6:3). The message of the cross is a "stone of stumbling, and a rock of offense" (1 Peter 2:8).

10. The story is found in John 8. We usually read only verses one to eleven, but we need to read the whole story. While some include the story as part of the original Gospel of John, many scholars leave it out for several reasons. The earliest and most reliable Greek manuscripts of John, dating back to the fourth century, do not include the pericope. It appears in

later manuscripts, but often in different places, suggesting it wasn't part of the original text. Early Church Fathers, including prominent figures like Origen and Chrysostom, don't mention the passage in their commentaries, despite commenting on surrounding verses. For this reason, many reputable modern translations like NIV and ESV include the passage but mark it with brackets or footnotes, indicating its disputed origins. And scholarly editions like the Nestle-Aland Greek New Testament usually omit the pericope within the main text, often offering it in an appendix.

11. Possibly referencing Jeremiah 17:13 KJV: "Those who depart from me shall be written in the earth, because they have forsaken the Lord."

12. In Exodus 31:18 ESV, the text explicitly states that God wrote the Ten Commandments on stone tablets with his own finger: "And when he finished speaking with him on Mount Sinai, he gave to Moses the two tablets of the testimony, tablets of stone, written with the finger of God."

13. The original Greek term used for "ground" in John 8:7 can refer to both earth and stone surfaces, although most translations have it "on the ground." When John 8:6–9 says that Jesus "wrote in the sand" or "wrote on the ground" it literally means "into the earth." Jesus wrote "into the earth" when sacred soil was not supposed to be written on.

14. Exodus 31:18.

15. Daniel 4.

16. After Jesus stops the stoning, and says he judges no one, the Pharisees attack him. Then they taunt him, bringing up his illegitimate birth, "Where is your father?" "You do not know me or my Father," Jesus replied. "If you knew me, you would know my Father also." Then in the same chapter, a few verses down, they taunt him again: "We are not illegitimate children," they protested. "The only Father we have is God himself."

Jesus said to them, "If God were your Father, you would love me, for I have come here from God. I have not come on my own; God sent me. Why is my language not clear to you? Because you are unable to hear what I say. You belong to your father, the devil, and you want to carry out your father's desires. He was a murderer from the beginning, not holding to the truth, for there is no truth in him. When he lies, he speaks his native language, for he is a liar and the father of lies. Yet because I tell the truth, you do not believe me! Can any of you prove me guilty of sin? If I am telling the truth, why don't you believe me? Whoever belongs to

God hears what God says. The reason you do not hear is that you do not belong to God" (John 8:42–47 NIV).

17. John 12:32.

SEMIOTIC TELL 14

1. 2 Timothy 1:12 KJV.
2. The reference to Issacharians, of course, draws from the biblical tribe of Issachar, known for their ability to understand the times (1 Chronicles 12:32).
3. William MacAskill, *What We Owe the Future* (2022).
4. Hebrews 6:16–20 NIV.
5. For more on this, see my *AquaChurch 2.0* (1999).
6. Sam Willitt, "Anchor Riddle," in his *New Light for the Old Dark* (2011).
7. The process of kedging is described in several historical naval manuals and texts. One of the earliest definitions can be found in the 1784 edition of the "Seaman's Vade-Mecum" by John Hamilton Moore, but a more detailed description is provided in the 1863 edition of "The Seaman's Manual" by Epes Sargent. The most comprehensive description of kedging can be found in the 1908 edition of "The Admiralty Manual of Seamanship" by the British Admiralty. This manual describes kedging as a method of moving a ship by dropping an anchor in a desired direction and then pulling the ship towards the anchor using a rope or cable.
8. For a whole book on this distinction, see Leonard Sweet and Len Wilson, *Telos* (2022).
9. Immanuel Kant, *Anthropology from a Pragmatic Point of View*, translated by Victor Lyle Dowdell (1996), 77.
10. *Letters from William Blake to Thomas Butts*, 1800–1803. Printed in Facsimile with an Introductory Note by Geoffrey Keynes (1926), Letter dated 25 April 1803.
11. As echoed in Jesus' departing futuristic words to his disciples "I have much more to say to you, more than you can now bear" (John 16:12 NIV).
12. For the "first fruits" of the final harvest, see Romans 8:23.
13. For the "down payment" of what is to come, see 2 Corinthians 1:22; 5:5; Ephesians 1:14.

NOTES

14. For the *arrabon* or "seal" of the future, see 1 Corinthians 1:21–22; Ephesians 1:13; 4:30.

15. Theologian Cynthia Campbell in a sermon, "What to Do about Deadwood," 08 December 2019, https://immanuelevanston.org/sermon/sermon-what-to-do-about-deadwood-december-8-2019/. Chittister's quote is on p. 104, but her discussion on hope continues on 105.

SEMIOTIC TELL 15

1. Seth Godin in *Tribes* (2008) discusses the life cycle of trends and how to identify where a trend is in its life cycle.

2. Malcolm Gladwell, in *The Tipping Point* (2000), explores the idea of trends reaching a critical mass, or "tipping point," where they rapidly gain widespread acceptance and become a trajectory.

3. The classic treatment of the trend life cycle is Everett Rogers' book *Diffusion of Innovations* (1962). He identifies five stages: Knowledge, Persuasion, Decision, Implementation, and Confirmation. He also proposed various stages of trend adoption: Innovators, Early Adopters, Early Majority, Late Majority, and finally Laggards. Geoffrey Moore in *Crossing the Chasm* (1991) applies Rogers' concept to the technology adoption life cycle, describing the stages as Early Market, Chasm, Bowling Alley, Tornado, and Main Street.

SEMIOTIC TELL 16

1. See the lawyer in his exchange with Jesus in Luke 10:25–37.

2. Ostranenie, often translated as "defamiliarization," is a term coined by Viktor Shklovsky. It refers to the artistic technique of presenting common things in an unfamiliar or strange way to enhance perception of the familiar. Jesus isn't changing the signs themselves (the covenant rituals) but altering their interpretation and significance. The frame (covenant) remains the same, but its context and meaning are shifted. Jesus' approach was not to overturn existing traditions, but to deepen their meaning and encourage a fresh, more profound understanding of them. For more on "Ostranenie," see my *Jesus Human* (2023), 310–314.

3. See for example Matthew 6:30, during the Sermon on the Mount; Matthew 8:26, when calming the storm; Matthew 14:31, to Peter when he was walking on water; Matthew 16:8, when discussing the yeast of the Pharisees; Luke 12:28, regarding anxiety.

4. John Wesley, Preface to Explanatory Notes upon the Old Testament (1765). In *The Works of John Wesley*, Volume 14 (1984).

5. C. S. Lewis, *An Experiment in Criticism* (1961). See the fourth chapter entitled "The Reading of the Unliterary."

6. Lewis, An *Experiment in Criticism*, 19.

7. This quote is from an essay by C. S. Lewis titled "Is Theology Poetry?" which was originally delivered as a talk at the Oxford Socratic Club in 1944. It was later published in Lewis's book *The Weight of Glory and Other Addresses* (1941), 140.

SEMIOTIC TELL 17

1. Crystal Downing, *Changing Signs of Truth* (2012).

2. Mary Douglas discusses "condensed symbols" in her book *Natural Symbols: Explorations in Cosmology* (1970) but most definitively in her classic *Purity and Danger: An Analysis of the Concepts of Pollution and Taboo* (1966).

3. Quoted in Jean Sulzberger, "The Touchstone" in *A Way of Working*, ed. J. M. Dooling (1979), 69.

4. This point is made by Anya von Bremzen in her wonderful book *National Dish: Around the World In Search of Food, History and the Meaning of Home* (2024).

5. Ben Lerner, *Angle of Yaw* (2006).

SEMIOTIC TELL 18

1. The annual conference of the National Justice and Peace Network of England and Wales (NJPN).

2. Scot McKnight, *The Letter to Philemon* (2017).

3. "Love Story," *The Economist*, 10 February 2024, 24.

4. Daniel Boorstin, *The Image* (1961).

5. For my critique of leadership culture, see my book *I Am A Follower* (2012).

6. For more on this, see my *Designer Jesus: The Lifestory of a Disciple* (2024).

7. David J. Baker, *On Demand: Writing for the Market in Early Modern England* (2010), 21. This is a quote attributed to the prominent merchant Edward Misselden (1608–1654).

NOTES

8. 2 Chronicles 6:6 TLV.

9. Nelly Sachs' poem "Sternenspiele" (Cosmic Plays or Cosmic Embrace) was published in Sachs' 1959 collection of poems entitled "*Teufel in Geschichte*" (Devil in History). Nelly Sachs (d. 1970), Nobel Prize in Literature winner in 1966, also said "I lack the necessary stillness to aim straight." She writes this in *Die gekrummte Linie des Leidens*, as quoted in Nelly Shanka, *Revelation Freshly Erupting*, translated by Andrew Shanks (London, 2023).

10. See the section on "The Dis-Uniting States of America" in my *Rings of Fire* (2020), 67–74.

11. Gellner wrote extensively about nationalism and its relationship to modernization in several works, most notably *Nations and Nationalism* (1983). He made a similar statement in his book *Thought and Change* (1964).

12. "Politics as a Vocation," lecture delivered at Munich University (1918) and published in a collection of essays called *From Max Weber: Essays in Sociology* (1991), 78, edited by H. H. Gerth and C. Wright Mills. Also find it in his magnum opus *Economy and Society* (1922), specifically in chapter I, section 17, "The State."

13. Chapter IV, "No Religion is an Island," in Abraham Joshua Heschel, *Moral Grandeur and Spiritual Audacity: Essays*, edited by Susanna Heschel (1996), 236.

SEMIOTIC TELL 20

1. The quote "Every artist draws himself" is often attributed to M. C. Escher, but there is no solid evidence that he actually said or wrote these exact words. They seem to be a paraphrased or interpreted summary of his ideas, rather than a direct quote.

2. There is evidence to suggest that autobiographical memory can be resilient in the face of cognitive decline, but I use this here in a more poetic than scientific sense. The concept of a life review as a non-linear, panoramic experience is widely reported in near-death experiences and other altered states of consciousness. While the scientific understanding of this phenomenon is still developing, it is a common theme in many cultural and spiritual traditions.

SEMIOTIC TELL 21

1. David Edwards, *Creating Things That Matter: The Art and Science of Innovations That Last* (2018), proposes seven "aesthetic dimensions" of the creative mind beyond the five physical senses: Passion, Empathy, Intuition, Innocence, Humility, Aesthetic intelligence, and Obsession.

2. Susan Gaidos, "Thanks," *Science News*, 21 June 2008, 27ff.

3. T. S. Eliot wrote this in his poem "Burnt Norton" (1935), which is the first of his "Four Quartets."

4. See Nietzsche's 1887 *Zur Genealogie der Moral: Eine Streitschrift (On the Genealogy of Morals)*, as reprinted in *Basic Writings of Nietzsche* (2009), 493.

5. Anthony Bale, *Times Literary Supplement*, 10 May 2013, 25.

6. Jude Rogers, *The Sound of Being Human* (2022).

7. So said US novelist John Gardner in *The Art of Fiction* (1984).

8. *Times Literary Supplement*, 08 March 2024.

9. In an NPR interview with Terry Gross, "Fresh Air Music Interviews," NPR, 01 November 2023. https://www.npr.org/2023/11/01/1209679558/david-byrne-talking-heads-stop-making-sense.

10. For the difference between "participant evidence" versus "spectator evidence," see the American philosopher Paul Moser's books like *Philosophy After Objectivity* (1993), *Knowledge and Evidence* (1989), and *The Elusive God: Reorienting Religious Epistemology* (2008).

11. Jason Swan Clark, "Are the Spiritual Exercises the Latest Evangelical Fad?" SpEx, 13 August 2023, https://www.spex.so/p/are-the-spiritual-exercises-the-latest.

12. The quote "God and the imagination are one" is from Wallace Stevens' 1942 poem "Asides on the Oboe" from his poetry collection *Parts of a World* (1985).

13. Kevin J. Vanhoozer, *Pictures at a Theological Exhibition: Scenes of the Church's Worship, Witness and Wisdom* (2021), calls for a return of biblical imagination. His chapter 7 on "cultural hermeneutics" outlines his style of teaching which bears resemblance to some of my ways of teaching semiotics.

14. Jean Leclercq O.S.B., *The Love of Learning and The Desire God: A Study of Monastic Culture* (1982), 75. Leclercq is writing on the biblical imagination.

NOTES

15. Agatha Christie, *The Mysterious Affair at Styles* (1920).
16. Oscar Wilde, *De Profundis*. Edited by Rupert Hart-Davis, complete and unabridged edition (1962).
17. Thomas H. Troeger, *Imagining a Sermon* (1990), 28. The word hermeneutical is inserted by me. Hermeneutical and homiletical are "horses" from the same stable. They run together.
18. W. H. Auden, *Making, Knowing and Judging*. Inaugural Lecture at the University of Oxford, 11 June 1956.
19. Jean Leclercq O.S.B., *The Love of Learning and The Desire God: A Study of Monastic Culture* (1982), 75. Leclercq's book is a lot like this one you are reading—a series of lectures given to young monks at the Institute of Monastic Studies at Sant'Anselmo in Rome during the winter of 1955–56.
20. Adolph von Harnack, *What is Christianity?* ("Das Wesen des Christentums") (1900).
21. "Because that, when they knew God, they glorified him not as God, neither were thankful; but became vain in their imaginations, and their foolish heart was darkened" (Romans 1:21 KJV).

    "Casting down imaginations, and every high thing that exalteth itself against the knowledge of God, and bringing into captivity every thought to the obedience of Christ" (2 Corinthians 10:5 KJV).
22. Leanne Payne explores the connection between imagination, faith, and spiritual growth in her book *Real Presence: The Christian Worldview of C. S. Lewis as Incarnated in His Life and Works* (1995). In *Mere Christianity* (1952), Lewis discusses the concept of holy imagination as a means to understand and connect with God. Biblical scholar and theologian Walter Brueggemann writes extensively on the role of imagination in faith, especially *The Prophetic Imagination: 40th Anniversary Edition* (2018), although I'm not aware he ever used the phrase "holy imagination" in his extensive exploration into how prophets are tasked with nurturing and sustaining the ministry of imagination, offering visions of hope and transformation. The grand-daddy of the "holy imagination" phrase is Jonathan Edwards, who wrote about the importance of imagination in the life of faith.
23. Wilda C. Gafney, *Womanist Midrash, Vol 1: A Reintroduction To The Women Of The Torah And The Throne* (2017).
24. J. D. Payne, *Apostolic Imagination: Recovering a Biblical Vision for the Church's Mission Today* (2022).

25. Wilda C. Gafney, *Womanist Midrash, Vol 1: A Reintroduction to the Women of the Torah and the Throne* (2017).

26. See chapter 1 in Iain McGilchrist, *The Master and His Emissary: The Divided Brain and the Making of the Western World* (2009).

27. *Calvin's Commentaries, Volume XXI: Galatians, Ephesians, Philippians, and Colossians* (1981), translated by William Pringle, 87–88.

28. *Luther's Works, Volume 1: Lectures on Genesis, Chapters 1–5* (1958), edited by Helmut T. Lehmann and Jaroslav Pelikan, 116–117.

29. Origen's sermons survived because he always preached extempore, but stenographers were allowed to take them down. Over 200 has survived. To be precise, Origen didn't allegorize his sermons, just his essays. He became very literal in his readings of Scripture. As an aside: We have so few sermons extant that we have very little understanding of preaching in the first three centuries. Except Origen.

30. As quoted by Ronald Lee Massanari, "The Sacred Workshop of God," *Religion in Life* (Summer 1971), 261.

31. In William Bradford's journal, *Of Plymouth Plantation*, he writes: "And thus they increased and multiplied, and the Lord was with them, and they enjoyed peace and plenty; and they became a great people, and their increasings were many." In the book *Mourt's Relation*, Edward Winslow writes: "By the blessing of God, our increasings are many." See William Bradford, *Of Plymouth Plantation* (1651), 120–121. Edward Winslow, *Mourt's Relation: A Journal of the Pilgrims at Plymouth, 1622–1623* (1622), 62.

32. Charles Foster *Times Literary Supplement*, 12 August 2022, 9.

33. For more on ostranenie, see the chapter on it in my *Jesus Human* (2023) 310–314.

34. See Samir Puri, *Westlessness: The Great Global Rebalancing* (2024).

SEMIOTIC TELL 22

1. 1 Chronicles 25.

2. Samuel Coleridge, *Biographia Literaria* (1817), chapter XIV.

3. Silas Weir Mitchell, *Rest in Nervous Disease: Its Use and Abuse*, (Series of American Clinical Lectures, ed. E.C. Seguin. Vol. 1, no.4, 94) (1879).

4. This is found in a collection of his personal notes and remarks compiled

NOTES

by his literary executors after his death titled *Culture and Value*, edited by G. H. von WRIGHT, translated by Peter Winch (1980), 86e.

SEMIOTIC TELL 23

1. Revelation 4:1–2 KJV.
2. Here are the main levels of holiness:
   10. Holy of Holies (Kodesh HaKodashim): The innermost sanctum, considered the most sacred space. Only the High Priest could enter, and only on Yom Kippur.
   9. Holy Place (Kodashim): The main sanctuary where priests performed daily rituals.
   8. Altar of Burnt Offering (Mizbeach HaOlah): Located in the Temple courtyard, where sacrifices were offered.
   7. Temple Courtyard (Azarah): The outer courtyard surrounding the Temple building.
   6. Women's Courtyard (Ezrat Nashim): A separate area for women. Temple Mount (Har HaBayit): The entire complex.
   5. Additionally, there were areas outside the Temple complex with decreasing levels of holiness:
   4. Jerusalem: Considered holy due to its association with the Temple.
   3. Walls of Jerusalem: Defined the city limits.
   2. Temple Mount ramparts: The outer walls surrounding the Temple Mount.
   1. Areas outside Jerusalem: The rest of the Land of Israel and beyond.
3. 1 Chronicles 9:17–27, 23:4–5; 2 Chronicles 35:15; Ezra 2:42; Nehemiah 7:45, 11:19, 12:25, 13:4–5, 7, 22.
4. Thomas Sebeok, *Communication Measures to Bridge Ten Millennia: Technical Report* (1984), osti.gov/servlets/purl/6705990/.
5. See See Rose's *Judaism and Modernity: Philosophical Essays* (1993, 2017), 222. See also Brett Gray, *Jesus in the Theology of Rowan Williams* (2016), 73, where he suggests "Rose's Miss Marple is just a little like Christ."

www.ingramcontent.com/pod-product-compliance
Lightning Source LLC
Chambersburg PA
CBHW072145070526
44585CB00015B/1001